A Critical Dictionary of...

Also by Andrew Samuels

Jung and the Post-Jungians
The Father: Contemporary Jungian Perspectives (ed.)

Also by Bani Shorter

An Image Darkly Forming: A Woman's
Experience of Initiation

A Critical Dictionary of Jungian Analysis

Andrew Samuels, Bani Shorter and Fred Plaut

London and New York

First published in 1986
Reprinted in 1987 by
Routledge & Kegan Paul Ltd
Reprinted 1991, 1992, 1993 by
Routledge
11 New Fetter Lane, London EC4P 4EE

Simultaneously published in the USA and Canada
by Routledge
29 West 35th Street, New York, NY 10001

Set in 10/12 Sabon
and printed and bound in Great Britain
by Butler and Tanner Ltd, Frome and London

© *Andrew Samuels, Bani Shorter and Alfred Plaut 1986*

British Library CIP data also available

Library of Congress Cataloging in Publication Data

Samuels, Andrew.

A critical dictionary of Jungian analysis.

Bibliography: p.
1. Psychoanalysis Dictionaries. 2. Jung, C.G.
(Carl Gustav), 1875–1961 Dictionaries. I. Shorter,
Bani, II. Plaut, Fred. III. Title.
BF173.J85S275 1986 150.19'54'0321 86–74

ISBN 0–415–05910–0

Contents

Acknowledgments

The authors would like to express their gratitude to the Scholarship Committee of the C. G. Jung Institute of San Francisco for a grant from the Ernst and Eleanor van Loben Sels Scholarship Fund.

Acknowledgments are due to Routledge & Kegan Paul and to Princeton University Press for permission to quote from the English translations of the *Collected Works of C. G. Jung*, edited by Read, H., Fordham, M., and Adler, G., translated by Hull, R.

Thanks are due to Jane Williams for her excellent typing; the problems of joint authorship created certain difficulties, but she overcame them with good humour. Catherine Graham-Harrison used her personal skills to keep the project moving steadily forward; gratitude is also due for her comments on the early drafts of several entries.

Introduction

Since the death of C. G. Jung in 1961, there has been a widespread growth of interest in analytical psychology and the work of those who have practised and developed it. However, Jungian terminology is unfamiliar to many readers and, therefore, many books about analytical psychology contain glossaries or a list of definitions of those terms employed by Jung himself. Yet these glossaries make use of Jung's own words, either extracted from the definitions given in Volume 6 of the *Collected Works*, from his autobiography (*Memories, Dreams, Reflections*, 1963) or from Jung's writings presented by one of his followers (e.g. Jaffé's commemorative volume, *C. G. Jung: Word and Image*, 1979). This is true, for instance, of Storr's *Jung: Selected Writings* (1983, published in the US as *The Essential Jung*) and the anthology entitled *Jungian Analysis* edited by M. Stein (1982).

It is reasonable to suppose that glossaries which depend on Jung's exact words may not perform the task of translation and summary that is needed. Maybe it is unfair to expect what is usually an addition to a book with a particular theme to fulfil this general educational function. There may also have been a fear of misinterpretation in a short explanation of terms with manifold meanings.

Those who want to find out more about the language of psychoanalysis are more fortunate. They can refer to Laplanche and Pontalis' *The Language of Psychoanalysis* (1980) or Rycroft's *A Critical Dictionary of Psychoanalysis* (1972). Both of these were inspirations for the present work – the former for its encyclopaedic, scholarly, historical perspective, and the latter for its blend of inspiration with responsibility.

Analytical psychology has not stood still since Jung's death and it was felt to be important for any dictionary to show how post-Jungian writers have adapted, amended or challenged Jung's concepts. A degree of recognition for objections from, and parallels to, psychoanalysis was also seen as desirable. Hence the appellation of 'critical'.

In many respects, the dictionary reflects a world-wide trend in which focus upon Jung is shifting from his esoteric interests to those

1

which inform a human psychology and underpin therapeutic endeavour generally. In all the helping professions, the clinical standing of analytical psychology is strengthening. There has been a tremendous growth in the number of therapists with a Jungian orientation and far greater academic attention is being paid to Jung's work than previously. In Britain, for example, the trend is shown by the number of analytical psychologists appointed as Consultant Psychiatrists or Psychotherapists in the National Health Service. The same is true in other Western countries.

This evolution is exemplified by the increase of the number of books by or about Jung in evidence on the reading lists of training courses. The number of eclectic programmes of training in psychotherapy and counselling is increasing and students on such courses have need of a book such as this dictionary. Psychoanalysts in training also require basic information, along with students of psychology, social work, counselling, religion and anthropology. Qualified practitioners, including psychiatrists, will, it is hoped, find something in the book for them as well. The authors are also interested in enabling scholars and those who are reading Jung for personal reasons to have recourse to an accurate reference book which summarises and explains difficult terms.

What are the difficulties in understanding which are associated with Jung? Jung was an empirical thinker and, at times, his deliberate eschewing of precise logic leads to confusion in the reader. In fact, Jung's intellectual development rested upon intuitive and tentative insights, often expressed differently in different contexts.

Sometimes, Jung's writing is best understood as a flow of images which necessitated the extensive use of analogy. Crucially, Jung was the sort of thinker who never abandoned anything. Unlike Freud, he did not undertake substantial (and official) revisions of his thought, preferring to use earlier formulations as a springboard for later formulations. When Jung *did* revise his books and papers, such revision often took the form of an insertion of more up-to-date material (e.g. CW 4, paras 693–744).

Jung was a man of his time. In some instances, this meant that he shared the cultural and conceptual approach of his day. For example, he tended to organise his thought into pairs of OPPOSITES, conflicting and combining according to context, and capable of producing a new synthesis. This Hegelian methodology is increasingly anachronistic. Today's paradigm is more fluid, oriented towards relations and feed-back, and concerned with process. The naming of hypothetical forces and elements, conceived as actual components of a structure, which was a feature of late nineteenth- and early twentieth-century thought, also sounds strange to us. Such a reification (or substantive abstraction) as 'ENERGY' comes to mind in this connection.

What is more, Jung had strong personal antipathies. Believing, as he did, in the 'personal equation' (the inevitable influence of personality upon ideas), his own life experience often furnished the raw material for his theoretical formulations. Though he regarded this as 'empirical', his personal input sometimes led him to take fairly extreme positions (about gender role, for instance).

There have been occasional problems of translation which have made understanding difficult. These are mentioned in the dictionary if they are relevant. Here, there seems to be less of a problem than there is with psychoanalysis, perhaps because of Jung's thorough and idiomatic grasp of English. An oral tradition of Jung's explication of his ideas in English was at the disposal of the translator of the *Collected Works*, in addition to certain lectures and papers delivered and/or written in English.

Each major definition includes several features, and cross-references are indicated by small capitals. The features are: the meaning or meanings of a term; its origin and place in Jung's thought; difference between analytical psychology and psychoanalysis when the same or similar terms are used; changes in use of the term within the field of analytical psychology; critical comment where applicable; quotations and references. Bibliographical references are gathered at the end of the book. Unless stated otherwise, references to Jung's writings are to his *Collected Works*, published by Routledge & Kegan Paul, London, and Princeton University Press. References are given by volume and paragraph numbers. Where the context does not make it clear, the authors have tried to indicate the orientation of writers whose names may be unfamiliar. A writer whose field of interest is not mentioned is an analytical psychologist.

It may be helpful to say something about what has been excluded from the scope of the book. The authors have confined themselves, insofar as it was possible, to the discipline of analytical psychology and to words with psychological implications. Likewise, they have not attempted to cover the basic terminology of psychodynamics or psychoanalysis. As previously mentioned, several psychoanalytic terms are included: where there is an overlap with analytical psychology, if a particularly sharp divergence, possibly of historical importance, has occurred, or when comparison might prove helpful to the reader.

The dictionary does include:

(a) terms and ideas introduced or developed primarily by Jung (e.g. INDIVIDUATION);

(b) terms and ideas in general usage in psychodynamics but used in a particular way by Jung (e.g. SYMBOL);

(c) ordinary words used by Jung in a particular way (e.g. WHOLE-NESS);

(d) major terms introduced and developed by other analytical psychologists (e.g. EGO-SELF AXIS). In general, only material of this kind which has appeared at some stage in English has been included;

(e) psychoanalytic terms (limited by the considerations mentioned in the previous paragraph – e.g. PROJECTION).

Another way for the reader to orientate her or himself is as follows. Some entries speak to Jung's ethos or ideology (e.g. REDUCTIVE AND SYNTHETIC METHODS). Others deal with themes which are central in analytical psychology (e.g. INCEST). Still others cover important theoretical ideas of Jung's (e.g. ARCHETYPE). Finally, technical terms are specifically defined (e.g. PERSONA).

It should also be recalled that analytical psychology, like psychoanalysis, is a knotting together of three main strands: an investigation and exploration of unconscious life, a body of theoretical knowledge, and a method of treatment.

Every discipline produces its own terminology, and depth psychology is not an exception. The hope is that, by explaining the meanings imprisoned in the jargon, the terminology will take on life. For words and ideas are alive; they grow, decay, change. They bind people together and they cause schism. They speak for psyche and they can damage psyche.

It was the authors' common and contrasting experiences as analysts, teachers and writers which led them to undertake this book. For their own wrestling with Jung's written word played a part in their motivation. So, beneath the surface of a serious didactic enterprise there lies a substratum of empathy with those who are struggling to understand.

A Critical Dictionary of
Jungian Analysis

abaissement du niveau mental A relaxation and an uninhibited letting go of psychic restraints; reduced intensity of CONSCIOUSNESS characterised by absence of concentration and attention; a state in which unexpected contents may emerge from the UNCONSCIOUS. The term was first used by Jung's teacher, the French Professor Pierre Janet, to explain the symptomatology of hysteria and other psychogenic neuroses (see NEUROSIS). In his early work on the WORD ASSOCIATION TEST, Jung found the same phenomenon observable in the spontaneous interventions into consciousness of contents connected with personal complexes (see COMPLEX). He subsequently used the term to describe a border condition in which consciousness of certain unconscious contents was imminent. He recognised it as an important state of pre-condition for the occurrence of spontaneous psychic phenomena. Hence, although it is usually a state that occurs involuntarily (as in cases of MENTAL ILLNESS), it may also be consciously fostered preparatory to ACTIVE IMAGINATION.

In such a condition the play of OPPOSITES, usually kept in check by the restraining EGO, is released; therefore every *abaissement du niveau mental* brings about a relative reversal of values. Such a lowering of the threshold of consciousness is also characteristic of the effects of certain drugs. Jung felt the state corresponded 'pretty exactly to the primitive state of consciousness in which myths were originally formed' (CW 9ii, para. 264) (see PRIMITIVES; MYTH). Negative possibilities at a time of *abaissement du niveau mental* have to do with the emergence of latent psychotic tendencies. Therefore, it is not necessarily a benign condition nor one to be encouraged, unless there is sufficient strength on the part of the ego, not only to withstand the encounter with the unconscious but also to do what is necessary for INTEGRATION of the archetypal symbolism which may erupt (see ARCHETYPE; INFLATION; POSSESSION; SYMBOL).

The imagery produced by such a condition shows discontinuity, is of a fragmentary character, reveals analogy formations, involves superficial ASSOCIATIONS of the verbal, clang, or visual type, may include condensations, irrational expressions, confusions. Like DREAMS, such fantasies are not necessarily sequential; neither do they appear to reveal purposeful symbolic content initially. By making perceptible psychic contents which are usually repressed, APPERCEPTION can be enriched, but there is no guarantee that these contents will become part of the general orientation of consciousness. This requires REFLECTION and ANALYSIS. In such a condition a person may become dissociated and unable consciously to re-orient himself.

Jung writes that a slackening of the tension of consciousness is felt subjectively as listlessness, moroseness, and depression, due to the fact that one can no longer command ENERGY to be used for ego purposes. Such a state was felt to correspond to that referred to as 'LOSS OF SOUL' by primitive peoples. *Abaissement du niveau mental* is descriptive of a psychic condition irrespective of what may produce that condition.

abreaction A dramatic replay of a traumatising moment, its emotional recapitulation in the waking or hypnotic state, an unbosoming, a retelling that 'depotentiates the affectivity of the traumatic experience until it no longer has a disturbing influence' (CW 16, para. 262).

The use of abreaction was linked to Freud's TRAUMA theory and early psychoanalytic experiments. Jung differed with Freud about the efficacy of using abreaction. Consideration of its inadequacy led to further definition of Jung's own method and clarification of the role that transference plays in treatment (see ANALYST AND PATIENT).

Used by itself (by suggestion or in the so-called cathartic method), Jung found abreaction to be insufficient, useless or harmful (just as Freud did later). He identified the aim of treatment as the INTEGRATION of the DISSOCIATION connected with trauma rather than its abreaction. This re-experiencing, in his view, should reveal the bipolar aspect of the NEUROSIS so that a person could once again relate to the positive or prospective content of the COMPLEX; hence, bringing AFFECT under control. The manner in which this could be effected, he thought, was by way of relationship to the therapist, a relationship which reinforced the conscious personality of the patient sufficiently so that the autonomous complex became subject to the authority of the EGO.

Abreaction is one form of ENACTMENT available in ANALYSIS. It is of central importance in some other therapies (e.g. Primal Therapy).

acting out Jung's concept of INFLATION to some extent parallels Freud's use of the term 'acting out' whereby 'the subject in the grip of his unconscious wishes and fantasies, relives these in the present with a sensation of immediacy which is heightened by his refusal to recognise their source and their repetitive character' (Laplanche and Pontalis, 1980). Here we note, as in cases of IDENTIFICATION with an ARCHETYPE, the compulsive, driven and repetitive character of action which is undifferentiated and not yet subject to EGO control. Such an absence of ego authority would appear to spring from a basic refusal or inability to acknowledge the existence of the motivating force and, thereby, conscious awareness is bypassed. The symbolic nature of the invasion of psychic contents is ignored (see ENACTMENT; INCEST).

active imagination   Jung used the term in 1935 to describe a process of dreaming with open eyes (CW, 6, para. 723 n). At the outset one concentrates on a specific point, mood, picture or event, then allows a chain of associated FANTASIES to develop and gradually take on a dramatic character. Thereafter the images have a life of their own and develop according to their own logic. Conscious doubt must be overcome and allowance made for whatever falls into consciousness as a consequence.

Psychologically, this creates a new situation. Previously unrelated contents become more or less clear and articulate. Since feeling is roused, the conscious EGO is stimulated to react more immediately and directly than is the case with DREAMS. Thereby, Jung felt maturation was quickened because the images that present themselves in active imagination anticipate dreams.

Active imagination is to be contrasted with day-dreaming which is more or less of one's own invention and remains on the surface of personal and daily experience. Active imagination is the opposite of conscious invention. The drama that is enacted appears to 'want to compel the viewer's participation. A new situation is created in which UNCONSCIOUS contents are exposed in the waking state' (CW 14, para. 706). Jung found in this evidence of the TRANSCENDENT FUNCTION at work; i.e. a collaboration between conscious and unconscious factors.

What becomes manifest can be dealt with in one of several ways. The process of active imagination itself may have a positive and vitalising effect but the content (as of a dream) may also be painted as well (see PAINTING). Patients can be encouraged to write down their fantasies in order to fix the sequence at the time of its occurrence and such records may be subsequently brought to ANALYSIS for INTERPRETATION.

Jung maintained, however, that the fantasy IMAGE has everything it needs for its subsequent development and transmutation in psychic life. While actively imagining he warned against having outside contact, comparing this to the alchemical process with its need for an 'hermetically sealed vessel' (see ALCHEMY). He did not recommend that active imagination be used indiscriminately or by everyone, finding it most useful in the latter stages of analysis when the objectivisation of images may replace dreams.

Such fantasies ask for the co-operation of conscious life. Active imagination may stimulate cure of a NEUROSIS but it achieves success only if it is integrated and does not become either a substitute for or an escape from the labour of conscious living. In contrast to dreams, which are experienced passively, this process of imagination demands the active and creative participation of the EGO (see Weaver, 1964; Watkins, 1976; Jaffé, 1979).

This method of raising to consciousness those contents which lie immediately below the threshold of the unconscious is not without its psychological hazards (see ABAISSEMENT DU NIVEAU MENTAL). Among these, Jung focused primarily upon three: (1) that the process may prove sterile if the patient remains caught in the circle of his own complexes; (2) that the patient becomes beguiled by the appearance of the fantasies and ignores their demand for confrontation; and (3) that the unconscious contents possess such a high level of ENERGY that, when afforded an outlet, they take possession of the personality (see INFLATION; POSSESSION).

adaptation Relating to, coming to terms with, and balancing internal and external factors. To be distinguished from conformism; a vital aspect of INDIVIDUATION.

According to Jung, failure to adapt is one definition of NEUROSIS. Sometimes this expresses itself in terms of external reality; sometimes in terms of internal reality. In ANALYSIS external problems may have to be dealt with first, thus freeing the person to face profound and pressing inner issues. Jung pointed out that adaptation *per se* also suggested a balancing of the needs of both internal and external worlds, which may make quite different demands upon a person. Initially, analysis may appear to destroy the adaptation a patient has achieved for himself; but later he may see that this was necessary, the previous adaptation having been spurious and gained at too great a cost.

There are many modes of adaptation, varying from person to person and according to TYPOLOGY. However, excessive dependence on one particular mode of adaptation, or excessive concentration on satisfying the requirements of either the internal or the external worlds may also be seen as neurotic.

The term 'adaptation' also relates to the tension between personal and COLLECTIVE demands. Here, Jung's opinion was that this depended on the individual; some individuals need to be more 'personal', others more 'collective' (CW 7, para. 462). See UNCONSCIOUS. A good illustration of the interpenetration of internal and external, personal and collective, may be found in relationships. Adaptation to one's partner in a marriage, say, may be looked at on all those levels.

Does adaptation equal 'normality'? With regard to the 'normal' person, Jung wrote that such a 'happy blend of character' is 'ideal' and a 'rare occurrence' (CW 7, para. 80). Such a point of view is similar to Freud's which described 'normality' as an 'ideal fiction' (1937).

aetiology (of neurosis) During the period of their psychoanalytic companionship, the search for the causes of psychological disturbance led both Freud and Jung to the conclusion that the aetiology of NEUROSIS was not traceable to the impact of specific traumatic experiences alone. For instance, Jung maintained that the personal attitude of the patient could be seen as a contributing factor. More importantly, he saw that aetiology lay not only in the traumatic effects produced by real figures (e.g. parents) but also in archetypal fantasy projections as well. The relative importance of these two could be assessed analytically, he realised, and the fascination of such compelling god-like images had to be taken into account (see IMAGE; IMAGO).

Jung suggested that, viewed psychotherapeutically, there are some cases in which the real aetiology of neurotic suffering becomes apparent only at the end of treatment and that there are others where aetiology is relatively insignificant. He contested the notion that all neurosis arises in childhood and that a patient must necessarily become conscious of the aetiological factor in order to be healed.

After 1912 Jung spoke of the need for a 'final' viewpoint in contrast to Freud's 'causal' standpoint (see REDUCTIVE AND SYNTHETIC METHODS). Later research and writing, especially on the subject of INDIVIDUATION, suggests that aetiology may be of other than pathological origin and play a more positive role in the development of the individual (see TELEOLOGICAL POINT OF VIEW). He stated that in the majority of cases the root cause of neurosis is connected with a loss of MEANING and worth.

Sandner and Beebe (1982) see neurosis as springing from 'the tendency of PSYCHE to dissociate or split in face of intolerable suffering'. Wheelwright (1982) speaks of both neurosis and psychosis as 'nature's attempt to initiate growth and development', a view pursued in psychiatric research and experiment by Perry (1974, 1976).

affect Synonymous with emotion; feeling of sufficient intensity to cause nervous agitation or other obvious psychomotor disturbances. One has command over feeling, whereas affect intrudes against one's WILL and can only be repressed with difficulty. An explosion of affect is an invasion of the individual and a temporary takeover of the EGO.

Our emotions happen to us; affect occurs at the point at which our ADAPTATION is weakest and at the same time exposes the reason for its weakness. This hypothesis was central to Jung's initial experiments with the WORD ASSOCIATION TEST. A key to the discovery of a COMPLEX is an affect-laden response. Affect reveals the locus and force of psychological values. The measure of a psychic wound is the affect aroused when it is touched (see ASSOCIATION).

alchemy Jung thought that alchemy, looked at from a symbolic and not a scientific eye, could be regarded as one of the precursors of modern study of the UNCONSCIOUS and, in particular, of analytical interest in the TRANSFORMATION of personality. The alchemists projected their internal processes into what they were doing, and, as they carried out their various operations, enjoyed deep, passionate emotional experiences along with spiritual ones. Crucially, they did not attempt to split off experience from activity and in this way, too, they link with a contemporary psychological attitude, at least as interpreted retrospectively. Like ANALYTICAL PSYCHOLOGY and PSYCHOANALYSIS in their time, alchemy can be seen as a subversive and underground force: its vivid and earthy imagery contrasting with the stylised and sexless expression of mediaeval Christianity, just as psychoanalysis startled Victorian prudishness and complacency.

As far as can be reconstructed, the alchemists of the fifteenth and sixteenth centuries had two interrelated aims: (a) to alter or transform base materials into something more valuable – variously referred to as gold, or a universal elixir or the philosopher's stone; (b) to transform base matter into SPIRIT; in short, to free the SOUL. Conversely, the attempt was also made to translate what was in the alchemist's own soul into material form – his unconscious projections serving this need. These various goals may be seen as METAPHORS for psychological growth and development.

The alchemist would carefully choose elements on the basis of a schema organised in terms of OPPOSITES. This was because the attraction of opposites led to their eventual conjunction and ultimately to the production of a new substance, arising out of, but different from, the original substances. The new substance would, after chemical combination and regeneration had taken place many times and in many different ways, emerge as pure. It is the fact that such a substance does not seem to exist in nature that led Jung to see that alchemy had to be approached from a symbolic viewpoint rather than as a by now discredited pseudo-science (see SYMBOL).

This last consideration becomes particularly relevant in connection with alchemical writing. There, as in our DREAMS, we may see the various elements represented either as persons or animals, and so-called 'chemical' processes (for alchemy was also the precursor of modern chemistry) depicted in the imagery of sexual intercourse or other bodily events. For instance, the combination of two elements may be represented by male and female figures which engage in intercourse, produce a baby, join as an HERMAPHRODITE, or become an ANDROGYNE. Male and female struck the alchemists as perhaps the most fundamental opposites (or, rather, as the most fundamental representation of the existence of psychological opposites). Because the outcome of intercourse is a new entity derived but also different from the parents, we can see that human beings and their development are being used *symbolically* to refer to intrapsychic processes and the way in which an individual personality develops.

But it should not be thought that the interpersonal factor is neglected. The alchemist (usually male) worked in relation to another person (sometimes real, sometimes a fantasy figure), referred to as his *soror mystica* or mystical sister (see ANIMA). The role of the 'other' in psychological change is, by now, well known – Lacan's 'stade du miroir' (1949), Winnicott's emphasis on the mother's reflection to the infant of his integrity and worth (1967) are only two examples of this. Alchemy, therefore, straddles the interpersonal/intraphysic divide and is a METAPHOR which illuminates how a relationship with another person promotes internal growth, and also how intrapsychic processes fuel personal relations.

Alchemy becomes a pertinent metaphor when we consider the relationship of ANALYST AND PATIENT. Jung's emphasis on the dialectical process and on the issue of mutual transformation can be illustrated from alchemy (*CW* 16, 'The psychology of the transference'). In the transference, the analyst stands in relation to the patient both as a person and as a projection of an inner content – parent, problem, potential. The task of ANALYSIS is to free the 'soul' (i.e. potential) from its material prison (i.e. NEUROSIS); what the modern psychotherapist sees in his patient's human psychology, the alchemist saw in chemical form. 'Personality is a specific combination of dense depressive lead with inflammable aggressive sulphur with bitterly wise salt with volatile evasive mercury' (Hillman, 1975, p. 186).

The conceptual heart of alchemy is the differentiation of PSYCHE and matter. The extent to which psychological factors such as MEANING, purpose, emotion, can be seen as operating in the natural, physical world has to do with the analysis of projections and varies according to context (see PSYCHOID UNCONSCIOUS; SYNCHRONICITY; UNUS MUNDUS). For some, Jung's interest in alchemy may seem questionable, even disreputable, and his linking of alchemy with a key clinical concept such as transference incomprehensible. Nevertheless, apart from lending Jung a degree of emotional support in the sense that he felt a fraternity with the alchemists, alchemy enabled him to survey psychological growth and change, psychological treatment and the question of psychological ubiquity in nature from a single, though flexible, vantage point outside either medicine or RELIGION.

Jung's writings are peppered with alchemical references and a brief glossary is appended together with suggestions as to the implications of certain terms.

Adept: The alchemist, his conscious participation in the work, hence symbolic of ego and of analyst.

Coniunctio: The mating in the *vas* (see below) of the disparate elements originally placed therein. When the alchemical metaphor is applied to analysis, several different kinds of CONIUNCTIO may be noted. (a) The conscious working alliance which develops between the analyst and his analytical 'opposite' the patient; the development of a joint goal for the analysis. (b) The *coniunctio* between the patient's CONSCIOUSNESS and his unconscious as he becomes more self-aware. (c) The same process within the analyst. (d) The growing integration within the patient's unconscious of warring and conflicting tendencies to be found there. (e) The same process within the analyst. (f) The gradual merging of that which was wholly sensual or material with that which was wholly spiritual to produce a less one-sided position.

Fermentatio: Stage in the alchemical process, a brewing of the elements. In analysis, evolution of the transference-countertransference.

Hierosgamos: Literally, 'sacred marriage'. Special form of *coniunctio* in which emphasis is placed on both 'sacred' and 'marriage'; hence, a linking of the spiritual and the bodily. In Augustinian Christianity, a *hierosgamos* is said to exist between Christ and his Church, brought to fruition on the marriage bed of the cross.

Impregnatio: Stage in the alchemical process, the soul is freed from its bodily (material) prison and ascends to heaven. In analysis, changes in the patient, possibly emergence of a 'new man'.

Lapis: Philosopher's stone, goal of the alchemist. Sometimes even alchemists regard the stone as a metaphor for the goal. Hence, *lapis* speaks of self-realisation and INDIVIDUATION.

Nigredo: Stage in the alchemical process, a darkening of the elements suggesting that something of import is about to take place. In analysis, may take the form of a depression just prior to movement or the end of an initial, honeymoon period. In general, refers to confrontation with the SHADOW.

Mercurius: The God's capacity to take innumerable forms and yet remain himself is precisely what is required in psychological change. In analysis, he is described by Jung as 'the third party in the alliance' and his infuriating, impish side is balanced by his transformative propensities (*CW* 16, para.384). For the alchemists, the importance of *Mercurius* lay in the fact that he was, at one and the same time, evil, base, smelly and also divine, the God of revelation and INITIATION – a personification of the *coniunctio* (see TRICKSTER).

Mortificatio: Stage in the alchemical process, the original elements are 'dead', do not exist in their original forms. In analysis, symptoms may acquire a new meaning and the analytical relationship a new importance.

Opus: The alchemical process and work. Also life's work, i.e. INDIVIDUATION.

Prima materia (massa confusa): The original elements in state of chaos.

Putrifactio: Stage in the alchemical process, a vapour is given off by the decaying elements which is the harbinger of transformation.

Soror: Real or symbolic figure to whom the adept relates. In analysis, patient and analyst adopt these roles.

Transmutation of elements: Idea, central to alchemy, that elements can be transformed and produce a new product. See ENERGY.

Vas: Alchemical vessel. In analysis, refers to containing aspects of analytical relationship.

ambivalence Jung used this term, which was introduced by Bleuler (see PSYCHOANALYSIS), in a number of ways which are detailed and discussed below.

(1) As referring to a fusing of positive and negative feelings about the same entity (person, image, idea, part of the self). These feelings derive from the same root and not from a mixture of qualities in the person to whom they are directed. For example, infantile ambivalence towards the mother stems from the existence of loving and hating capacities within the infant and not from lovable and hateful character traits in his mother (though these would undoubtedly heighten the ambivalence). Actually, Jung's use of 'ambivalence' is often in the sense of 'bivalence'; the positive and negative polarities are clearly adhered to. This reflects the tendency in his thought to see ever greater coherence arising out of the blending of apparently disparate psychic elements (see DEPRESSIVE POSITION; OPPOSITES).

(2) Sometimes the number of contradictory feelings is permitted to exceed two. Then Jung's use of the term reflects another (perhaps the other) side of his psychological speculation: interest in the fragmentation, plurality and fluidity of the psyche. Ambivalence would then be a kind of human condition.

(3) According to Jung, every position entails its own negation and ambivalence describes this phenomenon. For example, psychic ENERGY, theoretically neutral, may be seen as potentially ambivalent, serving life and death alike. In the first half of life, psychic energy strives for growth; in the second half of life, towards a different goal (CW 5, para. 681). See DEATH INSTINCT; STAGES OF LIFE.

(4) Ambivalence is an inevitability in relation to parental imagos (see GREAT MOTHER; IMAGO) and archetypal imagery in general (see ARCHETYPE).

(5) Ambivalence is a presence in the world: 'the forces of nature are always two-faced' and God, too, as Job found (CW 5, para. 165). In life itself, 'good and EVIL, success and ruin, hope and despair, counterbalance each other' (CW 9ii, para. 24). The most potent representative of this universal theme is Hermes/Mercurius (see ALCHEMY; MYTH).

amplification Part of Jung's method for INTERPRETATION (particularly of DREAMS). By way of ASSOCIATION he tried to establish the personal context of a dream; by way of amplification he connected it with universal imagery. Amplification involves use of mythic, historical and cultural parallels in order to clarify and make ample the metaphorical content of dream symbolism (see CULTURE; FAIRY TALES; METAPHOR; MYTH; SYMBOL). Jung speaks of this as 'the psychological tissue' in which the IMAGE is embedded.

Amplification enables the dreamer to abandon a purely personal and individualistic attitude toward the dream image. It emphasises a metaphorical (hence, approximate) rather than a literal translation of dream content and prepares the dreamer to exercise choice. This is done by acknowledging what is most immediately relevant for the dreamer and then allowing for further understanding as a consequence of REFLECTION. An additional possibility, though not one specifically formulated by Jung, is that, by way of amplification, one consciously experiences oneself within and as a part of archetypal energies rather than as their object (see final paragraph below).

There are dangers in the use of amplification. One is over-intellectualisation. Another is proliferation of meanings and consequent INFLATION. Jung's view was that by way of reflection and selection a person establishes a responsible and meaningful relationship to his own UNCONSCIOUS and, by way of such a dialogue, fosters the process of INDIVIDUATION.

Jung regarded amplification as the basis of his synthetic method (see REDUCTIVE AND SYNTHETIC METHODS). He stated its aim was to make both explicit and ample what is revealed by the unconscious of the dreamer. This then enables the dreamer to see it as unique but of universal significance, a synthesis of personal and COLLECTIVE patterns. In one of his earliest attempts at a formulation of a theory of the ARCHETYPE and its connection with the method of amplification, Jung speaks of the need to break down the personal psychological system into typical components during ANALYSIS. 'Even the most individual systems are not absolutely unique', he says, 'but offer striking and unmistakable analogies with other systems' (CW 3, para. 413). Here he speaks of amplification as widening the foundation upon which the construction of an interpretation rests. Such a formulation bears a resemblance to modern ideas of reality as 'holographic', inasmuch as amplification enables differing but simultaneous perspectives (Wilber, 1982).

analysis Jungian analysis is a long-term dialectical relationship between two people, ANALYST AND PATIENT, and it is directed toward an investigation of the patient's UNCONSCIOUS, its contents and processes, in order to alleviate a psychic condition felt to be no longer tolerable because of its interferences with conscious living. The disturbance may be neurotic in character (see NEUROSIS) or a manifestation of a more deep-seated psychotic tendency (see PSYCHOSIS). While beginning with disturbance, the practice of Jungian analysis may involve individuating experiences, whether with children and young people or persons in the second half of life (see STAGES OF LIFE), but these experiences may or may not be connected in such a way that a process of INDIVIDUATION can be said to occur. Distinguishing between analysis and PSYCHOTHERAPY, practising analysts have differentiated between the two on the basis of intensity, depth, frequency of sessions and duration of the work, coupled with a realistic assessment of the psychological capacities and limitations of the patient.

Among his own definitions (CW 6), Jung did not include one of analysis, but his original methodological model was PSYCHOANALYSIS. After the break with Freud in 1913, Jung introduced significant changes in this structure, changes consistent with his own experience and formulation of concepts. His personal point of view coloured his use of technique (for example, his preference for conversation conducted 'face to face'). When later analytical psychologists have deviated from his practices, they have had to reformulate ideas in support of their own procedures (see ANALYTICAL PSYCHOLOGY).

Jung's disagreements with the assumptions of psychoanalysis may be summarised as follows: (1) he saw much that happens as a play of OPPOSITES and from this perspective he derived his view of PSYCHIC ENERGY. This led to his insistence upon an analytic method which he called 'synthetic', since it eventually resulted in a synthesis of opposing psychological principles (see REDUCTIVE AND SYNTHETIC METHODS); (2) although he purported not to doubt that instincts motivated psychic life, he saw them as continually 'colliding' with something other which, for want of a better term, he called 'spirit'. He identified SPIRIT as an archetypal force personally encountered in the form of images. As a consequence, Jungian analysis involves work with archetypal imagery (see ARCHETYPE); (3) by his own admission, Jung preferred to 'look at a man in the light of what in him is healthy and sound rather than in light of his defects' (CW 4, paras 773–4). This accounts for his adoption of a prospective or TELEOLOGICAL POINT OF VIEW in analysis; (4) his attitude toward RELIGION was a positive one. While this does not necessarily lead to an emphasis upon religion itself, attention is given to the demands of the SELF as well as to the demands of EGO and implicit is the assumption that the experience of analysis is closely linked with the discovery of MEANING.

In addition to these differences set forth by Jung himself, Henderson (1982) has noted Jung's reliance upon MYTHOLOGY and universal myth-related patterns, his introduction of a dialectical procedure in contrast to Freud's model of 'closed-system analysis', a view of REGRESSION that goes beyond service to the ego but can also be seen in service to the self, a primarily symbolic method in which one is connected with archetypal sources of imagery by means of AMPLIFICATION and an analysis of transference/countertransference phenomena by way of the symbolic method.

Writing in 1929, Jung identified four aspects of analysis which he considered as 'stages' of analytical treatment. Lambert (1981) and M. Stein (1982) have pointed out that the four stages are not necessarily sequential but characterise various aspects of analytical work.

The first of the four stages is *catharsis* or cleansing (see ABREACTION). Jung spoke of this as the scientific application of an ancient practice, namely confession, and connected it with rites and practices of INITIATION. To unburden one's self to another human being breaks through personal defences and neurotic isolation; hence, preparing the way for a new stage of growth and a different status.

Jung identified the second stage as *elucidation*. Here, ties to unconscious processes are revealed and an awareness of this brings about a marked change of attitude, involving the individual in the SACRIFICE of the supremacy of his conscious intellect.

The third stage is *education* or a 'drawing forth' of the patient in response to new possibilities, similar to the psychoanalytic idea of working through – the often lengthy process of INTEGRATION.

The fourth stage is that of TRANSFORMATION. Transformation should not be thought of as connected with the patient only, however. The analyst must also change or transform his attitudes in order to be capable of interaction with his changing patient.

analyst and patient   Jung was emphatic that the analytical relationship was not to be viewed in terms of a medical or technical procedure. He referred to ANALYSIS as a 'dialectical process', implying that both participants are equally involved and that there is a two-way interaction between them. Thus the analyst cannot simply use whatever authority he might possess, for he is 'in' the treatment just as much as the patient and it will be his development as a person rather than his knowledge that will be decisive. For this reason, Jung was the first to initiate a compulsory training analysis for those wishing to practise (CW 4, para. 536; Freud, 1912). Jung's stress on equality is somewhat idealistic and it may be preferable to think in terms of analytical mutuality, to acknowledge the emotional involvement of the analyst while knowing that the roles of the two persons are not identical.

In Jung's conception, the analyst takes a flexible attitude towards the progress of the treatment and the evolution of the analytical relationship. Here again, the idealism needs to be tempered and Jung himself contributes to this with his idea that there are, typically, four stages to an analysis. What is highlighted, though, is the need to learn from the patient and adapt to his PSYCHIC REALITY.

From these remarks, it can be seen that Jung has underscored what would now be called the real relationship or therapeutic alliance of analyst and patient. This can be distinguished from transference and countertransference which are discussed below. In contemporary psychoanalysis, a similar movement has taken place so that the 'non-neurotic, rational, reasonable, rapport which the patient has with his analyst and which enables him to work purposefully in the analytic situation' is separately identified (Greenson and Wexler, 1969).

Jung's attitude to *transference* shows wide variance. On the one hand, transference is seen as the central feature of analysis, in any case unavoidable, and, in its blend of the sublime and the revolting, of great therapeutic usefulness (CW 16, paras 283–4, 358, 371). On the other hand, transference is sometimes conceived of as nothing but erotic and as a 'hindrance': 'you cure in spite of transference and not because of it.' This divided attitude of Jung's is reflected in the various schools of analytical psychology which have evolved since Jung's death in 1961. Some analysts regard transference analysis as a diversion from the more important elucidation of the symbolic content of the patient's material. Others see that, in the analysis of transference, they may meet those infantile traumas or deprivations which are still at work in their adult patients. Hence, the latter group do not seek to dissolve transference in favour of 'reality' but rather to allow it to deepen and to be worked with and within. Recently, it seems that this divide has become less marked than hitherto, as practitioners sense that content analysis (symbols) and process analysis (transference) are two sides of a single coin.

There are important differences of emphasis between the concept of transference which has evolved in analytical psychology and that of psychoanalysis. Jung separated transference into its personal and archetypal components in much the same way as he wrote of the personal and the collective UNCONSCIOUS. Personal transference included, not only those aspects of the patient's relationship to figures from the past such as parents which he projects onto the analyst, but also his individual potential and his SHADOW (see IMAGO; PROJECTION). That is, the analyst represents and holds for the patient parts of his psyche which have not yet developed as fully as they might and also aspects of the patient's personality he would rather disown.

Archetypal transference has two meanings. First, those transference projections which are not based on the personal, outer-world experience of the patient. For example, on the basis of unconscious fantasy the analyst may be seen as a magical healer or a threatening devil and this image will have a force greater than a derivation from ordinary experience would provide (see ARCHETYPE; MANA PERSONALITIES).

The second aspect of archetypal transference refers to the generally expectable events of analysis, to what the enterprise itself does to the relationship of analyst and patient. This pattern can be illustrated in schematic form, adapted from a diagram of Jung's (CW 16, para. 422).

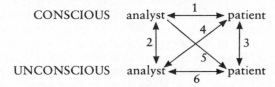

The double-headed arrows indicate a two-way communication and relatedness. (1) refers to the treatment alliance. (2) reflects the fact that, in analysis, the analyst both draws on his own unconscious for an understanding of his patient and also encounters whatever it is that has made him a WOUNDED HEALER. His own analysis will have made its impact here. (3) represents the patient's initial stage of awareness of his problems, interrupted by his resistance and his devotion to his PERSONA. (4) and (5) indicate the impact of the analytical relationship upon the unconscious life of each participant, an intermingling of personalities which will lead each to some kind of confrontation with the possibility of personal change. (6) proposes a direct communication between the unconscious of the analyst and that of the patient. This last hypothesis underpins various ideas about countertransference (see below). Jung felt that in ALCHEMY he had found a pertinent and potent METAPHOR for this aspect of archetypal transference.

Jung was one of the pioneers of the therapeutic use of countertransference. Until the 1950s, psychoanalysts, following Freud, tended to regard countertransference as invariably neurotic, an activation of the analyst's infantile conflicts and an obstacle to his functioning (Freud, 1910; 1913). In 1929, Jung wrote: 'You can exert no influence if you are not susceptible to influence ... The patient influences [the analyst] unconsciously ... One of the best known symptoms of this kind is the counter-transference evoked by the transference' (*CW* 16, para. 163). In sum, Jung regarded countertransference as 'a highly important organ of information' for an analyst (*ibid.*). Jung accepted that some countertransferences were not so benign, referring to 'psychic infection' and the dangers of identifying with the patient (*CW* 16, paras 358, 365).

Contemporary analytical psychology has deepened this interest of Jung's in countertransference. Fordham (1957) proposed that an analyst may be so in tune with his patient's inner world that he finds himself feeling or behaving in a way which he can see, with later understanding, is but an extension of his patient's intrapsychic processes projected into him. Fordham called this 'syntonic' countertransference. He contrasted that with 'illusory' countertransference (meaning neurotic responses to the patient on the part of the analyst). The central feature of this approach, and its similarity with present-day psychoanalysis, is that the analyst's emotions and behaviour become as much the object of scrutiny as the patient's (cf. Heimann, 1950; Langs, 1978; Little, 1957; Searles, 1968).

Jung's attitude to the patient's REGRESSION is of interest. He contended that analysis may have to support such regression to a very primitive form of functioning. Following that, psychological growth may be resumed. This can be contrasted with Freud's rather more stringent attitude – something which more recent psychoanalysts have redressed (Balint, 1968).

analytical psychology In 1913, the year when Jung left the psychoanalytic movement, he used the term 'analytical psychology' to identify what he called a new psychological science seen by him as having evolved out of PSYCHOANALYSIS. At a later date, when he was firmly established in his own right, he referred to the 'psychoanalytic method' of Freud and the 'individual psychology' of Adler, and said that he preferred to call his own approach 'analytical psychology' by which he meant a general concept embracing both, as well as other endeavours.

In the early days of analytic investigation, at the turn of the century, Bleuler had suggested the term DEPTH PSYCHOLOGY be used to indicate that this psychology was concerned with the deeper regions of the psyche, i.e. the UNCONSCIOUS. Jung found the term limiting because even then he saw his method as a symbolic one concerned as much with consciousness as with the unconscious (see SYMBOL).

Toni Wolff's term 'complex psychology' is not currently used because it emphasises only a limited, though primary, segment of Jung's conceptualisation.

Jung always asserted that his psychology was a science and empirically based. Therefore, in general usage today, analytical psychology embraces theory, writing and research as well as psychotherapeutic practice. The international professional association of Jungian analysts is called the International Association for Analytical Psychology.

Jung's statements on theory and method are now compiled and available in some twenty volumes of the *Collected Works* along with separate collections of correspondence, remembrances and interviews, as well as biographical writings. A short definition or précis of each of the main ideas of analytical psychology was printed as part of *Psychological Types* in 1921. These include the definitions of psychic ENERGY which Jung saw as having its source in the instincts, otherwise being comparable to and governed by the same principles as physical energy, with the exception that psychic energy has not only a cause but also an aim; the UNCONSCIOUS viewed as complementary to CONSCIOUSNESS and functioning both as a repository of former personal experiences as well as universal images (see ARCHETYPE; SYMBOL), referring to the way in which the unconscious communicates itself to consciousness, revealing the latent imagery which underlies and motivates an individual by way of the COMPLEX and evident in attitudes, actions, choices and DREAMS as well as illnesses; the human PSYCHE constellated in sub-personalities or archetypal representations (see PERSONIFICATION) identifiable as PERSONA, EGO, SHADOW, ANIMA, ANIMUS, WISE OLD MAN, GREAT MOTHER and the SELF; finally, INDIVIDUATION, seen as the process which in the course of a lifetime leads a person to a unification of his personality which is expressive of his basic wholeness. These are the underlying precepts upon which a psychotherapy has developed which employs a *synthetic* and hermeneutic as opposed to a *reductive* approach (see ANALYSIS; ANALYST AND PATIENT; REDUCTIVE AND SYNTHETIC METHODS).

Jung also wrote extensively in the field of the psychology of religion. At different times in his life he was interested in paranormal phenomena, individual TYPOLOGY, and ALCHEMY as well as other more widespread cultural subjects. Hence, analytical psychology has become a term of wide-ranging application as well as of professional significance.

androgyne A psychic PERSONIFICATION which holds male and female in conscious balance. In this figure the principles of male and female are conjoined without merger of characteristics. It was this metaphorical being and not the undifferentiated HERMAPHRODITE that Jung saw as symbolising the end product of the alchemical process. The IMAGE of the androgyne is, therefore, relevant to ANALYSIS, most especially in relation to work with ANIMA AND ANIMUS. In alchemical treatises there are not only references but frequent illustrations of this figure (see ALCHEMY). More than once, Jung drew attention to the historical person of Jesus as an example of one in whom the tension and polarity of sexual DIFFERENTIATION had been resolved in androgynous complementarity and unity.

The most comprehensive work on the androgyne is by Singer (1976). See CONIUNCTIO; GENDER; SEX.

anima and animus   The inner figure of woman held by a man and the figure of man at work in a woman's psyche. Though unlike in the ways in which they manifest, anima and animus have certain characteristics in common. Both are psychic IMAGES. Each is a configuration arising from a basic archetypal structure (see ARCHETYPE). As the fundamental forms which underlie the 'feminine' aspects of man and the 'masculine' aspects of woman, they are seen as OPPOSITES. As psychic components, they are subliminal to consciousness and function from within the unconscious psyche; hence, they are of benefit to but also can endanger consciousness by POSSESSION (see below). They operate in relation to the dominant *psychic principle* of a man or a woman and not simply, as is commonly suggested, as the contrasexual psychological counterpart of maleness or femaleness, however. They act as PSYCHOPOMPI or guides of soul and they can become necessary links with creative possibilities and instruments of INDIVIDUATION.

Because of their archetypal connections, anima and animus have been represented in many COLLECTIVE forms and figures: as Aphrodite, Athena, Helen of Troy, Mary, Sapientia and Beatrice; or as Hermes, Apollo, Hercules, Alexander the Great, Romeo. In projection, they attract attention and emotional fervour as public figures but also as friends, lovers, commonplace and ordinary wives and husbands. We meet them as consorts in our dreams. As personified components of PSYCHE they connect and involve us with life (see PERSONIFICATION). Complete realisation and integration of either image requires partnership with the opposite sex. The disentanglement and recognition of aspects of this SYZYGY between ANALYST AND PATIENT is a primary task in ANALYSIS.

Among his definitions (CW 6), Jung summarised anima/animus as 'soul-images'. He later elucidated this statement by calling each the not-I. Being not-I for a man most probably corresponds to something feminine and, because it is not-I, it is outside himself, belonging to his soul or spirit. The anima (or animus, as the case may be), is a factor which happens to one, an *a priori* element of moods, reactions, impulses in man; of commitments, beliefs, inspirations in a woman – and for both something that prompts one to take cognisance of whatever is spontaneous and meaningful in psychic life. Behind the animus, Jung asserted, lies 'the archetype of *meaning*; just as the anima is the archetype of life *itself*' (CW 9i, para. 66).

These concepts were devised empirically and enabled Jung to give coherence to a wide range of observable psychic phenomena and to differentiate it further when working with analysands. In analysis, separation of anima or animus is closely connected with the initial work of making conscious the SHADOW. The original images are illustrative of semi-conscious psychic COMPLEXES, autonomous and largely independent PERSONIFICATIONS until they acquire solidity, influence, and, finally CONSCIOUSNESS by encounter with the everyday world. Jung warned against conceptualising only (thereby losing touch with anima/animus as living forces) or to work in a manner which denies the PSYCHIC REALITY of such inner figures.

Possession by either anima or animus transforms the personality in such a way as to give prominence to those traits which are seen as *psychologically* characteristic of the opposite sex. Either way, a person loses individuality, first of all, and then in either case, both charm and values. In a man, he becomes dominated by anima and by the EROS principle with connotations of restlessness, promiscuity, moodiness, sentimentality – whatever could be described as unconstrained emotionality. A woman subject to the authority of animus and LOGOS is managerial, obstinate, ruthless, domineering. Both become one-sided. He is seduced by inferior people and forms meaningless attachments; she, being taken in by second-rate thinking, marches forward under the banner of unrelated convictions.

Speaking in non-professional terms, Jung said that men accepted the anima readily enough when she appeared in a novel or as a film star. But it was a different matter when it came to seeing the role she played in their own lives.

Had he made a corresponding statement on the animus, he might have said that until recently women have been only too ready and prone to let men do their fighting for them, secretly hoping for deliverance by a knight on a white charger. But now that it has come to their accepting their places not *as* men but alongside men, it is a different matter. Wanting to enjoy equal status, but, at the same time desiring to remain true to their identity as women, they have to come to terms with who is really boss in their lives and unmask their own sources of authority.

Hillman (1972, 1975) has investigated and elucidated anima psychology. He insists that it is she who personifies the unconsciousness of our entire Western culture and may be the image by which we will be liberated imaginatively.

There is no up-to-date work of corresponding depth on the animus. Moreover, because of the unfortunate connotations of animus possession that may have characterised pioneering women in a male-dominated society, very little attention has been given to the psychic interventions of the so-called positive or natural animus in contrast to the negative and acquired animus (Ulanov, 1981).

anxiety In Jung's use of the term, particular features may be distinguished:
(a) not all anxiety has a sexual base (see PSYCHOANALYSIS);
(b) anxiety can have a positive aspect by drawing a person's attention to an undesirable state of affairs;
(c) anxiety may be seen as an avoidance of becoming conscious of suffering.

There is little doubt that Jung did not deal adequately with the various defensive processes employed by the EGO to ward off anxiety. This may be partially attributed to his equating of 'ego' with 'CONSCIOUSNESS'. This meant that the possibility that parts of the ego's structure are themselves UNCONSCIOUS is not entertained. It is these unconscious ego defences which deal with anxiety. Also, because of his insistence that the content of a specific COMPLEX is more important than the name we give to the complex, Jung's work shows no parallel to Freud's discussions of the different kinds of anxiety. Anxiety for Jung always has a personal interpretation and significance.

apperception A process by which a new psychic content (recognition, evaluation, intuition, sense perception) is articulated in such a way that it becomes understood, apprehended or 'clear'. It is an inner faculty which represents external things as perceived by the registering, responding PSYCHE; therefore, the result is always a mixture of reality and fantasy, a blend of personal experience and archetypal IMAGO (see ARCHETYPE).

Jung distinguished between two modes of apperception, *active* and *passive*. The first, whereby the subject consciously decides to apprehend a new content, is initiated by the EGO. The other happens to the subject when a content intrudes upon his awareness and forces apprehension, as often occurs with dreams. Whether active or passive, the process is the same, however, involving the participation of the subject, willingly or unwillingly, and demanding REFLECTION. Jung also identified states of *directed* and *undirected* apperception corresponding to the degree of rational ego participation or irrational fantasy involvement in the operation (see DIRECTED AND FANTASY THINKING).

archetype   The inherited part of the PSYCHE; structuring patterns of psychological performance linked to INSTINCT; a hypothetical entity irrepresentable in itself and evident only through its manifestations.

Jung's theory of the archetypes developed in three stages. In 1912 he wrote of primordial images which he recognised in the unconscious life of his patients as well as by way of his own self-analysis. These images were similar to motifs repeated everywhere and throughout history but their main features were their numinosity, unconsciousness and autonomy (see NUMINOSUM). As conceived by Jung, the collective UNCONSCIOUS promotes such images. By 1917, he was writing of non-personal dominants or nodal points in the psyche which attract energy and influence a person's functioning. It was in 1919 that he first made use of the term archetype and he did so to avoid any suggestion that it was the content and not the unconscious and irrepresentable outline or pattern that was fundamental. References are made to the archetype *per se* to be clearly distinguished from an archetypal IMAGE realisable (or realised) by man.

The archetype is a psychosomatic concept, linking body and psyche, instinct and image. This was important for Jung since he did not regard psychology and imagery as correlates or reflections of biological drives. His assertion that images evoke the aim of the instincts implies that they deserve equal place.

Archetypes are recognisable in outer behaviours, especially those that cluster around the basic and universal experiences of life such as birth, marriage, motherhood, death and separation. They also adhere to the structure of the human psyche itself and are observable in relation to inner or psychic life, revealing themselves by way of such inner figures as ANIMA, SHADOW, PERSONA and so forth. Theoretically, there could be any number of archetypes.

Archetypal patterns wait to be realised in the personality, are capable of infinite variation, are dependent upon individual expression and exercise a fascination reinforced by traditional or cultural expectation; and, so, carry a strong, potentially overpowering charge of energy which it is difficult to resist (someone's ability to do so being dependent upon his stage of development and state of CONSCIOUSNESS). Archetypes arouse AFFECT, blind one to realities and take possession of WILL. To live archetypally is to live without limitations (INFLATION). To give archetypal expression to something, however, may be to interact consciously with the COLLECTIVE, historic image in such a way as to allow opportunities for the play of intrinsic polarities: past and present, personal and collective, typical and unique (see OPPOSITES).

All psychic imagery partakes of the archetypal to some extent. That is why dreams and many other psychic phenomena have numinosity. Archetypal behaviours are most evident at times of crisis, when the EGO is most vulnerable. Archetypal qualities are found in SYMBOLS and this accounts in part for their fascination, utility and recurrence. GODS are METAPHORS of archetypal behaviours and MYTHS are archetypal ENACTMENTS. The archetypes can neither be fully integrated nor lived out in human form. Analysis involves a growing awareness of the archetypal dimensions of a person's life.

Jung's concept of the archetype is in the tradition of Platonic Ideas which are present in the minds of the gods and serve as the models of all entities in the human realm. Kant's *a priori* categories of perception and Schopenhauer's prototypes are also antecedents.

In 1934 Jung wrote:

> The ground principles, the *archetypoi*, of the unconscious are indescribable because of their wealth of reference, although in themselves recognisable. The discriminating intellect naturally keeps on trying to establish their singleness of meaning and thus misses the essential point; for what we can above all establish as the one thing consistent with their nature is their *manifold meaning*, their almost limitless wealth of reference, which makes any unilateral formulation impossible (*CW* 9i, para. 80).

Ellenberger (1970) identified the archetype as one of the three main conceptual differences between Jung and Freud in defining the content and behaviour of the unconscious. Following Jung, Neumann (1954) saw the archetypes recurring in each generation but also acquiring a history of forms based upon a widening of human consciousness. Hillman, founder of the school of Archetypal Psychology, cites the concept of archetype as the most fundamental in Jung's work, referring to these deepest premises of psychic functioning as delineating how we perceive and relate to the world (1975). Williams argued that, since the archetypal structure remains skeletal without personal experience to flesh it out, the distinction between personal and collective dimensions of experience or categories of the unconscious might be somewhat academic (1963a).

Notions of innate psychological structure exist in present-day psychoanalysis, notably in the Kleinian school: Isaacs (unconscious fantasy), Bion (preconception), and Money-Kyrle (cf. Money-Kyrle, 1978). Jung's theory of the archetypes may also be compared to structuralist thought (Samuels, 1985a).

With increasing use of the term, we meet frequent references to such phenomena as 'a necessary shift in the paternal archetype' or 'the shifting archetype of femininity'. The word was included in the Fontana *Dictionary of Modern Thought* in 1977. The biologist Sheldrake finds relevance between Jung's formulation and his theory of 'morphogenetic fields' (1981).

association   The spontaneous linkage of ideas, perceptions, images, fantasies according to certain personal and psychological themes, motifs, similarities, oppositions or causalities. The word may designate the process of making such linkages (i.e. *by* association) or specify one item in such a chain (i.e. *an* association). Jung and Freud made different uses of association in dream interpretation and, at the outset of his career, Jung conducted extensive researches on association by way of the WORD ASSOCIATION TEST.

Associations, however freely arrived at, are seen to be psychologically bonded in meaningful sequence. This discovery, reached by means of researches made by others at the end of the last century, led to Freud's use of 'free association' in dream interpretation and Jung's applied researches using the word association test. This experimental work laid the basis for Jung's theory of the ARCHETYPES. Throughout his working life as an analyst he continued to use his own technique of association for the INTERPRETATION OF DREAMS.

Freud's initial work on hysteria led him to conclude: (1) random or free associations were seen as invariably referring back, whether consciously or not, to early experience and were linked so as to form memory networks; (2) he saw these networks or systems as organised into complexes of ideas split off from the psychic organism in such a way that consciousness of any particular association in a chain of associations might not necessarily imply a consciousness of the psychological meaning of the chain as a whole; (3) the force or energy charge of any one element or association condenses around a central nodal point; (4) such factors underlie the psychic conflicts specific to a person's *own* psychology.

Jung became acquainted with these ideas and during the period that he worked at the Burghölzli mental hospital (1900–1909) his main objective with the word association test was to detect and analyse the COMPLEX, a focus that led to a suggestion that his work be called 'Complex Psychology' (see ANALYTICAL PSYCHOLOGY). Initially, Jung explored his interest by way of associations. The main outcome of this was the verification of a linkage between association, AFFECT and ENERGY charge.

Though Jung soon abandoned experimental researches, he continued to work with and refine his understanding of association, aiming at 'a careful and conscious illumination of the inter-connecting associations objectively grouped round particular images' (CW 16, para. 319). These insights were later applied and became an integral foundation for his method of dream interpretation. He described the web of associations as the psychological context in which a dream is naturally embedded.

Jung maintained that proceeding by way of the patient's own associations was the opposite of interpretation by theory, because it requires the most careful, continuing attentiveness to a person's individual associative network. He compared such interpretative work to the translation of a text which permits one to enter a secret or well-guarded domain (i.e. the person's own psychic realm). Where there was resistance and blocking, Jung's method was to return again and again to associations surrounding the IMAGE of which the patient was both aware and unaware rather than to interpret the blockage. In this way he sought to make conscious the individual emotional context of the dream imagery (see IMAGO).

Jung's work on association was primary in establishing his theory of archetypes but in PSYCHOTHERAPY, he said, the individual complex and not archetypal knowledge is the goal. In ANALYSIS, association may be widened by application to universal themes by way of AM-PLIFICATION. This may be seen as an extension of the associative process to include an historical, cultural and mythological context and, thereby, both the universal archetypal pattern *and* the personal complex become evident during the process of association (see MYTH).

Assumption of the Virgin Mary, Proclamation of Dogma That the Blessed Virgin Mary, having completed her earthly life, was in body and soul assumed into heaven was proclaimed as dogmatic truth by Pope Pius XII in 1950.

Jung welcomed the Proclamation. In it he saw the elevation of the Christian version of the mother ARCHETYPE to the rank of dogma (CW 9i, para. 195). He felt it had been prepared for in popular imagination, reinforced by selective VISIONS and so-called revelations since the Middle Ages and most especially during the century preceding the Proclamation. Such phenomena represented to him the urge of the archetype to realise itself, an urge which in this instance culminated in the conscious and unavoidable issuance of the papal bull.

The proclamation could also be seen as a recognition and acknowledgment of *matter*, occurring at a time when the spiritual and psychic heritage of man was threatened with annihilation, he felt. Symbolically, this added a fourth, a feminine principle to what he saw as the essentially masculine Trinity. Not being divine initially, the Virgin Mary represents BODY and her presence thus heals the split between the OPPOSITES of matter and SPIRIT. She is seen as mediatrix, fulfilling in the divine IMAGE the role that the feminine ANIMA assumes in the human psyche. Her presence unites, he said, heterogeneous and incommensurate factors in a single image of WHOLENESS.

B

body There is a paradox in Jung's writings about the body. On the one hand, the body is seen as something in its own right, with its own ways, needs, joys and problems. On the other hand, the body is also seen as inextricably linked with mind, or with SPIRIT, and with PSYCHE.

Jung's later theories about the ARCHETYPE argued for a psychosomatic explanation. Archetypes may be seen as linking body (INSTINCT) and psyche (IMAGE). Instincts and images have the same PSYCHOID root. Hence, rather than devaluing body, Jung felt that his ideas revalued it and gave a new slant to the relationship of an individual to COLLECTIVE psychology.

The latter could be understood as expressing itself in and through the body which, because common to all, may be regarded in general terms as the locus of the collective UNCONSCIOUS (Stevens, 1982). Later writers (e.g. Henry, 1977) have taken Jung's hint seriously and have attempted to site the archetypes in the older, so-called 'reptilian' brain (the hypothalamus and brain stem). Similarly, Rossi (1977) argued that the bodily location of the archetypes lay in the right cerebral hemisphere.

Jung's own focus was somewhat different. The body may be regarded as an expression of the 'physical materiality of the psyche' (CW 9i, para. 392). What the body does, experiences, needs – all these reflect psychological imperatives. The body may then be regarded as a 'subtle body'. One example of the psychological import of bodily images may be found in motifs of resurrection or REBIRTH. Another would be the way sexual imagery has its own psychological meaning (see ANDROGYNE; INCEST; INFANCY AND CHILDHOOD).

Many aspects of the SHADOW are concentrated in the body. Jung wrote of 'Christian denial' concerning these. He discusses what is meant by an instinctual life and concludes that if a person tries to live exclusively through the body then he is unconsciously in the grip of spirit. Jung's position was that Nietzsche and Freud both fitted that description. An acceptance of the body, not one which is driven or compulsive, is different – and absolutely necessary for psychological development and INDIVIDUATION.

Contemporary analytical psychologists have emphasised connections between an infant's capacity to manage his bodily impulses, mediated and made sense of by the mother, and an evolving attitude toward him or herself and the SELF (Newton and Redfearn, 1977).

brain   See BODY.

C

catharsis   See ABREACTION; ANALYSIS.

causality   See AETIOLOGY (OF NEUROSIS); DEPTH PSYCHOLOGY; REDUCTIVE AND SYNTHETIC METHODS; SYNCHRONICITY; TELEOLOGICAL POINT OF VIEW.

circumambulation   Circumambulation means not only a circular movement but also the marking of a sacred precinct around a central point. Psychologically, Jung defined it as concentration upon and occupation with a point conceived as the centre of a circle. By AMPLIFICATION, he came to see this as a wheel motif, which suggested to him the containment of the EGO in the greater dimension of the SELF (CW 9ii, para. 352). He found the process reflected in the transformation symbolism of the mass as well as in the Buddhist MANDALA. He interpreted a clockwise movement as being in the direction of consciousness and a counter-clockwise circumambulation as a spiralling downward in the direction of the UNCONSCIOUS.

Circumambulatio was an alchemical term also used for a concentration upon the centre or place of creative change. The defined circle or TEMENOS is a metaphor for the containment necessary during ANALYSIS in order to withstand the tensions produced by the meeting of OPPOSITES and to prevent consequent psychotic disruption and disintegration. Manifesting unconscious processes, DREAMS can be observed to circumambulate or rotate around a point. Neumann (1954) substituted the term *centroversion* for circumambulation when applied as a principle of psychic INTEGRATION.

collective   The many in contrast to the one. From the distinction between CONSCIOUSNESS and the UNCONSCIOUS made by the forerunners of the psychoanalytic movement, Jung developed his own theories of the collective unconscious as the repository of man's psychic heritage and possibilities (see ARCHETYPE). He viewed the collective as the opposite of the individual, that from which the individual must differentiate himself as well as a repository of all that may have been at some time individually expressed, adapted or influenced.

The more a person becomes him or herself, i.e. the more he submits to INDIVIDUATION, the more distinctly he will vary from collective norms, standards, precepts, mores and values. Although he partakes of the collective as a member of SOCIETY and a particular CULTURE, he represents a unique combination of the potentials inherent in the collective as a whole. Such development and differentiation Jung saw as instinctive and essential. Although he supported his claim empirically, his position led him to adopt a TELEOLOGICAL POINT OF VIEW in relation to this.

When the collective is regarded as a reservoir of psychic possibilities, it is a gargantuan force capable of fostering grandiose delusions and mass psychoses. The opposite of individuality Jung viewed as IDENTIFICATION with the collective ideal, leading to INFLATION and ultimately to megalomania. He believed the real carrier of change to be the individual, since the mass as a whole is incapable of consciousness.

collective unconscious   See ARCHETYPE; COLLECTIVE; UNCONSCIOUS.

compensation   Jung asserted that he found an empirically demonstrable compensatory function operative in psychological processes. This corresponded to the self-regulatory (homeostatic) functions of the organism observable in the physiological sphere. Compensation means balancing, adjusting, supplementing. He regarded the compensatory activity of the UNCONSCIOUS as balancing any tendency towards one-sidedness on the part of CONSCIOUSNESS.

Contents repressed, excluded and inhibited by the conscious orientation of the individual lapse into unconsciousness and there form a counter-pole to consciousness. This counter-position strengthens with any increase of emphasis upon the conscious attitude until it interferes with the activity of consciousness itself. Finally, repressed unconscious contents gather a sufficient energy charge to break through in the form of DREAMS, spontaneous IMAGES or symptoms. The objective of the compensatory process seems to be to link, as with a bridge, two psychological worlds. That bridge is the SYMBOL; though symbols, if they are to be effective, must be acknowledged and understood by the conscious mind, i.e. assimilated and integrated (see EGO; TRANSCENDENT FUNCTION).

Normally, compensation is an unconscious regulator of conscious activity but where there is neurotic disturbance, the unconscious appears in such stark contrast to the conscious state that the compensatory process itself is disrupted (see NEUROSIS). If an immature aspect of the psyche is heavily repressed, the unconscious content overwhelms the conscious aim and destroys its intention. 'The aim of analytical therapy, therefore, is a realisation of unconscious contents in order that compensation may be re-established' (CW 6, para. 693 ff.). See ANALYSIS.

The standpoint of unconsciousness, being compensatory, will always be unexpected and appear differently from the point of view taken by consciousness. As Jung wrote, 'every process that goes too far immediately and inevitably calls forth compensations' (CW 16, para. 330). (See ENANTIODROMIA.) Therefore, we find evidence of compensation in such an obvious assertion as the infant's tantrum but also in such relatively sophisticated manifestations as those involved in the relationship of ANALYST AND PATIENT. Of this Jung observed: 'the intensified tie to the analyst is a compensation for the patient's faulty attitude to reality. This tie is what we mean by the transference' (CW 16, para. 282).

Extending the principle still further, and applying it collectively, Jung found in ALCHEMY a form of compensation for the point of view expressed in mediaeval Christianity. Alchemy can be seen as an endeavour to fill in (i.e. compensate) the gaps left by conventional religion. Because of this, analysts need to be careful lest they apply alchemical symbolism indiscriminately or consider it relevant without exception, especially in cases where there may have been a notable advance attributable to changes in the consciousness of the COLLECTIVE. In regard to INDIVIDUATION, a person must discriminate whether compensatory contents are related to his own individuality or merely appear as a balance to the other end of a spectrum of OPPOSITES.

In his remarks made at the time of the founding of the C. G. Jung Institute in Zurich, Jung challenged future analysts to undertake research into the *processes of compensation in psychotics and criminals*, and, in general, into the *goal of compensation* and *the nature of its directiveness* (CW 18, para. 1138). This is not a challenge which has been widely taken up. (See, however, Perry, 1974; Kraemer, 1976; Guggenbühl-Craig, 1980.)

complex The notion of a complex rests on a refutation of monolithic ideas of 'personality'. We have many selves, as we know from experience (see SELF). Though it is a considerable step from this to regarding a complex as an autonomous entity within the psyche,

Jung asserted that 'complexes behave like independent beings' (*CW* 8, para. 253). He also argued that 'there is no difference in principle between a fragmentary personality and a complex ... complexes are splinter psyches' (*CW* 8, para. 202).

A complex is a collection of images and ideas, clustered round a core derived from one or more archetypes, and characterised by a common emotional tone. When they come into play (become 'constellated'), complexes contribute to behaviour and are marked by AFFECT whether a person is conscious of them or not. They are particularly useful in the analysis of neurotic symptoms.

The idea was so important to Jung that, at one point, he considered labelling his ideas 'Complex Psychology' (see ANALYTICAL PSYCHOLOGY). Jung referred to the complex as the '*via regia* to the unconscious' and as 'the architect of dreams'. This would suggest that DREAMS and other symbolic manifestations are closely related to complexes.

The concept enabled Jung to link the personal and archetypal components of an individual's various experiences. In addition, without such a concept, it would be difficult to express just how experience is built up; psychological life would be a series of unconnected incidents. Furthermore, according to Jung, complexes also affect memory. The 'father complex' not only holds within it an archetypal image of father but also an aggregate of all interactions with father over time (see IMAGO). Hence the father complex colours recall of early experiences of the actual father.

Inasmuch as it has an archetypal aspect, the EGO also sits at the heart of an ego-complex, a personalised history of the individual's development of consciousness and self-awareness. The ego-complex is in a relationship with the other complexes which often involves it in conflict. It is then that there is a risk of this or any complex splitting off so that the personality is dominated by it. A complex may overwhelm the ego (as in PSYCHOSIS) or the ego may identify with the complex (see INFLATION; POSSESSION).

It is also important to remember that complexes are quite natural phenomena which develop along positive as well as negative lines. They are necessary ingredients of psychic life. Provided the ego can establish a viable relationship with a complex, a richer and more variegated personality emerges. For instance, patterns of personal relationship may alter as perceptions of others undergo shifts.

Jung developed his ideas via the use of the WORD ASSOCIATION TEST between 1904 and 1911 (see ASSOCIATION). The use of a psychogalvonometer in the test suggests that complexes are rooted in the body and express themselves somatically (see BODY; PSYCHE).

Though the discovery of complexes was of considerable value to

Freud as an empirical proof of his concept of the UNCONSCIOUS, few psychoanalysts now use the term. However, much psychoanalytic theory makes use of the concept of complex, particularly the structural theory – ego, super-ego and id are examples of complexes. Other systems of therapy such as Transactional Analysis and Gestalt Therapy also sub-divide the patient's psychology and/or encourage him to dialogue with relatively autonomous parts of himself.

Some psychoanalytic commentators have suggested that Jung's stress upon the *autonomy* of the complex provides evidence for serious psychiatric disorder in him (Atwood and Stolorow, 1979). Others confirm Jung's approach by stating that 'a person is a collective noun' (Goldberg, 1980).

In analysis, use may be made of PERSONIFICATIONS arising from complexes; the patient may 'name' the various parts of himself. Current interest in the theory of complexes arises from its usefulness in describing how the emotional events of earlier life become fixed and operative in the adult psyche. Finally, the idea of 'splinter psyches' is relevant to current re-working of the concept of the SELF.

coniunctio   An alchemical symbol of a union of unlike substances; a marrying of the OPPOSITES in an intercourse which has as its fruition the birth of a new element. This is symbolised by a child that manifests potential for greater wholeness by recombining attributes of both the opposing natures (see ALCHEMY).

From Jung's point of view, the *coniunctio* was identified as the central idea of alchemical process. He himself saw it as an ARCHETYPE of psychic functioning, symbolising a pattern of relationships between two or more UNCONSCIOUS factors. Since such relationships are at first incomprehensible to the perceiving mind, the *coniunctio* is capable of innumerable symbolic PROJECTIONS (i.e. man and woman, King and Queen, dog and bitch, cock and hen, Sol and Luna).

Because the *coniunctio* symbolises psychic processes, the REBIRTH and TRANSFORMATION that follow take place within the psyche. Like all archetypes, *coniunctio* represents two poles of possibility; one positive, the other negative. Hence, when it occurs, death and loss as well as rebirth are inherent in the experience. Bringing it to consciousness means the redemption of a previously unconscious part of the personality. But, Jung cautions, 'the kind of effect it will have depends to a large extent on the attitude of the conscious mind'. By use of the word *attitude* he implies that what is called for is the renewal of an ego position rather than the taking of outer action *vis-à-vis* the symbolic happening.

What the alchemists ultimately sought, according to Jung, was 'a union of form and matter'. Every potential *coniunctio* combines these elements. The failure of alchemists to distinguish between *corpus* and *spiritus* produced an imagery of *coniunctio* with body either able to take on a spiritual form or to draw SPIRIT into it. Within the context of ANALYSIS, the former can lead to the inflation that the relationship is a *hierosgamos* or wedding of the gods and the latter could become a sexual ACTING OUT (see INCEST).

Referring as they do to mysterious intrapsychic processes, such symbols as *coniunctio* have a particular fascination. Bedevilling logical explanation and interpretation, they tempt the therapist or patient to take a literal point of view. *Coniunctio* appears as a symbol of a goal, however; it is not attainable *as* a goal. Images of *coniunctio* are useful to ANALYST AND PATIENT as guidelines but cannot be considered as destinations on an inner journey.

consciousness This is one of the most important conceptualisations for an understanding of Jung's psychology. The distinction between conscious and UNCONSCIOUS was already a focus of attention in the early days of psychoanalytic inquiry, but Jung furthered and refined the theory by (1) positing the existence of a collective as well as a personal unconscious, (2) assigning to the unconscious a compensatory function in relation to consciousness (see COMPENSATION) and (3) recognising consciousness as a pre-condition for humanity as well as for becoming an individual. Conscious and unconscious were identified as prime OPPOSITES of psychic life.

Jung's definition of consciousness highlighted the dichotomy between conscious and unconscious and emphasised the role of EGO in conscious perception.

> By consciousness I understand the relation of psychic contents to the *ego*, insofar as this relation is perceived by the ego. Relations to the ego that are not perceived as such are *unconscious*. Consciousness is the function of activity which maintains the relation of psychic contents to the ego (*CW* 6, para. 700).

As a working concept, consciousness has been widely applied and, consequently, lends itself to misunderstandings. Perception in this sense is not the result of intellectualisation and cannot be achieved by the mind alone. It is the result of a psychic process in contradistinction to a thought process. At various times Jung equated consciousness with awareness, intuition and APPERCEPTION, stressing the function of REFLECTION in its achievement. Attainment of consciousness would appear to be the result of recognition, reflection upon and retention of psychic experience, enabling the individual to combine it with what he has learned, to feel its relevance emotionally, and to sense its meaning for his life. In contrast, unconscious contents are undifferentiated and there is no clarification about what belongs or does not belong to one's own person. DIFFERENTIATION 'is the essence, the *sine qua non* of consciousness' (CW 7, para. 339). SYMBOLS are seen as unconscious products referring to contents capable of entering consciousness.

Jung thought of the natural mind as undifferentiated. The conscious mind was capable of discrimination. Therefore, consciousness begins with control of the INSTINCTS, enabling man to adapt in an orderly way. But ADAPTATION and control of natural and instinctive behaviours can have dangers, leading to a one-sided consciousness out of touch with darker and more irrational components (see SHADOW).

Since whatever is split off becomes autonomous and uncontrollable, asserting itself negatively from the recesses of the SHADOW, Jung felt a one-sidedness of consciousness to be the current condition of Western man, recognisable in the neuroses of his own patients but also in COLLECTIVE psychic epidemics such as wars, persecution and other forms of mass repression (see NEUROSIS). The so-called Age of Enlightenment, emphasising as it did the rational attitude of a conscious mind and regarding intellectual enlightenment as the highest form of insight and, hence, of the greatest value, seriously endangered human existence in its totality. 'An inflated consciousness is always egocentric and conscious of nothing but its own existence' (CW 12, para. 563). Paradoxically, this leads to a REGRESSION of consciousness into unconsciousness. Balance can only be restored if consciousness then takes into account the unconscious (see COMPENSATION).

Despite the risk, however, consciousness must not and cannot be dispensed with. This would lead to an inundation by unconscious forces, undermining or obliterating the civilised ego (see ENANTIODROMIA). The hallmark of the conscious mind is discrimination; it must, if it is to be aware of things, separate the OPPOSITES, for in nature the opposites merge with one another. Yet, once separated, the two must be consciously related to one another.

Reaching the conclusion that the most individual thing about man was his consciousness, and based on the supposition that INDIVIDUATION is a psychic necessity, Jung's psychology became equated with increased consciousness and in ANALYSIS the assumption was that consciousness would shift from ego centredness towards a point of view more consistent with the totality of the personality (see SELF). Thus, the 'consciousness' of Jung's psychology ran foul of all the dangers identified with the pursuit of consciousness itself: one-sidedness, inundation, disintegration, INFLATION, REGRESSION, detachment, DISSOCIATION, splitting (see PARANOID-SCHIZOID POSITION), egocentricism and NARCISSISM, along with intellectualisation. It is within this context that the proliferations and schisms of analytical psychology can be seen (Samuels, 1985a).

In an attempt to show parallels between individual and collective processes of coming to consciousness, Neumann wrote *The Origins and History of Consciousness* (1954). Singer (1972) has given a classical exposition. Hillman (1975) defines consciousness as 'psychic reflection of the *psychic* world about us and part of adaptation to that reality'. He criticises analytical psychology for limiting itself to a much too narrow view of consciousness.

countertransference   See ANALYST AND PATIENT.

culture   Generally Jung used the word as roughly synonymous with SOCIETY, i.e. a somewhat differentiated and more self-conscious segment or group belonging to the COLLECTIVE. By and large he applied the word culture in reference to process; i.e. in phrases such as 'more cultured' or 'totally archaic and without culture'. From a psychological point of view, he suggests that culture carries the connotation of a group which has developed its own IDENTITY and CONSCIOUSNESS, together with a sense of continuity and purpose or MEANING.

cure   Generally accepted to mean the transformation from illness to health. Jung referred to the widespread prejudice that ANALYSIS provides something like a cure and that, when it is finished, a person can expect to be objectively 'cured'. But, he went on to say, such is not the case; for it is unlikely that there can ever be a form of PSYCHOTHERAPY that will effect 'cure'.

It is in the nature of life, Jung said, to present human beings with obstacles, sometimes in the form of illness, and these obstacles, if not excessive, provide us with opportunities for REFLECTION on inappropriate forms of an EGO adaptation so that we have a chance to discover more adequate attitudes and make the corresponding adjustments. He was aware, however, that such changes are valid only for a limited period of time, after which a problem may again assert itself. Over time, the INTEGRATION of problematic experiences can be seen to derive from promptings of the SELF, and to lead, eventually, to INDIVIDUATION (see WHOLENESS). Hence, the analyst's attitude towards cure may assist the patient to accept that a neurotic condition could be a potentially positive factor in his life (see ANALYST AND PATIENT; NEUROSIS).

Because of its dialectical nature, analysis is sometimes referred to as the 'talking cure' and, because of Jung's conceptual connection of PSYCHE and MEANING, it has also been referred to as 'cure of souls'.

Yet Jung took exception to this, for he strongly differentiated between the work of analysis and the pastoral cure of souls offered by clergymen. He saw analysis more as akin to a medical intervention for the purpose of exposing the contents of the UNCONSCIOUS and making them available for integration into CONSCIOUSNESS. Here he identified himself with Freud and the psychoanalytic tradition.

At the same time, however, because he saw neurotic suffering as potentially meaningful and accepted a TELEOLOGICAL POINT OF VIEW, he recognised the work of the analyst must minister to needs left unmet by both doctors and clergymen who were unwilling to accept the possibility of a spontaneous religious function operative in the psyche. Thus, he felt that those who came to him had to be apprised of the impossibility of a once-and-for-all cure but, simultaneously, be prepared to acknowledge the possibility of there being unconscious symbolic meaning in their suffering (see HEALING).

D

death instinct In *Beyond the Pleasure Principle* (1920), Freud proposed that the instincts could be divided into two broad groupings: the life instincts and the death instincts (see LIFE INSTINCT). The former class included the self-preservative instincts (hunger and aggression) and the sexual instincts. In Freud's earlier formulations, however, these two categories had been opposed. The death instinct exemplified the conservative and regressive character of instinct in general – i.e. the tendency of the instinct to seek discharge and hence reduce excitation to zero level. This takes the form of regression to ever more simple and archaic levels and ultimately leads to an inorganic state; hence, the 'death' instinct has taken over. Klein took these speculations of Freud's further, suggesting that aggression itself is a turning outward of the death instinct. But psychoanalysis as a whole has not emphasised these ideas of Freud's.

Jung, too, was suspicious of the notion, commenting on its dubious nature and asserting that Freud's formulation of his theory must have reflected a dissatisfaction with the one-sidedness of the libido theory (see ENERGY). Nevertheless, there are a number of features in Jung's own work which, taken together, suggest that concepts analogous to the death instinct have a place in ANALYTICAL PSYCHOLOGY.

The neutral nature of psychic energy means that it can be put to any use and this would not rule out the paradox of the application of energy to the search for a reduction of energic tension. The thesis can be demonstrated most clearly in the division in the human psyche between its progressive and regressive tendencies. Jung saw in REGRESSION an attempt to refuel or regenerate the personality by encounter and merger with a parental IMAGO or GOD-IMAGE, and hence as working in alignment with the SELF (see INCEST). This leads inevitably to a dissolution (or 'death') of the EGO in its old form with a consequent reduction in the tensions and excitations of a former way of life. This can be regarded metaphorically as a death from which ego potential reconstellates in a more adequate and conscious form. Even temporary loss of ego control is dangerous however, and it is only after the personality emerges enriched that the 'death' can be seen to have been a prelude to TRANSFORMATION (see ENANTIO-DROMIA; INITIATION; REBIRTH; WHOLENESS).

The conceptual weakness of such an argument is that the death instinct is viewed merely from the perspective of serving the life instinct. But instincts, of whatever kind, do work in the service of man; the un-pleasure they may occasionally cause should not disguise that fact. The death instinct provides a person with a frame for his life; images of death constitute a goal for its unfolding, and there is an intimate connection between death and creativity (Gordon, 1978). The death instinct is the means by which an impetus for further growth is incorporated into the PSYCHE (see MEANING).

These remarks about the death instinct have been couched in terms of the personality as a whole. But there is no reason why they should not also apply to sub-sections of the personality as well. In other words, an individual COMPLEX may pass through the death–REBIRTH process. The death instinct is experienced subjectively via imagery and emotional states – oneness, floating and oceanic, dreamy, a creative reverie, nostalgia. Crucial to this reading of the death instinct is that REGRESSION, whether benign or malign, is as much a part of life as growth and progress. Death, as a psychic fact, therefore occupies an individual all of his days and not just towards the end of his life. Repression of this may take place at any point (see STAGES OF LIFE).

defences of the self See SELF.

deintegration and reintegration See SELF.

delusion Jung defines delusion experientially. The patient *feels* something akin to a judgment based on intellect or feeling, or deriving from actual perceptions. But in fact this is based on unconscious factors within him. However, such an experience may not be wholly negative, provided it can eventually be understood. In a sense, delusions are as 'natural' as DREAMS or other psychological phenomena.

They exhibit the vigorous variety of the internal world and the way in which a delusion overwhelms a person's conscious standards and attitudes indicates its PSYCHIC REALITY (see PSYCHOSIS).

The idea that delusions can be interpreted may be attributed to Jung (see INTERPRETATION). This understanding can be either on a personal or collective level (see ARCHETYPE; UNCONSCIOUS), or it can be achieved by using a combination of both these perspectives. He calls attention to certain 'over-valued ideas' which are the fore-runners of paranoid delusions and he likens these to autonomous complexes (see COMPLEX). At such times he felt the aim of PSYCHO-THERAPY was to bring these into association with other complexes. Delusion is marked by ASSOCIATION of ideas to a limited and inflex-ible frame of reference.

As far as collective interpretation is concerned, Jung's emphasis was on the transpersonal aspect – that element in the delusion which has its history and place in man's psycho-cultural development. He therefore found MYTH and FAIRY TALES helpful, both to amplify clinical material and also to help organise it, portraying the essential psychological pattern (see CULTURE; AMPLIFICATION).

Jung enumerates several collective delusions (to be distinguished from collective interpretations of an individual's delusions). Amongst these would be the idea that we are exclusively rational creatures.

dementia praecox   See SCHIZOPHRENIA; WORD ASSOCIATION TEST.

depression   Jung's approach to depression concentrates on the ques-tion of psychic ENERGY rather than on OBJECT RELATIONS, object loss or separation. Analytical psychologists tend to borrow freely from PSYCHOANALYSIS in this area. Jung conceptualises depression as a damming up of energy which, when released, may take on a more positive direction. Energy is trapped because of a neurotic or psy-chotic problem but, if released, actually helps in the overcoming of the problem. A state of depression is one which should be entered into as fully as possible, according to Jung, so that the feelings involved may be clarified. Such clarification represents a conversion of a vague feeling into a more precise IDEA or IMAGE to which the depressed person can relate.

Depression is connected to REGRESSION in its regenerative and enriching aspects. In particular, it may take the form of 'the empty stillness which precedes creative work' (CW 16, para. 373). In such circumstances, it is the new development that has siphoned off energy from CONSCIOUSNESS, leading to the depression.

Jung warned that depression may be present in PSYCHOSIS and vice versa (see PATHOLOGY).

depressive position Term introduced by Melanie Klein to indicate a point in the development of OBJECT RELATIONS where the infant recognises that the good mother and the bad mother IMAGES to which he has been relating refer to the same person (said to be in the second half of the first year of life). Confronted with his mother as a whole person, he can no longer proceed as before (see GREAT MOTHER). Earlier functioning would have involved assigning and directing his negative feelings towards the negative mother, thereby protecting the positive mother from them (see PARANOID-SCHIZOID POSITION). Now he must face the fact that his hostile, aggressive feelings and his loving feelings also embrace the hitherto wholly positive mother (i.e. that he has ambivalent feelings). This, in turn, faces him with the fear of losing her via the operation of his own destructiveness, guilt at damaging her and, above all, with an evolving concern for her well-being (see INFANCY AND CHILDHOOD). In this latter regard, the depressive position is the forerunner of conscience in general and concern for other people in particular. Hence, Winnicott's name for the depressive position was 'the stage of concern'. (See AMBIVALENCE.)

Concurrent with this bringing together of a split object, there is also an integration of aspects of the personality itself which were previously experienced as good or bad. For instance, good parts of the personality may have been split off to protect them from bad parts or from a persecuting environment.

The depressive position is so named because for the first time fantasies of loss of the mother have to be faced on a personal level, a process analogous to mourning and therefore including the possibility of depression. At the time of the depressive position, the quality of anxiety changes from its being primarily a fear of attack from outside to a fear of losing whatever makes life livable and keeps one alive. Earlier on, experiences of loss can be fantasied away by illusions of omnipotence. From this angle, subsequent DEPRESSION in adulthood may be seen as originating in a failure to deal with depressive anxiety in infancy. The depressive position is a developmental hurdle to be overcome. Its achievement is a developmental milestone.

While the depressive position is contrasted with the PARANOID-SCHIZOID POSITION (in which the personality and the object are split), there is also a degree of two-way movement and, in adult life, evidence of the presence of both positions is usually to be found.

ANALYTICAL PSYCHOLOGY (especially the developmental school, see Samuels, 1985a) puts a further gloss on the depressive position in that its achievement towards the end of the first year of life may be regarded as one of the first conjunctions of OPPOSITES to be achieved (see CONIUNCTIO). This viewpoint has the advantage of linking the developmental perspective with one derived from the phenomenology of the SELF. Because of the purposive nature of much psychic functioning (see TELEOLOGICAL POINT OF VIEW; UNCONSCIOUS), the infant's aggression can be seen as operating in the service of INDIVIDUATION. As acceptance of the inevitability of aggressive feelings is a vital part of the depressive position, an integration of the SHADOW is taking place. What is more, the biting in oral aggression may be seen as an early attempt to discriminate opposites (infant and mother, mother and father). Such DIFFERENTIATION is regarded by Jung as a precondition for subsequent conjunctions of opposites.

depth psychology   In 1896 new departures in psychological theory and practice took place which marked the beginning of what is now called depth psychology. The significant events of that year were Freud's classification of neuroses and publication of a paper entitled 'On the Aetiology of Hysteria' (Ellenberger, 1970). This latter event, as it turned out, was as important for its failures as its success, leading as it did by way of second thoughts to Freud's realisation that in the UNCONSCIOUS it is very difficult to distinguish FANTASY from memory. From that time onward, he and his close associates (one of whom was Jung during the years from 1907 to 1913) paid less attention to uncovering suppressed memories than to exploring unconscious material.

Freud's innovations laid the foundations of what was to come, a fact well recognised by Jung (*inter alia*, CW 15, 'Sigmund Freud in his Historical Setting' and 'In Memory of Sigmund Freud'). Among these innovations in perspective and technique with patients, of primary importance was the introduction of dream INTERPRETATION as a tool of PSYCHOTHERAPY. This was combined with Freud's assertion that DREAMS have latent as well as manifest content; his contention that the manifest content is a distortion of the latent content of the dream resulting from unconscious censorship; and his application of free ASSOCIATION as a method in the analysis of dreams. Freud's theory of dreams and his awareness of parapraxes which resulted in publication of *The Psychopathology of Everyday Life* (1901) were formulations derived from his work on hysteria. In 1897 he started work on *Jokes and their Relation to the Unconscious* (1905), a book in which he is the first to investigate the psychological function of play. All of these changes claimed to furnish keys for the investigation of the unconscious with the aim of renewing the conscious mind and all were completed before he and Jung met.

Jung began an encyclopaedia entry on the subject of depth psychology, written in 1948 and published in 1951, with the words: '"Depth Psychology" is a term deriving from medical psychology, coined by Eugen Bleuler to denote that branch of psychological science which is concerned with the phenomenon of the unconscious' (*CW* 18, para. 1142).

In this article Jung is at pains to trace the sources of the main ideas but speaks of Freud as the 'true founder of the depth psychology which bears the name of PSYCHOANALYSIS'. He identifies Alfred Adler's *individual psychology* as a continuation of one part of the researches initiated by his teacher, Freud. Confronted with the same empirical material, Jung concluded that Adler had considered it from a different point of view from that of Freud, his premise being that the primary aetiological factor was not sexuality but the power drive.

As far as he himself is concerned, Jung acknowledges his own debt to Freud, emphasising that his early experiments with the WORD ASSOCIATION TEST confirmed the existence of the repressions encountered by Freud and the characteristic consequences, finding that in so-called normal persons as well as neurotics, reactions were disturbed by 'split-off' (i.e. repressed) emotional complexes (see COMPLEX). He identifies his differences in point of view as related to the sexual theory of neurosis which he found limited and a conception of the unconscious which he felt needed to be broadened since he saw it as 'the creative matrix of CONSCIOUSNESS', containing not only repressed personal contents but COLLECTIVE motifs as well. He rejected the wish-fulfilment theory of dreams, emphasising instead the function of COMPENSATION in unconscious processes and their teleological character (see TELEOLOGICAL POINT OF VIEW). He also attributed his break with Freud to a difference in point of view on the role of the collective unconscious and how that manifests in cases of SCHIZOPHRENIA, i.e. formulation of his theory of the ARCHETYPE.

In the same article, Jung goes on to outline his further independent observations and discoveries, now included in the body of works associated with ANALYTICAL PSYCHOLOGY. With further extension and proliferation of operational theories of personality and personality behaviour, the term depth psychology is little used today excepting in its original sense; namely, to identify and describe those who specifically investigate unconscious phenomena.

development Jung's views on the development of personality usually include a synthesising of innate, constitutional factors (see ARCHETYPE) with the circumstances in which an individual finds himself (see COMPLEX; INFANCY AND CHILDHOOD). Development may be looked at in terms of relation to oneself (see INDIVIDUATION; NARCISSISM; SELF) or to objects (see EGO; OBJECT RELATIONS) or to instinctual impulses (see ENERGY).

Regressive and progressive tendencies co-exist in development (see DEATH INSTINCT; INCEST; INTEGRATION; REGRESSION) and it is not a meaningless movement (see MEANING; SELF-REGULATORY FUNCTION OF THE PSYCHE; STAGES OF LIFE).

dialectical process   See ANALYSIS; ANALYST AND PATIENT.

differentiation   A word frequently used by Jung meaning to distinguish parts from a whole, to untangle, to separate what was formerly joined unconsciously, to resolve. It is then possible to speak of parts of the personality as more differentiated than others, meaning more firmly discriminated and embedded in CONSCIOUSNESS (see TYPOLOGY).

Differentiation is both a natural process of growth and a conscious psychological undertaking. It pertains to neurotic states of over- and inter-dependence upon parental figures and marriage partners, for example, as well as to inner states when one or more of the psychological functions may be contaminated by another, or when ego and shadow are 'undifferentiated'. In their original state the OPPOSITES exist in a fused or coalesced state. Their differentiation is required before conscious synthesis is possible.

INDIVIDUATION is a process that requires differentiation; a person dependent upon his projections has little or no recognition of *what* he is and *who* he is. However, Jung posited the idea that because discrimination and differentiation mean more to the rational intellect than WHOLENESS, there is a necessity for a compensatory symbolism in modern man which will stress the importance of his totality (see SELF). It is wrong to assume that whatever is 'earlier' is automatically less differentiated. For example, Jung was at pains to point out that tribal peoples as yet unadapted to industrialised society retain certain highly differentiated sensitivities no longer available to Western man (see PRIMITIVES).

directed and fantasy thinking   Terms introduced by Jung to delineate different forms of mental activity and the differing ways in which the PSYCHE expresses itself (*CW* 5, paras 4–46). *Directed thinking* involves the conscious use of language and concepts. It is based on, or constructed with reference to reality. Essentially, directed thinking is communicative, thinking outwards, to others, for others. It is the language of the intellect, of scientific exposition (though not, perhaps, of scientific discovery), and common sense. *Fantasy thinking*, on the other hand, employs images, whether singly or in thematic form, emotions and intuitions (see IMAGE). The rules of logic and physics do not apply, nor moral precepts (see MORALITY; PSYCHIC

REALITY; SUPER-EGO; SYNCHRONICITY). Such thinking may be said to be metaphorical, symbolic, imaginative (see METAPHOR; SYMBOL). Jung pointed out that fantasy thinking may be conscious but is usually pre-conscious or unconscious in its operation (see UNCONSCIOUS).

Fantasy and directed thinking may be compared to Freud's primary and secondary process respectively. Primary process activity is unconscious; single images may sum up great areas of conflict or refer to other elements; time-space categories are ignored. Crucially, primary process is an expression of instinctual activity (and, hence, amoral if not immoral); it is characterised by wishes, and governed by the pleasure principle. Secondary process is governed by the reality principle, is logical and verbal; it forms the basis of thought and is the expression of the EGO. Indeed, the ego itself cannot function without repression of primary process activity; primary and secondary process are therefore antipathetic. Though certain kinds of creative activity may contain a mixture of the two, there is a fundamental opposition.

For Jung, there was no reason why fantasy thinking should inevitably threaten the ego; his point was that the ego benefits from such contact. However, out-of-control fantasy is a part of states of INFLATION or POSSESSION. Directed and fantasy thinking are stated to co-exist as two separate and equal perspectives – though the latter is closer, as it were, to archetypal layers of the psyche (see ARCHETYPE).

This even-handedness brings Jung's ideas close to what we now know about the functioning of the two cerebral hemispheres, the interaction of which is central to human mental functioning. The left hemisphere is the site of brain activity connected with linguistic ability, logic, aim-directed action and obeys the laws of time and space; it may be characterised as analytical, rational, detailed in its operations. The right cerebral hemisphere is the site of emotions, feelings, fantasies, a general sensing of where one is in relation to everything else, and a holistic capacity to grasp a complex situation in one bound (in contrast to the left hemisphere's more piecemeal approach). The TRANSCENDENT FUNCTION has been described in terms of an intercommunication between the hemispheres – physiologically, the *corpus callosum* (Rossi, 1977). See BODY.

DREAMS may be seen as typical expressions of fantasy thinking or right hemispheric functioning – though elements of a logical outlook appear in dreams from time to time. Dream INTERPRETATION is sometimes said to bring in directed thinking but a more accurate summary would be that interpretation is really a combination of directed and fantasy thinking for imagination is involved in it (see REDUCTIVE AND SYNTHETIC METHODS).

Jung saw mythology as *the* expression of fantasy thinking and commented that the effort and attention we bring to science and technology today, the Greeks brought to the development of their myths. MYTH is a means of expressing a metaphoric view of the personal and physical worlds and cannot, therefore, be assessed by means of directed thinking. Not many analytical psychologists would agree with Jung's outdated evaluation of the thought of 'PRIMITIVES' as primarily fantasy thought. However, his observation that fantasy thinking may be clearly seen in the activity of children is still valid (though there, too, logic plays its part).

Jung's use of the word 'thinking', as described here, does present problems. He uses the word differently in his TYPOLOGY, for instance. When he writes of directed and fantasy thinking, is he doing anything more than simply particularising a difference between consciousness and the unconscious? Another point of view would be that the notion of fantasy thinking does point up the fact that the UNCONSCIOUS has its own structure, language and logic (psyche-logic); any attempt to elevate rationalism to too high a status is moderated (see PSYCHE; PSYCHIC REALITY). Similarly, Jung's twinning of directed and fantasy thinking serves as a caution to those who would dispense with rational thought altogether, accusing 'intellectuals' of being schizoid or 'heady'.

There is little doubt that personal preference, based on psychological type, plays a part in determining which kind of thinking comes more naturally to a person (see TYPOLOGY). During infancy and childhood, familial and social demands may cause distortions to occur. As this usually presents itself clinically in an account of fantasy thinking having been prohibited in the home, it is likely that a cultural factor is also at work. Indeed, Western society has tended to use and value directed thinking more than fantasy thinking.

dissociation   Refers to an UNCONSCIOUS fragmenting of what should be linked in the personality, a kind of 'disunion with oneself' (*CW* 8, para. 62). This suggests a collapse of a person's potential to embody WHOLENESS. Alternatively, dissociation may be used to describe a more or less conscious approach, one which fragments in order to 'analyse' when a holistic, all-embracing attitude would be more productive. Western society's dependence on science and technology and on a certain 'rational' style of thinking illustrate this point of view. Psychiatry may be a particularly relevant example, especially when the dynamics of the doctor–patient relationship are not adequately considered.

Dissociation is an important aspect of NEUROSIS. Here it may be seen as a 'discrepancy between the conscious attitude and the trends of the unconscious' (CW 16, para. 26). Repression is a special case of this; for instance, inability to come to terms with bodily impulses, or with the SHADOW generally, may be viewed as dissociation (see BODY). The ability to recognise that the psyche has parts and sub-systems, or the development of a capacity to dialogue with internal figures is different from dissociation by the EGO (see ACTIVE IMAGIN-ATION); in fact, such activities require the maintenance of a strong and conscious ego position.

Jung often described ANALYSIS as a healing of dissociations. Here, he was emphatic that neither technical knowledge nor ABREACTION were decisive. The transference-countertransference aspects of the relationship of ANALYST AND PATIENT are, in fact, more fundamental. In analysis, the intent is to facilitate the assimilation into conscious-ness of unconscious contents and hence overcome the dissociations. However, it must be recognised, said Jung, that in some psychoses the level of dissociation is too great for that goal to be achieved (see PATHOLOGY; PSYCHOSIS).

dominant   See ARCHETYPE.

dreams   Jung defined the dream in broad terms as 'a spontaneous self-portrayal, in symbolic form, of the actual situation in the UN-CONSCIOUS' (CW 8, para. 505). He saw the relation of the dream to CONSCIOUSNESS as basically a compensatory one (see COMPENSATION).

In contrast to Freud, whom he felt looked at dreams only from a casual standpoint, Jung spoke of them as psychic products that could be seen *either* from a causal *or* a purposeful point of view (see REDUCTIVE AND SYNTHETIC METHODS; TELEOLOGICAL POINT OF VIEW). The causal point of view tends toward uniformity of meaning, he wrote, a sameness of INTERPRETATION, and tempts one to assign a fixed significance to a SYMBOL, while the purposeful point of view 'perceives in the dream IMAGE the expression of an altered psycho-logical situation. It recognises no fixed meaning of symbols' (CW 8, para. 471).

The process of ASSOCIATION was used by both men when inter-preting dreams but Jung later varied his practice in accord with his findings on the COMPLEX, for he saw dreams as commentaries on personal complexes. To the technique of association he added AM-PLIFICATION from MYTH, history and other cultural material in order to provide as wide a context as possible for interpretation of dream imagery, allowing both its manifest and latent content to be explored. He distinguished between interpretation on the so-called subjective level in which the dream figures are conceived as PERSONIFICATIONS of features in the dreamer's own psyche and interpretation on the objective level whereby one investigates the dream images in their own terms (e.g. human figures who may be known to the dreamer).

Even though compensation was regarded as a fundamental principle, Jung emphasised that what is being compensated is not always immediately apparent and that patience and honesty play an important part in unlocking the enigmas of dream content. He believed that dreams have a prospective aspect, 'an unconscious anticipation of future conscious achievement'. Nevertheless, he recommended that the dream be taken as a *preliminary* sketch map or a plan *roughed out* in advance rather than as a prophecy or set of directions.

He emphasised that there are certain dreams (i.e. nightmares) whose purpose would appear to be to disintegrate, destroy, demolish. They fulfil their compensatory task in a necessarily unpleasant manner. Such impressive dreams may become so-called 'big dreams' that cause one to alter a life's course. Others may not portend or challenge but summarise the fulfilment of a condition. Dreams seen in sequence often disclose the path of one's INDIVIDUATION process and reveal a personal symbology. Dreams may also be looked at dramatically, like a play, with an introduction of a problem situation, development and conclusion.

Jung repeatedly cautioned against the danger of over-rating the unconscious and warned that such a tendency impairs the power of conscious decision. In this regard, an exceptionally beautiful or numinous dream may have an unhealthy seductive attraction until one looks more closely at it. The dream and the dreamer are inextricably linked and the unconscious functions satisfactorily only when the attitude of the conscious EGO is one of exploration and readiness for collaboration.

Dream images are seen as the best possible expression of still unconscious facts. 'To understand the dream's meaning I must stick as close as possible to the dream image,' Jung stated (CW 16, para. 320). There is a 'just-so' quality about dreams, he said, neither positive nor negative but a portrayal of the situation as it really is, rather than one conjectures or would like it to be. Understanding of the dream process is many-sided, involving the totality of a person and not simply the intellect alone (see SELF). Jung admitted to being mystified and baffled when confronted with dreams, particularly his own, and such an orientation seemed to him preferable when encountering any psychic phenomenon whose worth is not initially evident.

Jung's last work was on dreams and dream symbols, completed in 1961 and published in 1964. To read that now along with his other essays and early seminars on dreams is to be made aware of the changes that have taken place in COLLECTIVE attitudes towards dreams and dreaming since his time and that of Freud. For example, large numbers of people, whether in ANALYSIS or otherwise, now record their dreams and, even if unable to go farther, try to consider them in relation to the context from which they have arisen.

Symbolic awareness of dreams has increased markedly within the last few decades. The popularisation of Jung's teachings through the publication of *Memories, Dreams, Reflections* and *Man and his Symbols*, along with dream seminars and popular lectures on the subject, combined with the increasing numbers of people who enter analysis, have resulted in a widespread interest in symbolic and unconscious material. Other therapies (i.e. Gestalt and Psychodrama) have made contributions to the method and use of ACTIVE IMAGINATION for release of latent subjective dream content. Finally, there is now a conscious, collective fascination with 'journeying' or the undertaking of a difficult symbolic quest which involves wandering, estrangement, hazard, risk and lack of certainty – all attributes of the inner journey which is undertaken when one follows one's dreams.

Since Jung's death, continuing dream research has been conducted at the C. G. Jung Clinic, Zurich. Further medical and scientific evidence seems to refute certain of his early assumptions in regard to the action or penetration of somatic stimuli in the dream process. Hall (1977), Mattoon (1978) and Lambert (1981) have published on the clinical application of dream analysis.

drive See ARCHETYPE; DEATH INSTINCT; LIFE INSTINCT.

E

ego On his map of the PSYCHE, Jung was at pains to distinguish the place of the ego from that assigned to it by Freud. He perceived it to be the centre of CONSCIOUSNESS but he also stressed the limitations and incompleteness of ego as being something less than the whole personality. Though the ego is concerned with such matters as personal identity, maintenance of the personality, continuity over time, mediation between conscious and UNCONSCIOUS realms, cognition and reality testing, it also has to be seen as responsive to the demands of something superior. This is the SELF, the ordering principle of the entire personality. The relation of the self to the ego is compared to that of 'the mover to the moved'.

Initially, the ego is merged with the self but then differentiates from it. Jung describes an interdependence of the two: the self provides the more holistic view and is therefore supreme, but it is the function of ego to challenge or fulfil the demands of that supremacy. The confrontation of ego and self was identified by Jung as characteristic of the second half of life (see EGO-SELF AXIS; STAGES OF LIFE).

The ego is also regarded by Jung as arising out of the clash between a child's bodily limitations and environmental reality. Frustration promotes islets of consciousness which coalesce into the ego proper. Here, Jung's ideas about the dating of the emergence of the ego reflect a continuing dependence on Freud's early ideas. The ego, Jung asserts, comes into its full existence during the third or fourth year. Psychoanalysts and analytical psychologists now agree that an element of perceptual organisation is present at least from birth and that before the end of the first year of life a relatively sophisticated ego structure is in operation.

Jung's tendency to equate ego with consciousness makes it difficult to conceptualise unconscious aspects of ego structure, e.g. defences. Consciousness is the distinguishing characteristic of the ego but this is proportional to unconsciousness. In fact, the greater the degree of ego-consciousness, the greater the possibility of sensing what is not known. Ego's task in relation to SHADOW is to recognise it and integrate it rather than splitting it off via PROJECTION.

Jung conceived ANALYTICAL PSYCHOLOGY as a reaction to an over-rational and over-conscious approach which isolates man from his natural world, including his own nature and, so, limits him. On the other hand, he insisted that DREAMS and FANTASY images cannot be used directly to enhance life. They are a kind of raw material, a source of symbols, which must be translated into the language of consciousness and integrated by the ego. In this work the TRANSCENDENT FUNCTION links oppositions. The role of ego is to discriminate OPPOSITES, withstand their tensions, allow them to be resolved and, finally, to protect what emerges, which will expand and enhance the previous limitations of ego.

So far as PSYCHOPATHOLOGY is concerned, there are a number of recognisable dangers: (1) That the ego will not emerge from its primary identity with the self and hence be unable to meet the demands of the outer world. (2) That the ego will become equated with the self, leading to an INFLATION of consciousness. (3) That the ego may take up a rigid and extreme attitude, forsaking reference to the self and ignoring the possibility of movement via the transcendent function. (4) That the ego may not be able to relate to a particular COMPLEX because of the tension engendered. This leads to the splitting off of the complex and its dominating the life of the individual. (5) That the ego may be overwhelmed by an inner content arising out of the unconscious. (6) That the INFERIOR FUNCTION may remain unintegrated and unavailable to the ego, leading to grossly unconscious behaviour and a general impoverishment of the personality (see TYPOLOGY).

ego-self axis Though, as Jung wrote, 'the ego stands to the self as the moved to the mover, or as object to subject' (CW 11, para. 391), he also recognises that the two great psychic systems need each other. For, without the EGO's analysing powers and its capacity to facilitate independent living, separate from infantile and other dependencies, the SELF remains without a presence in the everyday world. With the aid of the ego, the self's valuable tendencies to foster life lived at greater depth and at a greater level of integration become available to a man or woman (cf. Edinger, 1972, who coined the phrase 'ego-self axis').

From a developmental viewpoint, a strong and viable ego-self axis arises in the individual out of a certain quality of relationship between mother and infant, a balance between togetherness and separation, between the evolution and approval of specific skills and acceptance of the baby as a whole, between outward exploration and self-reflection. But the reverse is also true and some of the dynamics inherent in the ego-self axis are projected onto the relationship between a baby and his or her mother (see DEVELOPMENT; INFANCY AND CHILDHOOD).

empiricism Jung regarded his psychology as empirical, meaning that it rests upon observation and experiment rather than upon THEORY. He regarded this as the opposite of speculation or ideology and described empiricism as having the advantage of presenting facts as accurately as possible even though it was limited, he felt, by its lack of appreciation for the *value* of ideas. He regarded empirical thinking as no less rational than ideological thinking and discussed the two approaches in relation to introversion, which he saw as expressive of empiricism, and extraversion which was applicable to ideologism (see TYPOLOGY).

Again, Jung's approach was relevant in relation to the ARCHETYPE, observed in the form of an IMAGE and, therefore, an empirical concept. Fordham (1969) and others insisted upon verification by observation of personal behaviour. Hillman and other archetypal psychologists have observed the functioning of the image instead (1975). Both groups have followed an empirical approach but this has led to different perspectives on clinical material (see Samuels, 1985a).

enactment To be distinguished from ACTING OUT, enactment can be defined as the recognition and acceptance of an archetypal stimulus, interacting with it while retaining EGO control and thereby allowing its metaphorical meaning to unfold in a personal and individual way. In contrast to acting out, enactment requires the exertion of the conscious ego so that invasive archetypal elements can be given individualised expression. Acknowledging the presence and power of unconscious motivation, one nevertheless withstands its pull, neither regressing nor allowing oneself to be overcome by it (see INFLATION; POSSESSION). The implication is that the invading stimulus is symbolic of something which the existing personality lacks and of which it is not yet aware. One tolerates or suffers the presence of the archetypal element until its implicit and symbolic meaning is made explicit (see SYMBOL).

See ACTIVE IMAGINATION; PAINTING.

enantiodromia 'Running contrariwise', a psychological 'law' first outlined by Heraclitus and meaning that sooner or later everything turns into its opposite. Jung identified this as 'the principle which governs all cycles of natural life, from the smallest to the greatest' (CW 6, para. 708). 'The only person who escapes the grim law of enantiodromia is the man who knows how to separate himself from the unconscious', he wrote (CW 7, para. 112). Without such separation there is an overdependence upon a self-regulating mechanism with consequent neglect and weakening of EGO control.

The ubiquity of his references to enantiodromia (clinical, symbolic and theoretical) emphasise that, for Jung, this was not a formula but a reality, not only of personal psychic development but of COLLECTIVE life as well. Over-emphasised therapeutically, it could lead, of course, to always looking on the bright side of things or, conversely, expecting the worst. Jung's recognition of the inevitability of enantiodromic change helped him anticipate psychic movement and he believed it was possible both to foresee and also to relate to it, such an attitude being the essence of CONSCIOUSNESS.

He applied the term to the emergence of unconscious OPPOSITES in relation to the points of view held or expressed by consciousness. If an extreme, one-sided tendency dominates conscious life, in time an equally powerful counter-position is built up in the PSYCHE. This first inhibits conscious performance and then, subsequently, breaks through ego inhibitions and conscious control. The law of enantiodromia underlies Jung's principle of COMPENSATION (see WILL).

energy Jung used this term and 'libido' interchangeably (CW 6, para. 778). It should be noted that psychic energy is said to be limited in quantity and indestructible. In this respect, Jung's ideas parallel Freud's libido theory. What is disputed is the exclusively sexual character which Freud assigned to libido or psychic energy. Jung's conception is closer to that of a form of life-energy, neutral in character (see INCEST; PSYCHOANALYSIS). He pointed out that psychic energy in the pre-oedipal phases of development takes many forms: nutritional, alimentary and so forth. Psychic energy can be used as a bridging concept between bodily zonal development and OBJECT RELATIONS (see INFANCY AND CHILDHOOD).

Though appearing to incorporate the terminology of physics, the concept of psychic energy, applied psychologically, is a complicated METAPHOR:

(1) There is a need to indicate the intensity of any particular psychological activity. This enables us to assess the value and importance of such activity to the individual. In general terms this can be achieved by referring to the amount of psychic energy invested, even though objective means to measure the amount of energy do not exist.

(2) There is a similar need to demonstrate a shifting focus of interest and involvement. This can be carried out by postulating a number of different channels in which psychic energy might flow. Jung suggests biological, psychological, spiritual and moral channels. The hypothesis is that, blocked in its flow in one channel, psychic energy will flow into another channel. Here energy itself does not change but takes a different direction.

(3) The alteration in the direction of flow is not random. That is, the channels themselves occupy a pre-existing structure (see ARCHETYPE). Specifically, a blocked flow will shift energy into the opposite channel; this can be illustrated by connection with incestuous, instinctual impulses which, when frustrated by the incest prohibition, take up a spiritual dimension (see ENANTIODROMIA; OPPOSITES).

According to Jung, this is an example of the natural tendency of the psyche to maintain a balance. Because of this tendency, psychic energy will change its direction and intensity when imbalance occurs and not only because of a blockage (see COMPENSATION). A shift in the flow of energy can be seen in terms of its outcome, as if such a shift were in the direction of a goal (see TELEOLOGICAL POINT OF VIEW). Jung's energic approach is concerned with patterns and MEANING and he paid particular attention to SYMBOLS as appearing both before and after transformations of psychic energy.

(4) Psychological conflict can be discussed in terms of disturbances in the flow of psychic energy. Thus, conflict itself is recognised as natural. When discussing the DEATH INSTINCT and the LIFE INSTINCT, both can be seen as manifestations emanating from a single energic source, though moving towards end and beginning respectively.

Eros   The principle of psychic relatedness; sometimes assumed by Jung to underlie the psychology of woman; recognised by himself as an intuitive formulation impossible to define accurately or prove scientifically. On this basis, the corresponding principle operative in man's psychology is LOGOS. But Jung, on many occasions, refers to Eros and Logos as capable of co-existing within a single individual of whatever sex.

The ambiguity of Eros, in contrast with the directedness of Logos, makes the concept difficult to grasp. As psychological principles, interpretations of both Eros and Logos have been subject to wide variation. The fallacious equation of Eros with 'feeling' has plagued ANALYTICAL PSYCHOLOGY throughout the years (see TYPOLOGY). It cannot be evaluated in quantitative terms; neither is it a neat label for one end of a spectrum of OPPOSITES, since it can be manifested in either positive or negative ways. Guggenbühl-Craig (1980) speaks of it as an attribute which makes both GODS and humans loving, creative and involved. One has to recognise it as an UNCONSCIOUS power whose strength increases in proportion to the degree that it remains unconscious.

Jung's supposition was that a woman's need for psychic related-ness characterised and outweighed her need for a purely sexual re-lationship itself; although he warned that this was not to be applied in an absolute sense and he was careful to give continuing analytic attention to how and where the principle applied. When he wrote about this, as whenever he addressed himself to controversial and public issues, it is difficult to ascertain to what degree he spoke as a psychologist or as Jung the person. He concluded, however, that Eros is not to be considered as synonymous with sex, but neither can it be divorced from sex and it 'participates' in or as an aspect of sex along with all other coupling or group activities of a psychic nature: human, aesthetic and spiritual.

At length, Freud came to hold the view that there were two basic instincts: the LIFE INSTINCT, which he identified as Eros, and the DEATH INSTINCT. He attributed to the former the establishment and preservation of fundamental relationships and to the latter the un-doing and destruction of those connections. Jung gave considerable attention to the refutation of such an opposition. 'Logically, the opposite of love is hate', he wrote, 'and of Eros, Phobos (fear); but psychologically it is the will to power' (CW 7, para. 78).

This background, which figured in Jung's interpretations of the work of both Freud and Adler, is useful for an understanding of his own use of Eros as a principle for he continued to assert that uncon-scious Eros inevitably finds expression in a power drive. With the supposition that the animus-possessed woman denies or is out of touch with Eros, one can then see her actions are not 'logical' so much as power-driven (see ANIMA AND ANIMUS; POSSESSION). Where

Logos is seen as 'eternal reason', the substitution of personal reason can be recognised as power.

There have been few clinical observations of the Eros principle in women and the corresponding principle of Logos in men and, therefore, there has been scant investigation or extension of the theory. The social breakthrough of women of today with corresponding changes in sexual behaviour, gender roles and definition have caused women analysts to re-investigate primary sources of feminine imagery in an attempt to find reflection or verification of how a modern woman breaks away from or manifests her Eros tendency in new and creative ways. Perhaps not surprisingly, attention now begins to focus more explicitly on father-daughter relationships and Jung's five stages of Eros expression; biological, sexual, aesthetic, spiritual and as a form of wisdom (*sapientia*).

See GENDER; REFLECTION; SYZYGY.

ethics   A system of moral demands. Neumann (1954) addressed himself to the ethical implications of depth psychology. For this volume Jung wrote a foreword in which he reiterated his point of view that a person's moral law expresses a psychic fact that may or may not have been subjected to REFLECTION and the arbitration of his own UNCONSCIOUS judgments. The development of consciousness requires careful consideration, involving a religious observation in the sense of seeing things from a universal as well as a personal perspective. This, for Jung, was an ethical undertaking (see MORALITY; RELIGION).

evil   Jung's attitude toward evil was pragmatic. As he said repeatedly, he was not interested in it from a philosophical perspective but from the point of view of EMPIRICISM. As a psychotherapist, it was the person's subjective judgment as to what constituted good or evil with which he felt he had to deal in the first instance. What may at one time appear as evil or at least meaningless and valueless may on a higher level of CONSCIOUSNESS appear as a source of good.

As a boy, Jung was brought face to face with the dark, unclean and (at that time) inadmissible side of God in a VISION (1963). Later, he conceptualised his vision and gave it psychological validity by identifying what he had seen as the SHADOW of the Christian God. In the empirical SELF, which he equated with a GOD-IMAGE, he maintained that light and shadow (good and evil) form a paradoxical unity.

'Good and evil are principles of our ethical judgment', Jung wrote, 'but, reduced to their ontological roots, they are "beginnings", aspects of God' (CW 10, para. 846). A principle is a supraordinate thing, more powerful than a person's own judgment, an attribute of the archetypal God-image (see ARCHETYPE). Therefore, in his view, the problem cannot be relativised. Humans have to deal with evil as such, recognising its power and daemonic ambivalence.

At different times in his career, Jung was severely criticised by theologians for his insistence upon the reality of evil and the paradoxical nature of the God-image. We cannot know what good and evil are in themselves, he insisted, but we perceive them as judgments and in relation to experience. He saw them not as facts but as human responses to facts and, therefore, neither, in his opinion, could be regarded as a diminution or privation of the other. Psychologically, he accepted both as 'equally real'. Evil takes its place as an effective and menacing reality in opposition to good, a psychological reality that expresses itself symbolically both in religious tradition (as the devil) and in personal experience (see OPPOSITES).

This view of evil was extensively explored in Jung's correspondence with Father Victor White, an English priest, but eventually the two friends found their perspectives irreconcilable (cf. Heisig, 1979).

See GUILT; RELIGION.

extraversion   See TYPOLOGY.

F

fairy tales   Stories representative of the collective UNCONSCIOUS, emerging from historic and pre-historic times, portraying the unlearned behaviour and wisdom of the human species. Fairy tales display similar motifs discovered in widely separated places and at different periods. Along with religious ideas (dogmas) and MYTH, they provide symbols with whose help unconscious contents can be canalised into consciousness, interpreted and integrated (see INTEGRATION; SYMBOL). In researches on SCHIZOPHRENIA, Jung found these typical forms of behaviour and motifs appearing in dreams, visions and the delusional systems of the insane independent of tradition. Such primordial images he identified as archetypes (see ARCHETYPE; IMAGE).

Fairy tales are stories developed around archetypal themes. Jung hypothesised that their original purpose was not for entertainment, but that they provided a way of talking about dark forces which were feared and unapproachable because of their numinosity and magical power (see NUMINOSUM). The attributes of these forces were projected into fairy tales along with legends, MYTHS and, in certain instances, into stories of the lives of historical personages. Such an awareness led Jung to state that archetypal behaviour could be studied in two ways, either by way of fairy tale and myth or in the analysis of the individual.

Applying Jung's dictum, analytical psychologists have used fairy tales as illustrative of psychological behaviour. Von Franz (1970) has focused most directly on the fairy tale as 'the purest and simplest expression of collective unconscious psychic processes'.

fantasy Flow or aggregate of images and ideas in the unconscious PSYCHE, constituting its most characteristic activity. To be distinguished from thought or cognition (but see DIRECTED AND FANTASY THINKING). Construed by Jung as initially taking place independently of ego-consciousness although potentially in relation to it (see EGO).

Unconscious fantasy is the direct result of the operation of archetypal structures (see ARCHETYPE). Though the raw material for unconscious fantasy may derive in part from conscious elements (such as memories of, or experiences with, real people), these are not objectively connected with the fantasy. One implication of this is that a distinction has to be drawn between the presence of real, external figures in fantasy functioning as raw material for the fantasy and figures who may bridge the internal-external divide (see below). Perhaps we can say that a true 'mating' of archetypal expectation with a personal correspondence in the environment is different and follows on from the use of external material by the psyche for the specific purpose of constructing unconscious fantasy.

This kind of fantasy may be said to 'colour' personal life, shaping it by means of the pre-existing unconscious schema. Jung writes of such fantasies as 'wanting' to become conscious and the individual is not required to do anything in relation to them to bring them about - indeed, they tend to 'erupt' into CONSCIOUSNESS. Hence, Jung called these 'passive' fantasies. (Cf. Isaacs, 1952, for an exposition of the Kleinian use of 'unconscious phantasy'.)

'Active' fantasies, on the other hand, do require assistance from the ego for them to emerge into consciousness. When that occurs, we have a fusion of the conscious and unconscious areas of the psyche; an expression of the psychological unity of the person. The relation between ego and fantasy was therefore of great importance to Jung both as an expression of the SELF and as a means of therapeutic endeavour (see ACTIVE IMAGINATION).

Jung's judgment that passive fantasies are usually pathological whereas active fantasies are highly creative seems suspect or at least contradictory. For another aspect of his definition of fantasy (CW 6, paras 711-22) is that of an imaginative activity, a completely natural, spontaneous and creative process of the psyche. This could hardly be pathological. It seems likely that, in order to sharpen the active/passive dichotomy, Jung paid too little attention to the eventual role of the EGO in relation to unconscious fantasy (see TRANSCENDENT FUNCTION).

Like DREAMS (which Jung compares to passive fantasies, a confirmation of the doubts expressed in the previous paragraph), fantasies may be interpreted. Jung stated that fantasy has its manifest and latent content and fantasy is susceptible to reductive and/or synthetic interpretation (see REDUCTIVE AND SYNTHETIC METHODS).

The main consituents of fantasy are images, but this is to be understood in an inclusive sense as referring to any elements active in the psyche when there is an absence of direct stimuli and not merely visualisations that originate in external stimuli. The term 'image' is used to indicate the gulf between fantasy and the external world (see IMAGE; IMAGO). In Jung's conception, it is fantasies and their images which lie behind and underpin feelings and behaviour rather than vice versa. Fantasies are not secondary, coded versions of emotional or behavioural problems. Jung's is a psychology of the UNCONSCIOUS and the unconscious is the primary and dynamic factor.

Again, some commentators would wish to moderate this, giving more weight to the quality of experience (and hence the characteristics) of the external world. At times, Jung's habitual concern to bridge logical or rational oppositions by means of a psychological, symbolic factor means that he, too, becomes aware of the over-rigidity of the divide. Then he refers to fantasy as linking an idea or image (which lacks tangible reality) and an entity in the physical world (which lacks mind or a place in mind). When fantasy performs this link, Jung refers to it as a 'third' factor (CW 6, paras 77–8). There is a parallel with Winnicott's (1971) use of the term 'third area' to indicate an infant's attempt to hold inner world fantasy and outer world reality in one frame (see OPPOSITES; PSYCHIC REALITY).

The problem is that we now have two disparate definitions of fantasy: (a) as different and separate from external reality, and (b) as linking inner and outer worlds. This difficulty can be resolved if we understand by 'inner world' something skeletal and present only in structural form. Then fantasy could be the bridging factor between archetype and external reality while at the same time being in oppositional relation to that reality.

Fantasy and artistic creativity are connected, though Jung made the point that artists do not simply reproduce their fantasies. Art of a 'psychological' nature may involve the artist utilising his personal situation – but that is something else. Jung also wrote of art as.

'visionary', going beyond the limits of the individual artist, a direct communication from the archaic wisdom of the psyche.

See SYMBOL.

father See ARCHETYPE; IMAGO; INFANCY AND CHILDHOOD; MARRIAGE.

female See SEX.

feminine See GENDER.

fixation Because the concept of fixation presupposes that there is an agreed line and timetable of psychological development to which any specific phenomenon may be referred, it does not often figure in ANALYTICAL PSYCHOLOGY (see DEVELOPMENT). Similarly, Jung's abandonment of a purely reductive approach to INTERPRETATION means that the idea of 'fixation points' is not emphasised either (see REDUCTIVE AND SYNTHETIC METHODS). It may be that the three major developments in PSYCHOANALYSIS since Freud's structural theory (ego-psychology, OBJECT RELATIONS and self-psychology) themselves demonstrate a move away from the notion of fixation. Psychoanalytically speaking, contemporary enthusiasm is more for the analysis of defences (ego-psychology), relationships (object relations) and MEANING (self-psychology).

fool See TRICKSTER.

G

gender A human and, therefore, a culturally influenced classification of the sexes as masculine and feminine. Jung often spoke and wrote as if he were unaware of the distinction between gender and SEX, which is, by contrast, biologically determined.

Although neither C. G. nor Emma Jung (1957) were unaware of the culturally based changes which were affecting both men and women of their times (note in this regard his acclaim of the Dogma of the ASSUMPTION OF THE VIRGIN MARY and her intuitive awareness of changes in a woman's self-image that would come with modern contraception), they were both more interested in the corresponding impact of these changes upon individuals and the resultant connections with the psychology of masculinity and femininity. In certain ways they anticipated and perhaps to some extent paved the way for today's changes in gender identity. In the main, their attitudes were consistent with the cultural mores of their own times in this regard but neither expressed a conscious preference for one as being superior to the other of the genders/sexes.

Their work on the SYZYGY was intended to be *gender*-oriented; but this is now questioned (Samuels, 1985a). Current work in ANALYTICAL PSYCHOLOGY proceeds along several lines of inquiry: the extent to which gender differences are sex linked; what psychological effects are manifested when there are shifts in gender role and status; whether an investigation of traditional imagery reveals anything about cultural forms more reflective of the feminine psyche in particular; and the possibility that there are linkages between gender definition and creativity.

God-image In psychological terms, Jung posited the reality of a God-image as a unifying and transcendent SYMBOL capable of drawing together heterogeneous psychic fragments or uniting polarised OPPOSITES. Like any IMAGE, it is a psychic product different from the object which it attempts to represent and to which it points. The God-image points to a reality that transcends CONSCIOUSNESS, is extraordinarily numinous (see NUMINOSUM), compels attention, attracts ENERGY, and is analogous to an idea that in similar form has forced itself upon mankind in all parts of the world and in all ages. As such, it is an image of totality and 'as the highest value and supreme dominant in the psychic hierarchy, the God-image is immediately related to, or identical with, the SELF' (*CW* 9ii, para. 170). Being an image of totality, however, the God-image has two sides; one good, the other EVIL.

Clarifying and differentiating *God* and the *God-image*, Jung wrote:

> It is the fault of the everlasting contamination of object and imago that people can make no conceptual distinction between 'God' and 'God-image', and therefore think that when one speaks of the 'God-image' one is speaking of God and offering 'theological' explanations. It is not for psychology, as a science, to demand a hypostatization of the God-image. But, the facts being what they are, it does have to reckon with the existence of a God-image ... the God-image corresponds to a definite COMPLEX of psychological facts, and is thus a quantity which we can operate with; but what God is in himself remains a question outside the competence of all psychology (*CW* 8, para. 528).

Viewed psychotherapeutically, the God-image functions as a church within, so to speak; as a psychic container, a frame of reference, a system of values and moral arbiter. Jung accepted as a

God-image whatever an individual claimed to experience as God, that which represented the person's highest value whether expressed consciously or unconsciously, and typical religious motifs which recurred in the history of ideas, dogma, MYTH, RITUAL and art.

See RELIGION.

gods and goddesses   See MYTH.

Great Mother   Jung's theory of archetypes led him to hypothesise that the influences which a mother exerts on her children do not necessarily derive from the mother herself as a person and her actual character traits. In addition, there are qualities which the mother seems to possess but which in fact spring from the archetypal structure surrounding 'mother' and are projected onto her by the child (see ARCHETYPE; PROJECTION).

The Great Mother is a naming of the general IMAGE, drawn from COLLECTIVE cultural experience. As an image she reveals an archetypal fullness but also a positive-negative polarity. An infant tends to organise his experiences of early vulnerability and dependence upon his mother round positive and negative poles. The positive pole draws together such qualities as 'maternal solicitude and sympathy; the magical authority of the female; the wisdom and spiritual exaltation that transcend reason; any helpful instinct or impulse; all that is benign, all that cherishes and sustains, that fosters growth and fertility'. In short, the good mother. The negative pole suggests the bad mother: 'anything secret, hidden, dark; the abyss, the world of the dead, anything that devours, seduces, and poisons, that is terrifying and inescapable like fate' (CW 9i, para. 158).

From a developmental perspective, this implies a splitting of the maternal IMAGO (see OBJECT RELATIONS). Jung points out that such contrasts are widespread in the cultural imagery of all peoples so that mankind as a whole does not find it odd or unbearable that the mother should be split. But eventually an infant has to come to terms with his mother as a person and bring opposite perceptions of her together, if he is to relate to her fully (see CONIUNCTIO; DEPRESSIVE POSITION; INFANCY AND CHILDHOOD).

In addition to the dualisms of personal/archetypal and good/bad, we must add that of earthy/spiritual: the Great Mother in her chthonic, agricultural guise and in her divine, ethereal, virginal form. This, too, has its reflection in the ordinary images of mother which an infant develops.

It is important to understand the use of terms like the Great Mother in developmental psychology in a metaphorical and not a literal sense. There is no question but that an infant knows his mother is not a fertility goddess or a destructive 'Queen of the Night'; however, he may relate to her *as if* she were such a figure.

Jung felt that the quality of the Great Mother image is different for males and females. Because what is female is alien to a man, it will tend to position itself in the UNCONSCIOUS and hence exert an influence made greater by the fact of its being hidden. But a woman shares the same conscious life as her mother and hence the mother image is both less terrifying and less attractive to her than it is to a male (see ANDROGYNE; ANIMA AND ANIMUS; ASSUMPTION OF THE VIR-GIN MARY; GENDER; SEX). Here Jung may idealise the mother-daugh-ter relationship, overlooking its competitive aspect and seeing it from the perspective of his time. Likewise, Jung draws a qualitative dis-tinction between the mother archetype and the father archetype which, it might be argued, also reflects his own culture.

The fundamental nature of the mother-infant relationship means that the Great Mother, as a cultural and historical phenomenon, offers many stimulating aspects for investigation (e.g. Neumann, 1955). Some of these are only now beginning to be explored by women.

group Jung's attitude to group psychology (and group psycho-therapy) reveals a certain AMBIVALENCE. For, while the group may give a person 'a courage, a bearing and a dignity which may easily get lost in isolation', there is a danger that the benefits of group life will prove so seductively inhibiting that individuality is lost (*CW* 8, para. 228).

There is a confusion in analytical psychology between a person's relationship to the COLLECTIVE, to SOCIETY, his own CULTURE, the mass, or to a group. That has perhaps been caused by Jung's ten-dency to see a person primarily in relation to his internal world, in contrast to an interest in personal relationships and social concerns.

Jung's main theoretical contribution to group psychology lies in his claim that it is the influence of insufficiently integrated archetypal tendencies that leads to mass phenomena such as fascism. See Jaffé (1971) and Odajnyk (1976) for observations on Jung's political orientation.

guilt This is to be taken as a psychological and not a moral or legal category. What is referred to is the presence of a feeling which may or may not have objective bases. Of course, irrationally based guilt may be more interesting from a clinical point of view, but Jung points out that there are enormous psychological consequences of a failure to recognise and acknowledge guilt feelings of a more rational nature.

Jung uses the term 'collective guilt' in contradistinction to 'personal guilt'. However, the division is not clear-cut. Jung is not suggesting that a sense of personal guilt arises *solely* from the specific circumstances of an individual; also present will be the archetypal factor. Similarly, collective guilt may strike on an individual level. Collective guilt may be compared to fate, or to a curse, or to a form of pollution (see COLLECTIVE; SELF; UNCONSCIOUS). Jung's example of collective guilt concerned what a non-Nazi German might feel after the end of the war and the revelation of Hitler's crimes against the Jews.

A sense of guilt may be necessary to avoid the projection outward of SHADOW contents so that it is the other's guilt that strikes one and excites moral condemnation. Jung is therefore rather at variance with Freud: the avoidance of neurosis may *require* a sense of guilt. Even if this is irrational, it will lead into charged areas of unconsciousness. Central to this idea of Jung's is the conviction that PROJECTION of the shadow diminishes the personality, even to the point of an annihilation of humanity.

The sense of guilt inspires reflection on what is EVIL – which is as important as reflection on what is good. 'In the last resort there is no good that cannot produce evil and no evil that cannot produce good' (CW 12, para. 36).

See SUPER-EGO; MORALITY.

H

---

healing   Often used by Jung to refer to the intent of ANALYSIS and implying something different from an objective 'CURE' (see Gordon, 1978). That is, the goal or end-product is defined in terms of the individual concerned and whatever form his potential WHOLENESS might take (see INDIVIDUATION). Similarly, Jung's wish to distinguish analysis from medicine in general, and his stress on the quality of the analyst's personality from what he saw as Freud's allegiance to technique in particular, led him to refer to healing as an art, sometimes a 'practical art'. He also linked healing with compassion – a view which finds resonances in modern attempts to characterise the effective elements in the therapeutic relationship as the therapist's warmth, genuineness and empathy. Symptoms may be looked at from a psychopathological viewpoint or as natural attempts at healing (see PATHOLOGY; SELF-REGULATORY FUNCTION OF THE PSYCHE).

The image of *the wounded healer* is sometimes introduced to illumine various aspects of analysis. Meier (1967) drew parallels between the ancient healing practices of the temples of Aesclepius and analytical treatment. Healing practices took place within a closed setting, the TEMENOS or temple precinct and fostered sleep in the hope of the 'patient's' having healing dreams. The teacher of the healing arts, Chiron the centaur, is depicted as suffering from an incurable wound. The analyst may be seen as the wounded healer, the analytic setting which permits regression and the giving up of over-consciousness functions as the temenos (see ANALYSIS; ANALYST AND PATIENT; REGRESSION).

This was developed further by Guggenbühl-Craig (1971). The wounded healer motif is a symbolic IMAGE of something archetypal. That is why it can contain two apparently contradictory elements. But, in our culture, we tend to split the image so that the analyst figure in any helping relationship becomes all-powerful; strong, healthy and able. The patient remains nothing but a patient; passive, dependent, 'hospitalised'. If all analysts have an inner wound, then for an analyst to present himself as 'healthy' is to cut off from part of the inner world. Likewise, if the patient is only seen as 'ill', then he is also cut off from his own inner health or his capacity to heal himself. Ideally, though the patient may *initially* project his self-healing capacities onto the analyst, later he will take them back. The analyst projects his own experience of being wounded into the patient in order to know the patient in an emotional sense (see Kohut's definition of empathy as 'vicarious introspection').

The institution of training analysis is an acknowledgment of the fact that, as a profession, analysis attracts 'wounded healers'. There is growing evidence that this pertains in all the therapeutic professions and may even be a qualification for such work (Ford, 1983). Jung emphasised that an analyst can only take a person as far as he has gone himself.

Jung made several further cultural observations concerning healing: (a) INITIATION points to healing; (b) religions function as 'great psychic healing systems' (CW 13, para. 478). See RELIGION; (c) SACRIFICE, literal or symbolic, bodily or financial, is necessary for healing – nothing is gained unless something is given up; (d) there is a universal need for, and interest in, healing.

hermaphrodite A primordial unity in which male and female are unconsciously conjoined. Among many images, the UROBOROS is strikingly symbolic of such an undifferentiated state.

Although the term is applied to a bisexual state, and alchemically it is frequently referred to as 'that for which the opus is undertaken', the final transformation, though hermaphroditic, is better defined as androgynous (see ANDROGYNE). As the initial substance, called the *prima materia* by alchemists, is one in which masculine-spiritual and feminine-corporeal aspects are merged, the end of the process, the *lapis*, will also contain the two but in differentiated form, co-existent and co-equal.

Jung found the figure of the hermaphrodite monstrous and felt that in no way did it do justice to the ideal and goal of the art of ALCHEMY. That such a lofty spiritual aim could be expressed by this crude SYMBOL he attributed to the fact that the alchemist was unable to free himself from the grip of unconscious and instinctive sexuality because he was separated from either a psychological or religious frame of reference. When we consider ALCHEMY as a projection of the modern processes of the UNCONSCIOUS, however, the extraordinary fascination and continuing emphasis upon the symbolism of the hermaphrodite provides a parallel for the difficulties of work with this particular pair of OPPOSITES, male and female, during the initial stages of ANALYSIS.

hero   A mythological motif that corresponds to man's unconscious SELF; according to Jung, 'a *quasi-human* being who symbolises the ideas, forms and forces that mould or grip the SOUL' (CW 5, para. 259). See MYTH. The image of the hero embodies man's most powerful aspirations and reveals the manner in which they are ideally realised.

The hero is a transitional being, a MANA PERSONALITY. His most approximate human form is the priest. Viewed intrapsychically, he represents the WILL and capacity to seek and undergo repeated transformations in pursuit of WHOLENESS or MEANING. Therefore at times he appears to be EGO; at other times, self. He is the EGO-SELF AXIS personified.

The wholeness of a hero implies not only the ability to withstand but also to hold consciously the tremendous tension of OPPOSITES. This is achieved, according to Jung, by risking REGRESSION and purposefully exposing oneself to the danger of being 'devoured by the maternal monster', not once but many times, a lifelong process beginning in infancy. The maternal monster Jung identified as the COLLECTIVE psyche.

When discussing the hero motif, Jung was at pains to point out dangers. A figure of such magnitude cannot be incorporated in its fullness but requires most careful analytic delineation and DIFFERENTIATION (see ANALYSIS). The value of the image lies in its intrapsychic functioning. The absurdity of IDENTIFICATION with the IMAGE of the hero is apparent but, when confronted with the ARCHETYPE, humour and a sense of proportion are often lacking. It is earnest pursuit of the hero image, when the destination is given precedence over the journey, that leads to over-intellectualisation and an artificially conscious striving for goals that are only realisable gradually and by way of dialogue with one's own UNCONSCIOUS (see ANALYST AND PATIENT; DREAMS; INDIVIDUATION).

As Jung rightly foresaw, an archetype with such widespread collective appeal will inevitably find collective expression and attract PROJECTION. Because of its youthfulness as a profession and the dynamism of its early interpreters, analytical psychology has had to confront this problem. Because of the numinous attraction and contagion, the tendency has been to downplay the motif in recent years.

homosexuality It is necessary to ascertain whether Jung is referring to homosexuality as an external sexual orientation leading to genital activity, or a latent version of that, or to an inner world tendency. There is little doubt that he saw homosexual practice as limiting, though he recognised the psychological necessity for some people to pass through a homosexual period. On the other hand, homosexuality as such is recognised as a component of sexuality. Jung commented that we would not need a dynamic conception such as libido or psychic ENERGY if sexuality simply consisted of a fixed quantum of heterosexuality. Homosexuality may be a residue of polymorphous infantile sexuality, but, as an inner world factor, it is inevitable and potentially psychologically valuable (see below).

Regarding the causes of homosexuality, Jung seemed to adopt *structural* and *developmental* perspectives, though these overlap. From the standpoint of psychic structure, homosexuality may be seen as an identification with the contrasexual components; ANIMA AND ANIMUS in men and women respectively (see PSYCHE). Jung's view was that the largely unconscious contrasexual component reflects the opposite of a person's anatomical sex. The personality of an anima-identified man takes on a feminine cast, that of an animus-identified woman, a masculine cast. In such circumstances, the feminised man will seek a male partner and the masculinised woman a female partner. Presumably the partners are attracted by the same psychology. The man may be seen as having projected his masculinity onto another man, the woman her femininity onto another woman. (The formulation is also applicable to heterosexual MARRIAGE.) This structural approach of Jung's is illustrated in the clinical situation. Some male homosexuals idealise or over-value the penis; it turns out, on analysis, to represent their own masculinity. Such men are prone to form father transferences in relation to older, more socially established men. Some female homosexuals idealise the sisterhood which they feel they have attained in relationship; an over-valuation of the femininity they have projected.

From the developmental standpoint, Jung saw homosexuality as an expression of a certain kind of relationship with the parent of the opposite sex. He was referring to an over-involvement, a more than usually strong tie, an over-developed mother-complex or father-complex (see COMPLEX). The incest taboo prevents the carrying through of heterosexual impulses and homosexuality would be the only way to discharge sexual energy, leaving all emotional vitality within the child's relationship with the parent of the same sex.

Furthermore, the child's identity as non-heterosexual opens the way and makes it safe for a kind of spiritual marriage between him or her and the parent of the opposite sex. A mutual admiration is fostered. This IMAGE of the sexless child-parent marriage was, according to Jung, a widespread motif, suggesting a kind of WHOLENESS and hence possessing its own attractive power. The mother, in particular, may gain an unconscious satisfaction from her son's homosexuality. Jung's view was that this fulfils her spiritually in spite of her conscious anxiety and sorrow about the situation.

Jung also commented on the role of the parent of the same sex. It is the image of that punishing parent which stands between the child and the parent of the opposite sex and forces a non-heterosexual pattern of attention.

The structural idea (PROJECTION of the man's MASCULINE elements and of the woman's FEMININE elements) may also be brought in here. The father image may be the carrier of this projection and hence he becomes the desirable object for the boy. This leads to homosexuality later on. And a similar phenomenon takes place between the girl and her mother. In addition, a woman's search for the good mother she may not have experienced may also lead her in the homosexual direction.

Turning to homosexuality as an inner tendency, Jung is explicit about its value, particularly if seen as part of a positive complex. He writes this passage from a man's point of view but, in the considerable amount of space devoted to female homosexuality, there is no suggestion that a corresponding possibility is out of the question. A man with a positive mother-complex and homosexual tendencies may also have

a great capacity for friendship, which often creates ties of astonishing tenderness between men and may even rescue friendship between the sexes from the limbo of the impossible. He may have good taste and an aesthetic sense which are fostered by the presence of a feminine streak. Then he may be supremely gifted as a teacher because of his almost feminine insight and tact. He is likely to have a feeling for history, and to be conservative in the best sense and cherish the value of the past. Often he is endowed with a wealth of religious feelings and a spiritual receptivity (CW 9i, para. 164).

Contemporary Jungian writers have argued that it is vital to recognise that homosexuality in and of itself is not psychopathological. Much theorising about homosexuality has been based on fear and prejudice and it should be realised that theory is not produced outside of a cultural context. Other writers have cautioned against an inadvertent idealisation of homosexuality. However, it seems that the category of 'homosexual' is itself problematic. There was once intense discussion about whether homosexuality should be regarded as a bar to participation in analytical training. Today, the major Jungian analytical trainings do not operate such a bar.

hysteria Though Jung adds his usual comment about Freud's over-estimation of the role of sexuality, he did not disagree with many of Freud's views on hysteria (see PSYCHOANALYSIS). These are that hysterical symptoms are a return of repressed memories in a different form, that they are symbolic and can be elucidated by means of ANALYSIS (see SYMBOL), that there is a problematic excess of psychic ENERGY (usually sexual), and that the aetiology of hysteria is to be found in the personal background of the patient. It is striking that Jung's habitual addition of the collective to the personal UNCONSCIOUS is muted when he discusses hysteria. Perhaps this reflects the fact that most of his writing on the subject dates from his earliest, psychiatric period when it was often Freud's theories which he was demonstrating or discussing. Jung's earliest psychiatric interests were in the general field of states of altered consciousness or semi-consciousness ('occult' phenomena, somnambulism, hysteria). See SPIRIT.

Jung's contribution may be summarised as follows:

(1) The WORD ASSOCIATION TEST (see ASSOCIATION) showed the central role of secrecy in hysteria (i.e. the forbidden, and, hence, sexual nature of the hysteric's fantasies is revealed).

(2) In hysteria, the natural tendency of the PSYCHE to divide itself into relatively autonomous complexes has gone out of control so that a complex/complexes have invaded and possessed the body (see COMPLEX POSSESSION). A form of personality disintegration has taken place and the somatic symptoms of hysteria may be seen as the symbolic representatives of such pathological complexes (see DISSOCIATION).

(3) Using TYPOLOGY, Jung concluded that hysteria may be seen as an extraverted disorder (SCHIZOPHRENIA being introverted). The reason why hysterics tend to need to involve other people in their difficulties

is that they have projected these difficulties onto the outside world (hence, extraverted). The effect the hysteric has on the immediate world is an indication of that person's internal state. A simple example of this would be that a hysterical paralysis of the legs would require the patient to seek assistance of others in walking. What could be a clearer demonstration of the patient's regressed state and his/her unmet infantile needs?

(4) Because of (3), hysterics often manifest as leader figures. Hitler was an example of this, in Jung's view. Apropos of Nazism, Jung wrote of a 'collective hysteria' (see GUILT) in which a large group splits off a part of itself which then functions 'out of control'. Hitler's dissociations and those of the German people at that time coincided.

I

idea Jung uses this term in two ways. On the one hand, the word refers to the MEANING that springs from an IMAGE. Here, the idea would appear to be a secondary phenomenon. On the other hand, 'idea' suggests a primary psychological factor, without which there can be no concrete emotion or conceptualisation.

The first usage was developed to avoid giving the impression that imagery was purely visual. The second usage reflects Jung's Platonic lineage and his interest in Kant.

A benefit of Jung's usage is that it emphasises that there is no need to make a rigid division between the products of intellect and those of imagination; these may be accepted as evidence of *different* kinds of thinking. Here, as in certain other respects, Jung anticipates the post-Cartesian paradigm shift in scientific methodology (CW 6, 1921).

See DIRECTED AND FANTASY THINKING.

identification An UNCONSCIOUS PROJECTION of one's personality onto that of another, whether person, cause, place or other figure, able to provide either a reason for being or a way of being. Identification is an important part of normal DEVELOPMENT. In extreme form, identification takes the form of IDENTITY or may lead to an INFLATION. Identification with another person, say an analyst, does by definition preclude individuation. Fortunately, identifying and dis-identifying processes can go on simultaneously on different levels of development even in the adult.

See OBJECT RELATIONS.

identity An unconscious tendency to behave as if two dissimilar entities were in fact identical. These could both be internal entities, or both external, or the identity could be between an internal and an external element. (Jung does not use the word in the sense of 'personal identity'; see EGO.)

Jung's view of the psychology of an infant was that he exists in a state of identity with his parents and, in particular, with his mother. That is, he shares in the psychic life of his parents and has little or none of his own. This is clearly not the case (and Jung contradicted it himself with the observation that the neonate has a complicated psychology; see INFANCY AND CHILDHOOD). Because of this, subsequent analytical psychologists have retained the idea only in modified form.

Identity is now used as a general term to cover the whole range of phenomena in infancy when a clear conscious differentiation between subject and object has not yet arisen. It is used metaphorically to indicate the infant's positive and negative images, fantasies and feelings of his being fused (at one) with his mother. Identity is seen as somewhat of an achievement; a state which the mother-infant dyad, led by the infant's active approach behaviour, must enter prior to attachment-separation processes taking place (Fordham, 1976). See PARTICIPATION MYSTIQUE, which is a state of less than total identity.

Jung's insistence that identity is a pre-existent state ('original' identity) is also adapted so that reference is being made to innate, archetypal *capacities* to enter a state of identity (see ARCHETYPE). In plain language, one cannot become personally attached without having been very close – just as one cannot separate without having been attached. The order of events is: (a) at birth, mother and infant are psychologically separate. Both have innate capacities to enter a state of identity; (b) a state of identity is reached; (c) out of this, personal attachment develops; (d) out of that, separation commences.

Jung's *a priori* conception of identity is retained in connection with the theory of OPPOSITES. Such identity underpins what we perceive as opposites (Hillman, 1979).

Jung also used the term to summarise the outcome of his speculations about the ultimate links between psyche and matter (see PSYCHIC REALITY; PSYCHOID UNCONSCIOUS; SYNCHRONICITY; *UNUS MUNDUS*).

image Although it is possible to assign a particular time and setting to Jung's definition of SYMBOL, it is less easy to describe the evolution of his ideas about image. Perhaps it is true that the progression from speaking of symbol to concentration upon image is a phenomenon of analytical psychology in its post-Jungian period (cf. Samuels, 1985a), but a close observation of Jung's personal writings appears to substantiate a definition of *image* which contains or amplifies the *symbol*, being the context within which it is embedded, whether personal or collective.

Jung's life work, along with his writing, seems to be dominated by certain psychic configurations around which he moves in CIRCUM-AMBULATION, seeing them ever more deeply and clearly, thus enabling him to fill out or give shape to a basic form. Therefore, although he intermingled the words symbol and image at different times in his professional career, using these words almost as synonyms for one another, in the long run it would appear that he conceived of the image as both prior to and greater than the sum of its symbolic components. In his own words: 'The image is a *condensed expression of the psychic situation as a whole*, and not merely, or even predominantly, of unconscious contents pure and simple' (*CW* 6, para. 745).

Jung's understanding of the image changed in the course of a lifetime. Originally formulated as a concept, the image was experienced as a companionate psychic presence. His most telling discovery, verified empirically, could be that psyche itself does not proceed 'scientifically', that is, by way of hypothesis and model, but imagistically, that is, by way of MYTH and METAPHOR. However, Jung says of the image:

> It undoubtedly does express unconscious contents, but not the whole of them, only those that are momentarily constellated. This constellation is the result of the spontaneous activity of the UNCONSCIOUS on the one hand and of the momentary conscious situation on the other.... The INTERPRETATION of its meaning, therefore, can start neither from the conscious alone nor from the unconscious alone, but only from their *reciprocal relationship* (*ibid*, emphasis added).

This highlights the place of emotion and AFFECT in regard to imagery. Whereas, looked at from a causal, a theoretical or a scientific point of view, imagery is supposedly objective, of its nature it is highly subjective as well (see REDUCTIVE AND SYNTHETIC METHODS). Because the image is a *container* of opposites, in contradistinction to the symbol which is a *mediator* of opposites, it does not adhere to any one position but elements of it can be found in either. As an example, the image of the ANIMA is both an inner and an outer experience at one and the same time; likewise 'mother' or 'queen'. In part, the work of ANALYSIS consists of differentiation in preparation for a re-unification of OPPOSITES as part of a renewed and more conscious imagery. That is to say, life for being real is no less psychological.

The image is always an expression of the totality perceived and perceivable, apprehended and apprehensible, by the individual. Whereas, especially late in his life, Jung delineated between the archetypal image and the ARCHETYPE *per se*, in practice it is images which stir the beholder (e.g. the dreamer) to the degree that he is able to embody or realise (make conscious) what he perceives. According to Jung, the image is endowed with a generative power; its function is to arouse; it is psychically compelling.

In summary, images have a facility to beget their like; movement of images toward their realisation is a psychic process which happens to us personally. We both look on from the outside and also act or suffer as a figure in the drama. 'It is a psychic fact', Jung writes, 'that the FANTASY is happening and it is as real as you – as a psychic entity – are real. If this crucial operation of entering in with your own reaction is not carried out, all the changes are left to the flow of images, and you yourself remain unchanged' (*CW* 14, para. 753). Psychological life emphasises above all the need for a subjective reaction to imagery, thereby establishing a relationship, a dialogue, an involvement or give and take which results eventually in a CON-IUNCTIO in which both person and image are effected (see ACTIVE IMAGINATION; EGO; TRANSCENDENT FUNCTION). This relationship is the focus of current attention among analytical psychologists, symbolised by an emphasis upon empathy, relatedness and EROS.

Although a great deal of attention has been given to individual symbols, Hillman (1975) has also attempted to clarify the concept of *image*. The appropriate relationship between the individual and image is expressed by the Islamic scholar Corbin (1983): 'the image opens the way itself to what lies beyond it, toward what it symbolises with.' Corroborating this, we have Jung's statement: 'When the conscious mind participates actively and experiences each stage of the process, or at least understands it intuitively, then the next image (an enlargement of the original image) always starts off on the higher level that has been won and purposiveness develops' (*CW* 7, para. 386). See IMAGO; PSYCHIC REALITY; TELEOLOGICAL POINT OF VIEW.

imago Term introduced by Jung in 1911–12 (*CW* 5) and adopted in psychoanalysis. When 'imago' is used instead of 'image', this is to underline the fact that images are generated subjectively, particularly those of other people. That is, the object is perceived according to the internal state and dynamics of the subject. There is the additional specific point that many images (e.g. of parents) do not arise out of actual personal experiences of parents of a particular character, but are based on unconscious fantasies or derived from the activities of the ARCHETYPE (see COMPLEX; FANTASY; GOD-IMAGE; GREAT MOTHER; IMAGE; SYMBOL).

incest Unlike Freud, Jung did not view the incest impulse from a literal perspective, although he could not avoid remarking on the concrete way children express it (in *CW* 17, 'Psychic conflicts in a child'). However, he saw incest FANTASY as a complicated METAPHOR for a path of psychological growth and development (see ACTING OUT; ENACTMENT). His ideas both applied and extended the work of the anthropologist/analyst Layard (1945, 1959).

Jung's view is that when a child experiences incestuous feelings or fantasies, he or she can be seen as attempting unconsciously to add enriching layers of experience to his or her personality by close emotional contact with the parent (see TELEOLOGICAL POINT OF VIEW). The sexual aspect of the incestuous impulse ensures that the encounter is deep and meaningful – sexual feelings cannot be ignored. The incest taboo prevents physical expression, however, and has its own psychological purpose (see below).

When an adult regresses in an incestuous manner, he can be seen as attempting to recharge his batteries, to regenerate himself spiritually and psychologically. REGRESSION has, therefore, to be valued as something more than an EGO defence. For an adult, incestuous regression need not necessarily be towards a particular figure or IMAGE, though it often is (as in a 'crush'). The state in which a person finds him or herself also signals such regression: serene, floating, dreamy, at one. This is the state of the mystic or the creative reverie which those who study the processes of artists have noted.

Out of the *temporary* giving up of adult ego-ic behaviour comes a new and refreshing encounter with the internal world and with the grounds of being. For a child (or for an adult fixated incestuously on one person), the sexual element is a symbolic entry to such a state and its rewards. Reflecting upon the symbolism, the two bodies which might engage in the sex act represent different parts of the psyche which are not, as yet, integrated. Intercourse marks such integration and the baby which might result symbolises growth and regeneration (see ALCHEMY; SYMBOL).

Sometimes incestuous regression becomes a search for a different kind of oneness – power and control over others. Jung stressed that it was vital to emerge from the state of merger with a parent (see IDENTITY; *PARTICIPATION MYSTIQUE*). This is both an ordinary developmental task and, for an adult, a necessary confrontation with adult realities. Luckily, there are disadvantages in the state of oneness; it may be felt as dangerously devouring and unending (see DEATH IN-STINCT; GREAT MOTHER).

Jung developed these ideas on incest from a man's point of view (CW 5), in terms of incestuous entanglement with, or regression to, the mother. There is no reason why the model should not apply to the daughter's relationship with her father. For a girl, this implies that she has to experience a deep connection to her father that has an erotic tone. For the adult woman, her experience may take the form of a kind of paternal regression. But what if this symbolically eroticised relation fails to take place? Then a father cannot, as it were, initiate his daughter into a deeper psychology for she will be too distant from him for their relationship to have a profound effect on her (see INITIATION).

The father could not be more different from the daughter; he is male and from another generation (see OPPOSITES). This gives him potential for stimulating an expansion and deepening of her person-ality. But he is also part of the same family as his daughter; and this makes him 'safe' as far as physical acting out is concerned. Yet, the familial and loving link encourages an emotional investment in his daughter's maturation while father/daughter union is prohibited.

Cases of actual incest result when the symbolic nature of these interactions is bypassed, perhaps because of unresolved incestuous longings on the part of the father. Equally damaging to the psycho-sexual development of the child is erotic withdrawal or indifference on the part of the parent. This is perhaps a greater problem for girls than for boys. The mother will have experienced and become accus-tomed to a close, physical contact with her children with its attendant excitement. The father may find this kind of experience with a daughter too much to bear and repress the eroticism – displaying a mockery of her sexuality or setting far too rigid boundaries for it. There may also be a greater cultural inhibition as well, i.e. men may be barred from emotional expression.

The incest taboo was given a specifically psychological value and function by Jung. This is in addition to his recognition of its role in the maintenance of a healthy SOCIETY – marital relationships have to be outside the designated family lest CULTURE itself stagnate or re-gress. But it would be a mistake to see the incest taboo as an encul-tured or SUPER-EGO prohibition against a 'natural' incest impulse. The incest impulse and the incest taboo are natural to each other. To respond only to the taboo but ignore the impulse may well suggest to us a frustration-based boost to CONSCIOUSNESS which will be spurious, desiccated, intellectual. On the other hand, to act on the impulse and ignore the taboo leads to a focus on short-lived pleasure and the exploitation of the child's vulnerability by the parent. However, in cases of incest, the child may be capitalising on his or her more than special relationship to a powerful figure.

We might add that it is one function of the incest taboo to force an individual to consider with whom he may or may not mate. He has, therefore, to regard a potential mate *as an individual*. The moment choice is limited, choice is highlighted (and this is true even in a system of arranged marriages). The incest taboo, thought of like this, underpins I-Thou relating (R. Stein, 1974).

In ANALYSIS, feelings of sexual attraction between ANALYST AND PATIENT occur in very many instances. Jung's ideas about the psychological aspects of incest fantasy may be used in addition to understandings of Oedipal dynamics to underscore the symbolic aspects of the feelings, leading to a lessening of the possibility of hurtful acting out. But the goal is not merely to assist the analyst's adherence to the rule of abstinence. For, locked up in what might seem to be an infantile sexualisation of a state of mind, may be the seeds of important psychological development.

See ENERGY; PSYCHOANALYSIS.

individuation A person's becoming himself, whole, indivisible and distinct from other people or collective psychology (though also in relation to these).

This is the key concept in Jung's contribution to the theories of personality development. As such, it is inextricably interwoven with others, particularly SELF, EGO and ARCHETYPE as well as with the synthesis of CONSCIOUSNESS and UNCONSCIOUS elements. A simplified way of expressing the relationship of the most important concepts involved would be: ego is to INTEGRATION (socially seen as ADAPTATION) what the self is for individuation (self-experience and -realisation). While consciousness is increased by the analysis of defences (e.g. PROJECTION of the SHADOW), the process of individuation is a CIRCUMAMBULATION of the self as the centre of the personality which thereby becomes unified. In other words, the person becomes conscious in what respects he or she is both a unique human being and, at the same time, no more than a common man or woman.

Because of this inherent paradox, definitions abound, both throughout Jung's work as well as that of the 'post-Jungians' (Samuels, 1985a). The term 'individuation' was taken up by Jung via the philosopher Schopenhauer but dates back to Gerard Dorn, a sixteenth-century alchemist. Both speak of the *principium individuationis*. Jung applied the principle to psychology. In *Psychological Types*, published in 1921 but in the writing since 1913, we find the first published definition (CW 6, paras 757–762). The attributes emphasised are: (1) the goal of the process is the development of the personality; (2) it presupposes and includes COLLECTIVE relationships, i.e. it does not occur in a state of isolation; (3) individuation involves a degree of opposition to social norms which have no absolute validity: 'The more a man's life is shaped by the collective norm, the greater is his individual immorality' (*ibid*). See MORALITY.

The unifying aspect of individuation is emphasised by its etymology. 'I use the term "individuation" to denote the process by which a person becomes "in-dividual", that is a separate indivisible unity or "whole"' (CW 9i, para. 490). The phenomena described by Jung in a variety of contexts are always close to his own personal experience, his work with patients and his researches, especially into ALCHEMY and the minds of the alchemists. The definitions or descriptions of individuation therefore vary in emphasis according to whatever source Jung was closest to at the time.

A much later book (CW 8, para. 432) refers to the difficulty which apparently persisted in distinguishing between integration and individuation: 'again and again I note that the individuation process is confused with the coming of the ego into consciousness and that the ego is in consequence identified with the self, which naturally produces a hopeless muddle. Individuation is then nothing but ego-centredness and auto-eroticism.... Individuation does not shut out from the world, but gathers the world to oneself.' Clearly it is as important to describe what the manifestations of individuation are as it is to say what they are not (the references to autoeroticism, i.e. NARCISSISM). Again, '*Individualism* means deliberately stressing and giving prominence to some supposed peculiarity, rather than to collective considerations and obligations. But *individuation* means precisely the better and more complete fulfillment of collective qualities' (CW 7, para. 267, emphases added). Or: 'The aim of individuation is nothing less than to divest the self of the false wrappings of the PERSONA on the one hand, and the suggestive power of primordial images on the other' (CW 7, para. 269). See ARCHETYPE.

We know that Jung started to paint MANDALAS about 1916 during a stormy period of his life, not long after the break with Freud. A whole chapter in CW 9i is called 'A Study in the Process of Individuation' and is based on a case study in which the patient's PAINTINGS played a prominent role. It is not surprising that, what with Jung's introversion and the early emphasis on intrapsychic material, the impression may have come about that experiencing the inner psychic world was taking precedence over interpersonal relationships during the process. Jung further illustrates Christ's individuation in 'Transformation symbolism in the mass' (CW 11) and this, as well as statements to the effect that individuation was not for everybody, may have led to the notion that one was dealing with an elitist concept.

Jung may unwittingly have added to this misunderstanding by stating that the process is a relatively rare occurrence. Although the process may be more easily demonstrated by choosing dramatic examples, it frequently occurs in unobtrusive circumstances. The transformation brought about may result both from a natural event (e.g. birth or death) or at times from a technical process. The dialectical procedure of ANALYSIS offers in our day and age a prominent example of the latter kind whereby the analyst becomes no longer the agent but a fellow participant in the process. In that case, the appropriate handling of the transference can be of crucial importance (see ANALYST AND PATIENT).

One danger of an intense involvement with the inner world and its fascinating images is that it may lead to a narcissistic preoccupation. Another danger would be to consider all manifestations, including antisocial activities and even psychotic breakdowns as justifiable results of an individuation process. Inasmuch as the transference in analysis plays a decisive part, it has to be added that individuation is, in the language of alchemy, a work against nature (*opus contra naturam*). That is to say, the INCEST or kinship libido must not be yielded to. On the other hand, it is not to be despised because it is an essential driving force.

As regards methodology, individuation cannot be induced by the analyst nor, of course, demanded. Analysis merely creates a facilitating environment for the process: individuation is not the outcome of a correct technique. It means, however, that the analyst must have more than an inkling about individuation (and/or the lack of it) from his personal experience in order to have an open mind towards the possible meaning to the patient of his unconscious productions ranging from physical symptoms to DREAMS, VISIONS or paintings (see ACTIVE IMAGINATION). One can certainly speak of a *psychopathology of individuation* which Jung clearly does (e.g. see CW 9i, para. 290). The common dangers during individuation are INFLATION (hypomania) on the one hand, and DEPRESSION on the other. Schizophrenic breakdowns are also not unknown.

Jung refers to psychotic ideas which, unlike neurotic contents, cannot be integrated (CW 9i, para. 495). They remain inaccessible and may swamp the ego; their nature is baffling. It is conceivable that the centre of the personality (the self) is expressed by ideas and imagery which, in this sense, are 'psychotic'. Individuation is regarded as an inescapable issue and the analyst can do little more than stand by with all the patience and sympathy he can muster. The outcome in every case is uncertain. Individuation is no more than a potential goal, the idealisation of which is easier than its realisation.

Mandalas and dreams point to the symbolism of the self wherever a centre and a circle (usually squared) appear. And symbols of the self, many of which are recorded and illustrated in Jung's work, occur wherever the process of individuation 'becomes the object of conscious scrutiny, or where, as in PSYCHOSIS, the collective unconscious peoples the conscious mind with archetypal figures' (CW 16, para. 474). Symbols of the self are sometimes identical with the deity (both Eastern and Western) and there are religious overtones to the individuation process just as there are 'religious' overtones to some psychotic contents, though the distinction may be subtle. At one point, Jung answered a question put to him by replying: '*Individuation is the life in God*, as mandala psychology clearly shows' (CW 18, para. 1624, emphasis added).

Analysis and marriage are specific examples of settings of an interpersonal nature which lend themselves to the work of individuation. Both require devotion and are arduous journeys. Some analysts would regard the psychological type of each partner as of crucial importance (see TYPOLOGY). No doubt there are other interpersonal relationships which, combined with a more or less conscious observation of intraphysic events, could facilitate individuation. The most important theoretical development since Jung wrote that individuation belonged to the second half of life has been the extension of the term towards the beginning of life (Fordham, 1969).

An unanswered question is whether integration must of necessity precede individuation. Obviously, the chances are better for the ego that is strong (integrated) enough to withstand individuation when this erupts suddenly, rather than entering quietly into the personality. Great artists whose self-realisation can hardly be doubted (e.g. Mozart, van Gogh, Gauguin) sometimes seem to have retained infantile character formation and/or psychotic traits. Were they individuated? In terms of perfection of their talents which had become amalgamated with their personalities the answer is, yes; in terms of personal completeness and relationships, probably not.

Finally, there is a question relating to individuation which concerns every thorough analysis, and society as a whole: will it make any difference to the rest of mankind if an infinitesimally small number undertake this arduous journey? Jung answers positively that the analyst is not only working for the patient but also for the good of his own soul and adds that 'small and invisible as the contribution may be it is yet a *magnum opus*.... The ultimate questions of PSYCHOTHERAPY are not a private matter – they represent a supreme responsibility' (CW 16, para. 449).

infancy and childhood Jung's reticence in drawing together his ideas about infancy and childhood may have stemmed from a reluctance to enter theoretical areas marked out by Freud as his own. Jung's stated interest was in the second half of life. He was also concerned to balance the reductive and synthetic approaches (see REDUCTIVE AND SYNTHETIC METHODS). Nevertheless, a coherent approach can be discerned.

Jung's views revolve around a central question: are we to see a small child as an extension of the psychology of its parents and subject to their influences, or more as a being recognisable from the first as possessing his or her own personality and intraphysic organisation? At times, Jung contradicts himself on this matter, but the advantage of his vacillation is that the tension between what seem to be 'real' parent figures on the one hand, and images constructed out of the interaction of ARCHETYPE and experience, on the other, is highlighted. For, while it is not disputed that the character and life experience of the parents will be important to the developing child, the parents are also 'not the "parents" at all but only their imagos: they are representations which have arisen from the conjunction of parental peculiarities with the individual disposition of the child' (CW 5, para. 505). See IMAGO.

The implication of this for ANALYSIS is that all the events of infancy, inner and outer, may be regarded as 'real', without undue concern whether the material is factual (see PSYCHIC REALITY).

Jung was among the first to spell out the primary importance of the relationship of infant and mother in terms recognisable today. This has to be compared with Freud's insistence that it was the Oedipal triangle that most imposed its aura and vicissitudes on later relationship patterns. Jung wrote in 1927: 'The mother-child relationship is certainly the deepest and most poignant one we know ... it is the absolute experience of our species, an organic truth.... There is inherent ... (an) extraordinary intensity of relationship which instinctively impels the child to cling to its mother' (CW 8, para. 723).

Jung stressed three aspects of the child's relation to the mother. These are: first, that throughout maturation there will be REGRESSION towards her or her IMAGE; second, that separation from the mother is a struggle (see HERO); third, that nutrition is of prime importance (see OBJECT RELATIONS).

Regarding the psychopathology of the mother-infant relationship, Jung describes the result of archetypal expectations not being met. If personal experience does not meet the expectation, then the infant is forced to try to achieve a direct connection to the archetypal structure which underlies the expectation, to try to live on the basis of an archetypal image alone. PATHOLOGY also results from confirmation by experience of only one pole of the negative/positive possibilities. Thus, if bad experiences predominate over good in infancy, then the 'bad mother' pole of the range of expectations is activated, and there is no counterbalance. Similarly, an idealised image of the mother-infant relationship can lead to only the 'good' end of the spectrum's being experienced, and the individual will never come to terms with the disappointments and realities of life (see PARANOID-SCHIZOID POSITION).

As far as the father is concerned, the following themes appear in Jung's work:

- father as the opposite of mother, incarnating different values and attributes.
- father as an 'informing spirit' (CW 5, para. 70), as a representative of the spiritual principle and as the personal counterpart of God-the-Father (see GENDER; LOGOS; SEX).
- father as a model PERSONA for his son.
- father as that from which the son must differentiate himself.
- father as the first 'lover' and animus image for his daughter (see ANIMA AND ANIMUS; INCEST).
- father as he appears in transference in analysis (see ANALYST AND PATIENT).

The PRIMAL SCENE may also be looked at with a combination of the empirical and the symbolic. What the child internalises of his parents' marriage and their attitude to each other will affect his later experiences in adult relationships. But, from the symbolic viewpoint, the image he develops of his parents' marriage is also a representation of his own inner world situation – the parents standing for opposite or conflicting tendencies within himself (see OPPOSITES; SYMBOL).

Jung's ideas about INDIVIDUATION have been applied to infancy, strengthening the view of individuation as a life-long process (Fordham, 1969, 1976). By the end of the second year, all the essential ingredients are there: opposites, such as good and bad images of mother, have been brought together; symbols are being used in play; the rudiments of MORALITY are in operation; the child has differentiated himself from others (see DEPRESSIVE POSITION).

The concept of COMPLEX links the events of infancy and childhood to adult life.

In analysis, images of babies or children may be taken as referring to the emergence of hitherto unconscious potentials (see INITIATION).

inferior function   See TYPOLOGY.

inflation   Refers to a greater or lesser degree to an IDENTIFICATION with the collective psyche caused by an invasion of unconscious archetypal contents or as a result of extended consciousness (see ARCHETYPE; POSSESSION). There is disorientation accompanied either by a feeling of immense power and uniqueness or a sense of non-worth and being of no account. The former represents a hypomanic state; the latter, depression.

Jung wrote that 'inflation is a regression of consciousness into unconsciousness. This always happens when consciousness takes too many conscious contents upon itself and loses the faculty of discrimination' (CW 12, para. 563). An archetypal content 'seizes hold of the PSYCHE with a kind of primeval force and compels it to transgress the bounds of humanity. The consequence is a puffed-up attitude, loss of free will, DELUSION and enthusiasm for good or evil alike' (CW 7, para. 110). He added that it is always dangerous when the EGO becomes inflated to the point when it is identified with the SELF. This is a form of hybris and INDIVIDUATION is not possible since there is no longer any DIFFERENTIATION between person and GOD-IMAGE.

initiation Initiation occurs when one dares to act against natural instincts and allows oneself to be propelled toward CONSCIOUSNESS. From time immemorial, initiation rites have been devised which prepare for and parallel the significant transitions in life involving both body and spirit; as, for example, at puberty (see RITUAL). The complexity of such ceremonies suggests the breadth and depth of the ritual container that is needed when psychic ENERGY must be diverted from acquired habit into new and unaccustomed activity. What occurs for the initiate is an ontological change which is later reflected in a recognised change in outer status as well. Again, using puberty as an example, a boy becomes a man, takes over or moves away from his father's house. Significantly, one is initiated not into knowledge but into mystery and the 'knowledge' so acquired may be termed *gnosis*.

All initiations involve the death of a less adequate and the REBIRTH of a renewed and more adequate condition (i.e. TRANSFORMATION); hence, the rites are both mysterious and terrifying for one is brought face to face with the numinosity of the GOD-IMAGE or SELF, while being propelled by the UNCONSCIOUS toward CONSCIOUSNESS (see NUMINOSUM). SACRIFICE is involved and it is this sacrifice rather than any torments or tortures that produces suffering. Rites therefore anticipate a liminal or transitional state, corresponding to temporary loss of EGO. Because of this, the initiate must be accompanied by someone, priest or mentor, a MANA PERSONALITY, capable of taking the projected TRANSFERENCE of what the initiate will become, although at first the content of the projection may take the form of one who is preventing that same initiate from becoming it. The relationship between the two, initiate and initiator, is a symbolic one. During the initiatory process a re-combination of OPPOSITES, a CONIUNCTIO involving spirit and matter, takes place in the individual.

Initiation is of central importance in psychological life and all outward ceremonies conform to an inborn psychological pattern of change and growth. The rite or ceremony simply safeguards either person or society from disintegration while deep-seated and pervasive change takes place. Therefore, it is not surprising that Jung writes:

The transformation of the unconscious that occurs under ANALYSIS makes it a natural analogue of the religious initiation ceremonies, which do, however, differ in principle from the natural process in that they anticipate the natural course of development and substitute for the spontaneous production of symbols a deliberately selected set of symbols prescribed by tradition (CW 11, para. 854).

It is not surprising, either, when he claims 'The only "initiation process" that is still alive and practised today in the West is the analysis of the unconscious as used by doctors for therapeutic purposes' (CW 11, para. 842). See PSYCHOTHERAPY.

Initiation was a potent image for many of the first generation of analytical psychologists and, perhaps because of this, the dichotomy between psychological and dogmatic approaches became apparent. Gradually reliance upon initiation as an unpredictable and unforeseen process indicated by the unconscious gave way to the outlining of stages of ANALYSIS, the sketching out of phases in the process of INDIVIDUATION, and, in addition assigning levels in the training of analysts (see ANALYTICAL PSYCHOLOGY).

After Jung's death, Eliade, an anthropologist and scholar of comparative religions, who was a close friend and former associate, continued to work on parallels between psychology, anthropology and comparative religion (1968). Jung had called attention to the fact that initiation is connected with HEALING; i.e. when a psychological orientation outlives its usefulness but is not allowed to transform, it putrefies and infects the entire psychic organism. Writers on initiation and its purely psychological function are Henderson (1967), Sandner (1979), Micklem (1980) and Kirsch (1982).

instinct See ARCHETYPE; DEATH INSTINCT; LIFE INSTINCT; TRANSFORMATION.

integration Term used by Jung in three main ways:

(1) As a description (or even diagnosis) of the psychological situation of an individual. This implies an examination of the interaction of CONSCIOUSNESS and the UNCONSCIOUS, the masculine and feminine parts of the personality (see ANIMA AND ANIMUS; SYZYGY), the various

pairs of OPPOSITES, the position taken up by the EGO in relation to the SHADOW, and movement between the functions and attitudes of consciousness (see TYPOLOGY). Diagnostically, integration is the converse of DISSOCIATION (see PROJECTION).

(2) As a sub-process of INDIVIDUATION, roughly analogous to 'mental health' or 'maturity'. That is to say, integration as process suggests the groundwork for individuation without the sharp emphasis upon uniqueness and self-realisation implied in the latter term. It would also follow that integration may lead to a sense of WHOLENESS, resulting from an in-gathering of the various aspects of the personality.

(3) As a stage of development, typically during the second half of life, in which the various dynamics referred to in (1) above achieve some kind of balance (or, rather, optimal level of conflict and tension). See COMPENSATION; STAGES OF LIFE.

interpretation The act of making clear in one language what has been expressed in another. All translators know the difficulties of interpreting the subtleties and nuances of another language, expressive as it is of another culture, its way of life, its values, its sense of time and timing. It is even more difficult when an interpreter attempts to translate a psychological utterance whose origin, meaning and purpose are obscure. Yet, this is what doctors, psychiatrists, analysts or other psychotherapists attempt to do: for DREAMS, VISIONS and FANTASY are indistinct METAPHORS. Expressed in symbolic language, they communicate by way of imagery (see IMAGE; SYMBOL).

Jung's direct commentaries on the techniques of interpretation are very few, although most of his work was interpretative. In specific reference to his method of interpretation of dreams, the following points emerge:

(1) Interpretation should bring something new to consciousness and neither reiterate nor moralise. Only if it reveals an unfamiliar, unexpected or alien content does an interpretation do justice to the compensatory psychological intent of the dream process (see COMPENSATION).

(2) Interpretations must take into account the personal context of the dreamer's life and his psycho-biographical experience. These and the influence of his social milieu (sometimes spoken of as collective consciousness) are arrived at by the process of ASSOCIATION (see COLLECTIVE).

(3) Likewise, wherever relevant, the symbolic content of a dream is enhanced by comparisons with typical cultural, historical and mythological motifs. These enlarge the personal context of the dream and connect it with the 'collective unconscious'. Making such compari-

sons involves the painstaking work of AMPLIFICATION (see FAIRY TALE; MYTH; UNCONSCIOUS).

(4) Interpreters are admonished to 'stick to the dream image', to stay as close as possible to that which has been dreamed. Association and amplification are seen as ways of making the original image more vivid, available and meaningful. Nevertheless, the dream image belongs to the dreamer himself and must be referred back to his own psychological life.

(5) The ultimate test of an interpretation is whether it 'works', i.e. enables a shift in the attitude of CONSCIOUSNESS held by the dreamer.

In dream seminars (1928–30, pub. 1984) Jung spoke of interpretation on two levels which he called subjective and objective. The terms are confusing. What he meant by 'subjective' was 'in depth' or at the level of intrapsychic change within the person. His use of the word 'objective' suggests on the surface level and was applied to the actual world of real happenings which a person inhabits and that affects him. Jung asserted that most dreams could be interpreted at either level although some clearly speak of one or the other level.

The patient needs to know how to relate to symbolic content but has little use for terminology and cannot be expected to follow the theoretical path of the psychotherapist. The therapist needs to interpret the material psychologically in order to analyse psychic and archetypal phenomena. However, if he moves too quickly in the articulation of interpretations in depth, he is in danger of bypassing the potential involvement of an individual in his own process. Attracted by the numinosity of archetypal figures or impressed by the therapist's expertise, the patient is tempted to explain and not take seriously the need to integrate unconscious contents (see point 5 above). His own understanding of imagery may remain purely intellectual and without either personal or psychological relevance. No dialectical relationship is established between him and his own inner processes. The fostering and maintenance of such a dialectical relationship is the function of interpretation.

introjection The opposite of PROJECTION; an attempt to internalise experience. Referred to by Jung far less frequently than projection. This may be for typological reasons (see TYPOLOGY). As an introvert, Jung would invest LIBIDO in his internal world. In order to encounter the external world, to vivify it, as it were, he would need to project. (An extravert invests libido in his external world. He must introject that investment to spark his internal processes.)

Jung's approach to empathy makes explicit use of introjection rather more than of projection. Empathy is said to involve the taking of the other's personality or situation inside oneself, rather than the projection of one's ego, say, into another person's PSYCHE.

introversion   See TYPOLOGY.

L

libido   See ENERGY; INCEST; PSYCHOANALYSIS.

life instinct   When Jung writes of the life instinct, it is invariably linked with the DEATH INSTINCT. This is because his interest was in the way progressive and regressive forces mingle in the PSYCHE. For example, symbols and images of death may be understood in terms of their significance and meaning for life, while experiences and intimations of life need to be construed as leading towards death. Life viewed as a preparation for death, death as integral to life, summarises his perspective (see INDIVIDUATION; INITIATION; REBIRTH).

Jung's use of 'life instinct' is not as precise as Freud's. There is little stress on the tension between the self-preservative instincts and sexuality. (Jung's 'life instinct' is more reminiscent of Freud's 'eros' – i.e. a more broadly based observation of man's tendency towards in-gathering, consolidation, unity and, hence, progress.) However, Jung's references to the life instinct refer more to a general life ENERGY, an *élan vital*, or animation. However, this leads to a conceptual problem; for, if energy is *equated* with the life instinct, but at the same time *fuels* the death instinct, then the conclusion would have to be that it is the life instinct which fuels the death instinct. The dualism would be replaced by a model in which the life instinct was primary. To avoid this, Jung usually returned to the idea of energy as neutral, serving life and death instincts alike – and both instincts are then seen as serving the psyche and/or man (see EROS).

Logos   A Greek word defined as 'word' or 'reason'. The term, used both in pagan and Jewish antiquity, also appears in writings of the early Christians. Heraclitus conceived of 'the Logos' as universal reason governing the world and it is in this sense that Jung seems to have adopted and applied it. It is important to bear in mind, however, that it was referred to as a principle and does not have the status of a GOD-IMAGE nor is it an archetypal metaphor (see ARCHETYPE). Logos is 'essential reason', the transcendent idea which finds expression in individual lives. Each person, therefore, has his *own*

Logos which connects him, ultimately, with meaning (see INDIVIDUA-TION).

As a principle, Jung spoke of Logos as spirit, not matter, and attributed to it maleness. He used the words *judgment, discrimination* and *insight* as synonyms for Logos, differentiating it from what he saw as the corresponding female principle of Eros for which he used such words as *love, intimacy* and *relatedness*. Logos and Eros are posed as OPPOSITES and, since, according to the law of ENAN-TIODROMIA, over-dependence on one principle constellates its opposite, the man rigidly defensive of a Logos position is besieged by the corresponding psychic principle activated in his unconscious by images of anima (see ANIMA AND ANIMUS; COMPENSATION). Logos includes the idea of universality, of spiritual impregnation, of clarity and rationality. It may therefore be identified with animus. All this is in contrast to the personal feeling-infused and bedevilling qualities of anima. Yet both motivate human behaviour (see PSYCHOPOMP).

Jung admitted that Logos, like Eros, was a concept that could neither be defined accurately not observed empirically. From a scientific point of view he found this regrettable but, from a practical point of view, conceptualisation of a field of experience was essential. He would have preferred, he said, to use names for the images of Logos and Eros, names like Sol and Luna, which the alchemists used, hence personifying these abstractions. But the use of images, he admitted, requires an alert and lively FANTASY and is not always congenial to those who must intellectualise. The IMAGE is more full but is not apprehensible to the mind alone. 'Concepts', he wrote in this regard, 'are coined and negotiable values; images are life' (CW 14, para. 226).

For those who find in Logos (and Eros) something too defined and neatly conceptualised, it may be useful to approach them as terms which summarise aspects of living imagery. Being male in Jung's definition, Logos has been culturally equated with man, husband, brother, son and father. Jung saw the father as exerting a natural and often unconscious influence upon the mind and spirit of his daughter in particular. This sometimes increased her reliance upon reason to a pathological degree, he felt, and both he himself and his wife (1957) described this condition as 'animus POSSESSION'.

Jung made certain cogent observations about what happens collectively when Logos dominates (see COLLECTIVE). His view was that the paternal principle, Logos, struggles to extricate itself from the primal warmth and darkness of the womb. But the spirit that dares this inevitably suffers the disadvantage of an over-emphasis upon patriarchal CONSCIOUSNESS. Nothing can exist without its opposite, however, and, therefore, consciousness is unable to exist without unconsciousness, nor Logos without its compensatory counterpart, Eros. His observations have been applied both by defenders of a patriarchal position and advocates of woman's liberation.

At another point, Jung defines Logos as 'the dynamic power of thoughts and words' (CW 9ii, para. 293). Looked at in this manner and apart from notions of male or female complementarity, it is perhaps easier to conceptualise. Jung warned that there was a danger of over-valuing that which empowers creation and under-valuing the creation itself. Here he saw the problems of an Age of Reason.

See SYZYGY.

loss of soul An unnatural, neurotic and pathological condition that has threatened man from the beginning of time; the severance of relationship with one's individual psychic life. It is marked by, though not synonymous with ABAISSEMENT DU NIVEAU MENTAL. Often manifesting at midlife, the condition may be the prelude to further INDIVIDUATION. Viewed from a TELEOLOGICAL POINT OF VIEW, Jung was convinced that at such a time 'the values which the individual lacks are to be found in the NEUROSIS itself' (CW 7, para. 93). The condition is accompanied by lack of energy, loss of a sense of MEANING and purpose, a diminished sense of personal responsibility, preponderance of AFFECT and eventual DEPRESSION or REGRESSION with a disintegrating effect upon CONSCIOUSNESS (see UNCONSCIOUS). Jung spoke of the term as one used by primitive peoples (see PRIMITIVES) and said that, if unchecked, the condition eventually resulted in the dissolution of an individual's personality in the collective PSYCHE (see COLLECTIVE; STAGES OF LIFE).

M

magic An attempt to intercept or become one with UNCONSCIOUS forces in order to use, propitiate or destroy them; thereby to counteract their remarkable potency or to ally with their competitive purposes. The more limited a person's field of CONSCIOUSNESS, Jung stated, the more often psychic contents will be met as quasi-external apparitions, either in the form of SPIRITS or as magical powers projected upon living people, animals or inanimate objects. He identified such a PROJECTION as being an autonomous or semi-autonomous COMPLEX not yet subject to INTEGRATION.

Belief in magic, therefore, implies unconsciousness over which the individual has little or no mastery and the performance of magical rites gives the person concerned a greater sense of security. The purpose of these rites is to maintain psychic balance. The person capable of intervention (magician, shaman, witch, priest or doctor) is himself recognised as one having some kind of supernatural power, a liminal and archetypal figure corresponding to a MANA PERSONALITY.

male See SEX.

mana See MANA PERSONALITIES.

mana personalities Mana is a word derived from anthropology, being Melanesian in origin; it pertains to the extraordinary and compelling supernatural power which emanates from certain individuals, objects, actions and events as well as from inhabitants of the SPIRIT world. The modern equivalent is 'charisma'. Mana suggests the presence of an all-pervading vital force, a primal source of growth or magical healing that can be likened to a primitive concept of psychic ENERGY. Mana can attract or repel, wreak destruction or heal, confronting the EGO with a supraordinate force. It should not be confused with numinosity which pertains only to the divine presence (see NUMINOSUM). This is the quasi-divine power which adheres to the magician, mediator, priest, doctor, trickster, saint or holy fool – to anyone who partakes of the spirit world sufficiently to conduct or radiate its energy (see MAGIC).

Since Jung's death, studies of transitional states confirm that during liminal periods or borderline states a person such as an initiate, novice, patient or analysand is particularly susceptible to attraction by so-called mana personalities. The effect of such images, real or projected, is that they give the individual a feeling of direction toward a realisable heightening of CONSCIOUSNESS. The extraordinary mana personality, Don Juan, portrayed by Carlos Castaneda is an example. Because one is convinced that such a figure has attained a higher state of consciousness, the possibility of achieving it is established and, consequently, one has confidence that he himself can make the transition in their company.

Unfortunately, scientific analysis of the transference relationship between ANALYST AND PATIENT has lost touch with the efficacy of such images. As transitional personages, they are of immense value, since the projection of power is essential at that time; its integration comes later when the ego is able to wrest that power from them and claim it on behalf of the individual and his own purposes. At a still later stage when ANIMA AND ANIMUS have been divested of their own semi-magical attraction and force, the analysand has a second confrontation with mana personalities, but this time they are projected inward and usually take the form of spiritual presences of the per-

son's own sex – personifications of God the Father or the GREAT
MOTHER, WISE OLD MAN or WISE OLD WOMAN, as the case may be (see
ENERGY; MAGIC). (Jung enjoyed a life-long relationship with such a
figure whom he painted and with whom he dialogued repeatedly:
Philemon.) Mana adheres to 'the desired mid-point of the personality', Jung writes, 'that ineffable something betwixt the OPPOSITES, or
else which unites them, or the result of conflict, or the product of
energic tension: the coming to birth of personality, a profound individual step forward, the next stage' (CW 7, para. 382).

Mana personalities appear whenever the ego is consciously confronted with the SELF. To see them as mere father or mother IMAGOS
is to reduce them to 'no more than' or 'nothing but', according to
Jung. The mana personality as an ideal and incorruptible image is
essential to the process of INITIATION after which one has a renewed
sense of individuality. The danger inherent in transitional periods is
that one identifies with the mana figures, however, and there is a
consequent INFLATION (see IDENTIFICATION; IDENTITY).

mandala Sanskrit word meaning 'magic circle'. Refers to a geo-
metric figure in which the circle is squared or the square encircled;
it has more-or-less regular sub-divisions, is divided by four or
multiples thereof, radiates from or moves into a centre, depending
upon one's perspective. Jung interpreted it as an expression of the
PSYCHE and, in particular, the SELF. Mandalas may appear in dreams
or paintings during Jungian ANALYSIS. Though mandalas can express
a potential for WHOLENESS or represent cosmic wholeness (as is true
of the great mandalas of religious tradition), they can also function
defensively for people who are fragmented.

See MEANING; RELIGION.

marriage The context usually makes it clear whether Jung is referring to marriage as a prolonged *relationship* between a man and a
woman, or to an *internal* marriage of masculine and feminine parts
of an individual's psyche, or to CONIUNCTIO, or, finally, to the *hierosgamos* (sacred marriage, see ALCHEMY).

Jung's belief was that OPPOSITES attract and he saw marriages (in
the external sense) as likely to involve personalities of a different
cast. In particular, he developed a model (CW 17, paras 324–45) in
which it is assumed that one partner in a marriage will have a more
complicated personal psychology than the other. The sex of the partners involved does not come into this. The complex personality will,
as it were, *contain* the simpler personality and, for a while, all may
be well. But the more complex partner will find him/herself unsti-
mulated by the less complex one and will look elsewhere for what is

imagined to be fulfilment (see PROJECTION). This makes the contained, more simple, personality even more dependent and likely to invest everything in the relationship. Jung's observation was that the partner who functions as container is in secret need of containment and this is sought in experimentation with other people. The remedy for that partner is to recognise his or her dependency needs. The contained partner has to see that salvation is not to be found in the shape of the other partner.

It is difficult to assess this model. In so far as the experiential evidence can be trusted, this suggests that it is not a case of opposites attracting, nor, in fact, of similars. Rather, partner choice in marriage seems to depend on the perception of a manageable balance between difference and similarity. Jung's container-contained model is an attempt to describe what is now referred to as 'collusion'. It is also helpful to see the partners in a marriage as operating sometimes under the aegis of a shared fantasy. The partners may have elements in their backgrounds which promote such a shared fantasy. Jung was not offering a complete analysis of marital dynamics but he was interested in the psychological factors involved.

The container-contained model should not be considered in isolation from the activity of the ANIMA AND ANIMUS. These archetypal structures influence relationships and, hence, the features in the other which determine partner choice may be regarded, to some extent, as anima and animus projections (see ARCHETYPE). Because these PERSONIFICATIONS are influenced somewhat by childhood relationships with the parent of the opposite sex; choices of marriage partners often reflect the psychological condition of the parent with whom the child is unconsciously bonded (see INCEST).

The idea of an *internal* marriage rests on Jung's conviction that the entire range of psychological possibilities is available to everyone (see GENDER; SEX). It follows that personality can be described in terms of a balance between masculine and feminine factors. When 'masculine' and 'feminine' are used to refer to internal tendencies, external gender role is not directly involved. However, Jung often overlooked this and, at times, a confusion between sex and gender becomes apparent.

Recently, attention has been paid to the question of INDIVIDUATION within a marriage relationship. 'Individuation marriages' do not adhere to the standards of the COLLECTIVE but serve the deepest interests of the partners by fostering a style of relating specific to two people (Guggenbühl-Craig, 1977).

For 'marriage' in analysis, see ANALYST AND PATIENT.

masculine   See GENDER.

meaning   The quality ascribed to something that gives it value.

The question of meaning was central to Jung and to all that he undertook as person, doctor, therapist; as someone who wrestled constantly with problems of good *and* EVIL, light *and* dark, life *and* death; as a scientist and as a man of deeply religious temperament. He concluded that the *locus* of meaning is in PSYCHE and psyche alone is capable of discerning the meaning of what is experienced. This underlines the crucial function of REFLECTION in psychological life and emphasises that CONSCIOUSNESS is not confined to the intelect.

Meaning was fundamental to Jung's concept of the AETIOLOGY OF NEUROSIS since the recognition of meaning appears to have a curative power. 'A psychoneurosis must be understood, ultimately, as the suffering of a soul which has not discovered its meaning,' he wrote (*CW* 11, para. 497). At the same time, however, though intent upon the discovery of meaning, Jung remained open to the possibility of life's meaninglessness. He perceived meaning to be paradoxical in nature and conceived it as an ARCHETYPE (see OPPOSITES).

Consistent with this approach, Jung considered each answer to the question of meaning to be a human interpretation, a conjecture, a confession or a belief. Whatever may be the answer given to the ultimate question of life's meaning, he maintained that the answer is created by a person's own consciousness and its formulation is, therefore, a MYTH, since man is not capable of uncovering absolute truth. Without a means of establishing objective meaning, we rely upon subjective verification as our ultimate measure and it is upon this that ANALYST AND PATIENT must also rely psychotherapeutically. But the discovery of meaning is at the same time an experience attended by numinosity and accompanied by a sense of the awesome, the mysterious and the terrifying which are always connected to an experience of the divine, in whatever lowly, unacceptable, obscure or despised form it may appear (see NUMINOSUM).

Jung's own myth of meaning seems to be inextricably linked to consciousness. Meaning is revealed by consciousness and, therefore, consciousness has a spiritual as well as a cognitive function (see SPIRIT). 'Without the reflecting consciousness of man the world is a gigantic, meaningless machine, for as far as we know man is the only creature that can discover "meaning"', he wrote in a letter in 1959. After intensive work upon SYNCHRONICITY he concluded that, in addition to cause and effect, there is another factor in nature which is shown by the arrangement of events; this appears to us in the guise of meaning. But when asked who or what creates that meaning, his answer was not God but rather a person's own GOD-IMAGE (see SELF).

Jaffé, Jung's secretary, has drawn together an account of his encounters with meaning and the conclusions on the subject that he drew from his life and work (1971). See RELIGION.

mental illness Jung, following his teacher Janet in France, and along with Forel in Switzerland and Freud in Austria, pioneered in establishing public awareness that the root cause of NEUROSIS is psychogenic in nature. Until World War One the prevailing assumption, both medical and psychiatric, was that this and all so-called mental illnesses were diseases of the brain.

From the outset of his career, Jung disagreed with the emphasis upon anatomical researches into mental illness and turned his attention instead to the *content* of PSYCHOSIS (along with neurosis). He adopted a standpoint which affirmed the role of psychogenesis in relation to SCHIZOPHRENIA and, by analysis of the delusions and hallucinations which accompanied it, established the fact that these were significant psychic products (see SYMBOL). Thus, he could go on to concern himself further with the psychology of the illness and to adopt a psychotherapeutic approach to its treatment. It is important to note, however, that although bringing relief to the patient, this approach was not considered sufficient as a CURE (see PSYCHO-THERAPY). Jung's life-long emphasis was upon the interaction between illness and its psychological manifestations (see CW 3, paras 553–84).

Mercurius See ALCHEMY; TRANSCENDENT FUNCTION; TRICKSTER.

metaphor The definition and exploration of one thing by reference to the IMAGE of another. Metaphor is used as a conscious poetic device and has always been employed by story-tellers and writers to suggest the subtleties of mystery or as an aid when trying to 'express the inexpressible'. MYTH, RITUAL and RELIGION make use of metaphor.

Jung's acknowledgment of a deep reservoir of irrepresentable images called ARCHETYPES in the PSYCHE, his definition of SYMBOL as the best possible expression of an as yet undisclosed fact, his insistence that INTERPRETATION should remain faithful and as close as possible to the dream image, his likening of the psychic functioning of the SELF to a GOD-IMAGE, and his affirmation that it is MEANING rather than treatment that relieves the suffering induced by a NEU-ROSIS are all based on the supposition that the psyche reasons imagistically and that the closest rational equivalent is analogy or metaphor. Thus, his method of AMPLIFICATION involves more than the provision of a more complete frame of reference for interpretation; it is a search for relevant metaphor. From this metaphor the rational

EGO may ascertain or approximate to an understanding of a psychic message, while the psyche can re-orient itself by way of an enlarged image in CONSCIOUSNESS (see IMAGO).

midlife   See STAGES OF LIFE.

morality   Jung's contribution to the field of ETHICS and morality was from the point of view of an analyst and psychiatrist: 'Behind a man's action there stands neither public opinion nor the moral code, but the personality of which he is still unconscious' (CW 11, para. 390). In other words, the moral problem is posed psychologically when a person faces the question of what he *may* become in contrast to what he *will* become if certain attitudes are maintained, decisions taken or actions fostered without REFLECTION. Jung stated that morality is not society's invention but inherent in the laws of life. It is man acting with awareness of his own moral responsibility to himself that creates CULTURE rather than the other way around.

In contrast to the Freudian SUPER-EGO, Jung suggested that it was an innate principle of individuality which compels each person to make moral judgments in accord with himself. This principle, compounded of a primary responsibility to the EGO on the one hand and, on the other, in relationship to the supraordinate demands of the SELF (what a person *may* become), is capable of making the most arbitrary and trying demands. These may appear to have little or no bearing upon the standards of the COLLECTIVE and yet maintain an equilibrium within SOCIETY. The result of making a conscious decision to surrender or to renounce (to SACRIFICE) an ego position may bring apparently little personal and immediate outward satisfaction but it sets things right psychologically; i.e. it 'works', to use Jung's word. It restores a balance between conscious and UNCONSCIOUS forces.

Any encounter with an archetype poses a moral problem. This becomes the more difficult when the EGO is weak and indecisive in relation to the numinous attraction exerted by the archetype itself. The archetype of the self conveys a strong and authoritative summons. What Jung appears to say is that it is possible to say a conscious 'no' to the authority of the self; it is also possible to work in conjunction with the self. But to try to ignore or to deny the self is immoral because it denies one's unique potential for being. These ideas are consistent with Jung's basic theory of OPPOSITES; fundamentally, it is the conflict of opposites that poses a moral problem to the personality (see EGO-SELF AXIS).

mother   See ARCHETYPE; GREAT MOTHER; IMAGO; INFANCY AND CHILDHOOD; MARRIAGE.

mundus imaginalis Imaginal world. Term introduced by the Islamic scholar Corbin (1972) and taken up in analytical psychology by Hillman (1980) and Samuels (1985b). 'Imaginal' is used in preference to 'imaginary' to indicate a mode of perception or being and not an evaluation. Refers to a precise level or order of reality situated midway between the sense impressions of the body and developed cognition (or spirituality). May be thought of as the locus of archetypal imagery (Hillman) or as an interactive and intersubjective field of images fostering a two-person relationship such as that of ANALYST AND PATIENT (Samuels).

See ARCHETYPE; IMAGE.

myth Jung's investigations of the contents of DREAMS as well as the hallucinations of his psychotic patients led him to the conclusion that there were innumerable psychic interconnections for which, he said, he could find parallels only in mythology. Ruling out previous ASSOCIATIONS on the part of his patients or any kind of 'forgotten knowledge' of such connections, he felt that he was presented with elements separate from any conscious influences. Consequently, he reached the conclusion that the pre-conditions for myth-formation must be present within the structure of the PSYCHE itself. He hypothesised the existence of a collective UNCONSCIOUS or reservoir of archetypal structures, experiences, and themes.

Myths are stories of archetypal encounters. As the fairy tale is analogous to the workings of the personal COMPLEX, the myth is a METAPHOR for workings of the ARCHETYPE *per se*. Like his ancestors, Jung concluded, modern man is a myth-maker; he re-enacts age-old dramas based upon archetypal themes and, through his capacity for CONSCIOUSNESS, can release himself from their compulsive hold.

In a sequence of myths, the earliest of the gods and goddesses are representative of a basic design that unfolds or is differentiated in the stories of their descendants. Mythic tales illustrate what happens when an archetype has free rein and there is no conscious intervention on the part of man. By contrast, individuality consists of confrontation and dialogue with such fateful powers in recognition of their primal force, but without submission to it.

Modern psychology, Jung concluded, must treat the products of unconscious fantasy, including mythological motifs, as statements of psyche about itself. We do not invent myths; we experience them. 'Myths are original revelations of the pre-conscious psyche, involuntary statements about psychic happenings' (*CW* 9i, para. 261). For example, Jung wrote that they did not *represent*, but rather *were* the psychic life of PRIMITIVES. When such motifs crop up during an ANALYSIS, they convey a vital meaning. The analyst should not assume that they simply correspond to certain COLLECTIVE elements but be aware that for better or worse these elements are re-activated in the SOUL of a present-day person.

Not only does the behaviour of the unconscious resemble the workings of myth, but we ourselves participate in 'living and lived myth'. PATHOLOGY is mirrored in myth, while consciousness has the opportunity to extend or enhance mythic themes. Hence, Jung's view of mythology is in direct contrast to that held by Freud and has a bearing upon REGRESSION. Regression, which always involves archetypal behaviour, can be seen not only as an attempt to avoid reality, but also as a search for new mythologems with which to reconstruct reality. Again, Jung felt that analysts misuse mythological motifs if they attach them only as labels for certain patterns of psychic behaviour rather than see them as symbols dynamically activating and enabling the discovery of new possibilities (see INCEST; SYMBOL).

There is also danger in taking myth literally. Myth is analogous to certain aspects of personal experience but it cannot be seen as a substitute without consequent INFLATION. It provides a metaphorical perspective; but is not an explication or a portent to be fulfilled. It is a non-personal image which provides psychic space for individual expression. See REDUCTIVE AND SYNTHETIC METHODS.

N

narcissism Jung is seldom explicit on the subject of narcissism, generally concentrating on demonstrating how this psychopathological term has been incorrectly applied to healthy psychological activity. For instance, meditation and contemplation are decidedly not narcissistic in a pathological sense (CW 14, para. 709) and, as for the accusation that artists are narcissistic, well, 'every man who pursues his own goal is a narcissist' (CW 15, para. 102). In short, Jung accepted that there was a pathological usage (with which he was familiar) but sought to restrict it to what he described as 'masturbatory self-love' (CW 10, para. 204).

It is the enormous change in psychoanalytic attitude to narcissism since about 1970 that has brought about a situation in which numerous writers have developed an interest in the subject. These changes in psychoanalysis stimulated analytical psychologists to examine their own concepts and, when they did so, they found that many of Jung's ideas not only paralleled the psychoanalytic evolution (though worked out earlier), but that there is a particular 'Jungian' contribution to consider (see below).

For Freud, *primary* narcissism was a love of oneself, or an investment of one's own body with libido, which preceded the capacity to relate to and love others. *Secondary* narcissism is the gathering into the self of the entire object world, or a failure to recognise the separateness of self and objects from each other. This would justify the popular conception of a narcissistic person as cut-off from others, self-absorbed, vain and somewhat superior in manner. The naming of the condition after the beautiful Greek youth who fell in love with his reflection, thinking it was another person, is also explained. Of course, used clinically, secondary narcissism (or narcissistic personality disorder) refers to fantasy life as much as observable behaviour. Many narcissistic patients seem at first to function rather well on the social level.

Narcissism is now regarded by many psychoanalysts as something which persists throughout life and which may take on a healthy or unhealthy tone depending on circumstances. This is in distinction to a restriction of health to an overcoming of narcissism in its primary form, its continued presence in secondary form being castigated as pathological. Narcissistic disorders are seen as resulting from unempathic parenting, leading to a failure to develop authentic self-love out of the love of others and to the erection of a personality structure in which apparent preening camouflages feelings of emptiness and lack of self-esteem (cf. Kohut, 1971, 1977).

According to Kohut, narcissistic development proceeds along its own separate pathway, in the same way as object relations are conceived of as having a distinct path of development. It is important to note that there is no fundamental reason why narcissistic development and object relations should be opposed. Quite the reverse; they complement each other. However, the self-psychology to which Kohut's ideas about narcissism led him and the object relations perspective are rather different. The former uses empathy ('vicarious introspection', in Kohut's phrase) to find out what it is like to be a person from inside that person, as it were. Object relations is somewhat more detached, 'experience-distant', in Kohut's words. The main problem seems to be over *conflict*. The detached observer may see all kinds of inner conflicts but the person concerned will feel himself to be all of a piece (a self) in spite of this. This is now a heated debate in psychoanalysis (cf. Tolpin, 1980). We shall discuss below a contribution which might be made here by ANALYTICAL PSYCHOLOGY.

Narcissistic development implies positive involvement and investment in oneself, the development and maintenance of self-esteem, and the construction and attainment of ambitions and goals. In addition, there is the question of the evolution of values and ideals. Narcissistic development then becomes a life-long task.

It is the issue of relation to the SELF that energises some analytical psychologists, for that relation is archetypally structured and hence imbued with a fascinating and compelling quality, a certain numinosity (see NUMINOSUM). In a sense, the relation to the self *is* the self, and a link is established between narcissism and INDIVIDUATION (cf. Gordon, 1978; Schwartz-Salant, 1982). Kohut developed the concept of the self from his point of view because of the need for a construct which would assist in the exploration of *feelings* rather than of phenomena. But this attitude of his is not the only aspect of his work which appeals to analytical psychologists. Kohut disputes Freud's psychobiological approach; it seems to him mechanistic and to concentrate over much on modification of the pleasure principle. According to Kohut, Freud was in the grip of a 'maturation morality' and required of us that we grow up even at the cost of our humanity. Kohut was also in reaction to ego-psychology, sensing its limitations as a means of exploring the whole personality.

Because analytical psychology has undergone a different historical evolution to psychoanalysis, the twin-perspective problem caused by the existence of self-psychology and object relations is much less of a problem. The main reason for this is that archetypal theory permits the idea that the self is a given and is already in existence and operation at (or before) birth. In psychoanalysis, the self is viewed more as something arrived at or achieved and the concern is to state exactly how this happens; hence the dispute. On the other hand, some commentators feel that 'Kohut's self' is similar to Jung's idea (Jacoby, 1981) in that it seems to have an unknowable, cosmic aspect.

There seems to be general agreement that the narcissistically disordered patient requires careful use of a modified technique. His tendency to incorporate the object world interferes with the capacity to symbolise. Moreover, transference interpretations may only be effective after a long period of empathic relationship, allowing the omnipotence and grandiosity of the narcissistically disordered patient time and space to erode (cf. Ledermann, 1979). The point is that his omnipotence and grandiosity are a distorted version of the selfhood he might have attained in relation to his parents, but did not.

When we recall that narcissistic personality disorder is said to result from poor parenting, the reason for the excitement within analytical psychology becomes clearer. We can see that the self, the totality of the personality, the supraordinate personality, the GOD-IMAGE, archetypal at its core, depends for its individual incarnation on the feeling experiences of infancy. The analysis of early experience via the transference can touch the depth and majesty of the self, in fact enable it to be released.

See ANALYST AND PATIENT.

neurosis   Jung was resistant to the tendency in the psychiatry of his time to devote immense effort to the correct classification of mental illness (see MENTAL ILLNESS; PATHOLOGY). Thus, save for a broad distinction between neurosis and PSYCHOSIS (specifically between the position and strength of the EGO in HYSTERIA and SCHIZOPHRENIA respectively), a well-developed categorisation does not exist in his writing (CW 2, para. 1070). There is no parallel, for instance, to Freud's distinction between the actual neuroses, deriving from sexuality itself, and the psychoneuroses (such as hysteria), deriving from unmanageable psychical conflict. However, as Laplanche and Pontalis attest, 'it is scarcely possible to claim that an effective distinction has yet been established between the structures of neurosis, psychosis and perversion. As a consequence, our own definition of neurosis is inevitably open to the criticism that it is too broad' (1980).

Jung's overall attitude was that the person with the neurosis was a more fit subject for attention than the neurosis itself. A neurosis should not be isolated from the rest of the personality but rather seen as the whole of the psychopathologically disturbed PSYCHE. Hence, in ANALYSIS, the content of the complexes is what is crucial, not a refined clinical assessment (see COMPLEX).

Inasmuch as he defined neurosis, Jung's reference was to one-sided or unbalanced development. Sometimes, the imbalance is between the ego and one or more complexes. Sometimes Jung uses his outline of the psyche to refer to the ego's difficulties in relation to the other psychic agencies such as the anima or animus and the SHADOW (see ANIMA AND ANIMUS). Neurosis is therefore a (temporary) failure of the psyche's natural capacities for SELF-REGULATORY FUNCTION OF THE PSYCHE (see COMPENSATION).

At the same time, neurotic symptoms may be seen as something more than emanations of underlying disturbance or imbalance. They may be regarded as attempts at self-healing (see HEALING) in that they draw a person's attention to the fact that he is out of balance, is suffering from dis-ease (see TELEOLOGICAL POINT OF VIEW).

The clinical picture of neurosis often, but not always, contains the feeling of meaninglessness. This led Jung to refer metaphorically to a typical neurosis as a religious problem (CW 11, paras 500–15). See MEANING; RELIGION.

Jung's reluctance to use reduction to infantile factors as an explanation means that he has left no comprehensive theory of the AETIOLOGY OF NEUROSIS. However, the idea of the complex may be used descriptively to make clear the make-up of a neurosis. Sometimes, however, Jung seems to suggest that neurosis is a matter of inherent constitution (see ARCHETYPE; PSYCHIC REALITY; REDUCTIVE AND SYNTHETIC METHODS).

numinosum   In 1937 Jung wrote of the *numinosum* as

> a dynamic agency or effect not caused by an arbitrary act of will. On the contrary, it seizes and controls the human subject, who is always rather its victim than its creator. The *numinosum* – whatever its cause may be – is an experience of the subject independent of his will. ... The *numinosum* is either a quality belonging to a visible object or the influence of an invisible presence that causes a peculiar alteration of CONSCIOUSNESS (CW 11, para. 6).

It defies explanation but seems to convey an individual message which, though mysterious and enigmatic, is also deeply impressive.

Jung felt that belief, conscious or unconscious, that is, a prior readiness to trust a transcendent power, was a pre-requisite for experience of the *numinosum*. The numinous cannot be conquered; one can only open oneself to it. But an experience of the *numinosum* is more than an experience of a tremendous and compelling force; it is a confrontation with a force that implies a not-yet-disclosed, attractive and fateful MEANING.

This definition was consistent with that given by Otto in *The Idea of the Holy* (1917) and Jung saw an encounter with the *numinosum* as an attribute of all religious experience. Numinosity is an aspect of a supraordinate GOD-IMAGE, whether personal or COLLECTIVE. Investigations of religious experiences convinced him that at such times previously UNCONSCIOUS contents break through the constraints of the EGO and overwhelm the conscious personality in the same way as do invasions of the unconscious in pathological situations. However, an experience of the *numinosum* is not habitually psychopathological. Presented with reports of individual encounters with the 'god-like', Jung maintained that he did not necessarily find proof of the existence of God; yet, in all instances, the experiences were of such profundity that mere descriptions could not convey their effects.

Contemporary humanistic psychology speaks of such impressive happenings as 'peak experiences'.

See RELIGION; SPIRIT; VISION.

O

objective psyche   A term used by Jung in two ways: first, to denote that the PSYCHE has objective existence as a source of knowledge, insight and imagination (1963). See PSYCHIC REALITY. Second, to indicate that certain of the contents of the psyche are of an objective rather than a personal or subjective nature. In this regard, he equated the objective psyche with what he called 'the collective unconscious' (*CW* 7, para. 103 n.).

See ARCHETYPE; IMAGE; UNCONSCIOUS.

object relations   Theory developed in psychoanalysis of understanding psychological activity on the basis of human relating to 'objects' (that is, an entity which attracts attention and/or satisfies a need and not a 'thing'). This can be contrasted with understandings based on instinctual drives which seem to object relations theorists to be mechanistic.

Although he did not employ the term, Jung's approach makes implicit use of object relations. Jung's view of the PSYCHE is characterised by (a) emphasis on relations between the various components of the psyche; (b) relations between those components and the external world; and (c) a working out of the implications of the psyche's tendency to fragment, split, dissociate, personify and so forth (see DISSOCIATION; PERSONIFICATION). There is, therefore, a parallel with the psychoanalytic concept of part-objects. These are treated by the subject solely as agencies for the satisfaction of need. The equivalent of the psychoanalytic concept of the whole object is to be found in Jung's speculation on the conjunction of opposites (see CONIUNCTIO; OPPOSITES). Jung's descriptions of certain psychological processes give further indications of the similarity between his perspective and that of object relations theorists. For example, Jung describes the basis of the infant's splitting of the object in his depiction of the GREAT MOTHER as invariably possessing two contrary aspects. See ARCHETYPE; DEPRESSIVE POSITION; IDENTITY; PARANOID-SCHIZOID POSITION; *PARTICIPATION MYSTIQUE*.

Though object relations possesses no explicit equivalent of the SELF, it has been suggested that this concept is implicit or that such an idea is compatible with object relations (Sutherland, 1980). On the other hand, Kohut has argued that the object relations approach and that of self-psychology are incompatible (Tolpin, 1980). This is because the former is constructed as if by a detached observer; it is experience-distant. The latter, on the other hand, is experience-near, derived from empathy, and respecting the fact that though we may speak of a person in terms of his internal and external objects that is not how he experiences himself. This psychoanalytic debate has not been paralleled in ANALYTICAL PSYCHOLOGY (see NARCISSISM; SELF).

Oedipus complex   See INCEST; PSYCHOANALYSIS.

opposites   'The opposites are the ineradicable and indispensable preconditions of all psychic life,' Jung wrote in one of his last works

101

(CW 14, para. 206). An acquaintance with the principle of opposition is essential to an understanding of his point of view. It was a foundation for his scientific endeavours and lay at the root of many of his hypotheses. Jung was expressing the dynamism of the psyche in terms of the first law of thermodynamics which states that energy demands two opposing forces. At different times he made reference to several philosophical sources for his thesis but none was acknowledged as primary.

From the time of his conceptualisation of the role of the UNCONSCIOUS as a counterpole to CONSCIOUSNESS (and, therefore, capable of exercising a compensatory function), Jung applied the concept of intrinsic duality to an everwidening field of psychic research, observation and insight (see COMPENSATION). He did not discuss or attempt to verify the theory so much as to apply it. Whether aware of it or not, from the beginning analytical psychologists have relied upon the theory of opposition.

Applying Jung's theory, pairs of opposites are considered to be of their nature irreconcilable. In the natural state they co-exist in an undifferentiated way. The faculties and needs of a human life contained in a living BODY furnish rules and limitations of their own that prevent excess of psychic disproportion; conscious and unconscious states are harmonious in 'the balanced person'. But the dissolution of any 'compromise' reached between two halves of a pair renders the activity of opposition ever more intense and brings about psychic disequilibrium such as that which is noticeable at times of neurotic disturbance. Alternation, or the experience of being at the mercy of now one and then the other of a pair of opposites is the hallmark of an awakening consciousness. When the tension becomes intolerable, a solution must be discovered and the only viable relief is to be found in a reconciliation of the two at a different and more satisfactory level.

Fortunately, out of collision between two opposing forces, the unconscious psyche tends to create a third possibility. This is of an irrational nature, unexpected and uncomprehensible to the conscious mind. Presenting itself as neither a straight *yes* or *no* answer, in consequence the third will not be immediately acceptable to either of the opposing points of view. The conscious mind comprehends nothing, the subject feels nothing excepting the oppositions and, so, has no knowledge of what will unite them. Therefore, it is the ambiguous and paradoxical SYMBOL which is capable of attracting attention and eventually reconciling the two. The conflict situation which offers no rational solution to the dilemma is the situation in which the opposition of the 'two' produces an irrational 'third', the symbol.

'Science seems to stop at the frontiers of logic, but ... [nature] does not halt at the opposites; she uses them to create, out of opposition, a new birth' (CW 16, para. 534). Jung uses these words to describe the problematic resolution of the transference which involves ANALYST AND PATIENT in seemingly irreconcilable demands for relationship. The resolution of this conflict between the opposites may be symbolised first of all by union (CONIUNCTIO) and then by the appearance of a reconciling motif such as that of the orphan or abandoned child. Rather than opposition, there now appears a newborn configuration, symbolic of a nascent whole, a figure possessing potentials beyond those that the conscious mind has yet been able to conceive.

This motif, along with all other uniting symbols, is of redemptive significance; i.e. it redeems the subject from the divisiveness of conflict. Similarly, all symbols can be said to be potentially redemptive in that they transcend slavish obedience to divisive opposition (see TRANSCENDENT FUNCTION). However, symbols that transcend the human condition by uniting the opposites of spirit and matter can be said to be part of the GOD-IMAGE or SELF.

Logically, the opposites are always split and perpetually in conflict, one against the other (i.e. good against EVIL and vice versa); but, illogically, they coalesce in the unconscious PSYCHE. The ARCHETYPE is perceived as containing an inherent and opposed duality which can be expressed as a spectrum (for example, considering the archetype of the GREAT MOTHER, the good or nourishing mother would be at one end of the spectrum and the bad or devouring mother at the other end). Analytically speaking, an archetypal content can be said to be integrated only when the full range of its spectrum has been made conscious.

If left to itself, the coincidence of unconscious opposites would cancel itself out and stasis would result. However, the principle of the coincidence of opposites is counter-balanced by that of absolute opposition or ENANTIODROMIA. Paradoxically, at the point of greatest fullness, that which lies at one end of a spectrum turns into its opposite and the possibility of a new synthesis is released. Psychic ENERGY is then concentrated upon resolution of the conflict and there is an attempt at reconciliation. Therefore, all psychic conjunction or synthesis must be thought of as temporary; lasting unification is impossible. Jung believed that it was only the discovery of MEANING in human existence which made it possible to withstand the shifting demands of the opposites (see INDIVIDUATION; TRANSFORMATION; WHOLENESS).

Jung has been much criticised in connection with the implications of his position, not only by scientific colleagues but also by clergy who have found the concept of a dark as well as a light side inadmissible as part of the image of the Christian God. Building upon such a theoretical basis has itself led to a wide spectrum of approaches, oppositions and shifts among analytical psychologists themselves.

P

painting In analysis or self-analysis, the portrayal of inner imagery in visual form. The imagery may derive from DREAMS, ACTIVE IMAGINATION, VISIONS or another form of FANTASY.

During the late nineteenth century in Central Europe, interest was aroused in the paintings of the insane; undoubtedly Jung was aware of this. Early in his career he began to paint or sculpt himself and he continued the activity throughout his lifetime. He also encouraged his patients to paint and interpreted the paintings in certain of his articles (see especially 'A Study in the Process of Individuation', CW 9i; 'The Philosophical Tree', CW 13). An archive of the paintings of analysands is maintained at the C. G. Jung Institute, Zurich.

Jung's comments on the psychological value of such painting placed emphasis both upon process and product. The picture mediates between the patient and his problem. With the production of a painting, a person achieves distance from his psychic condition. For the disturbed patient, whether he be neurotic or psychotic, incomprehensible and unmanageable chaos is objectified by painting.

Often, differentiation between the person and his painting can be regarded as the beginning of psychological independence. While portraying a fantasy, one goes on imagining it in ever more complete form and greater detail. In this instance, one does not depict the vision or dream itself but is painting *out of* that vision or dream; hence, the conscious PSYCHE has an opportunity to interact with what has erupted unconsciously (see TRANSCENDENT FUNCTION; UNCONSCIOUS).

Initially, the approach to painting is the opposite to that of active imagination. One does not strive to uncover or release unconscious contents but to assist them in reaching full and conscious expression. The less the initial material is shaped, Jung warns, the greater is the danger that matters will be regarded as settled too early or judgments formulated in moral, intellectual or diagnostic terms.

Great care must be taken in the handling of paintings and their INTERPRETATION, both on the part of the painter and the analyst. Jung worked consistently from the point of view that the painting was the patient's own (like the dream) and the primary relationship to be fostered was between the painter himself and his own imaginative interpretation of the figures portrayed.

Followers of Jung have used painting as a way to encourage release of repressed AFFECT along with or as well as for purposes of diagnosis. Series of paintings can often be seen to have a sequential or narrative development expressive of a changing psychological condition.

See MANDALA.

paranoid-schizoid position Term introduced by Melanie Klein to indicate a point in the development of OBJECT RELATIONS before the infant has recognised that the images of the good mother and the bad mother to which he has been relating refer to the same person (see DEPRESSIVE POSITION; GREAT MOTHER; IMAGE). While the paranoid-schizoid position is contrasted with the depressive position (in which splits in the personality and in the object are healed), there is also something of a two-way movement and, in adult life, evidence of both positions is usually to be found.

In developmental schema, the paranoid-schizoid position follows on whatever state of primary identity might be thought to exist (see IDENTITY). Splitting, the characteristic of the paranoid-schizoid position, is not the same as a 'deintegration' of the primary self (see SELF). In the latter, the various splits carry within them an intimation of wholeness and tend to work towards personality enhancement.

The quality of anxiety at this time is *paranoid* (i.e. the infant's fear may be of persecution and attack). His means of defence is to split the object (i.e. a *schizoid* manoeuvre). The infant splits the image of the mother so as to possess the good and control the bad versions of her. He also splits within himself because of the intense anxiety caused by the presence of apparently irreconcilable feelings of love and hate. It has been suggested that the capacity to withstand this split is a pre-requisite for any later synthesis of OPPOSITES. But as Jung emphasised, first these must be differentiated; that is, split apart.

The paranoid-schizoid position reflects a style of CONSCIOUSNESS which Jung termed 'heroic' in that the infant tends to behave in an overly determined and goal-directed manner.

See HERO; *PUER AETERNUS*.

participation mystique Term borrowed from the anthropologist Lévy-Brühl. He used it to refer to a form of relationship with an object (meaning 'thing') in which the subject cannot distinguish himself from the thing. This rests on the notion, which may be prevalent in a CULTURE, that the person/tribe and the thing – for instance a cult object or holy artifact – are *already* connected. When the state of *participation mystique* is entered, this connection comes to life.

Jung used the term from 1912 onwards to refer to relations between *people* in which the subject, or a part of him, attains an influence over the other, or vice versa. In more modern psychoanalytic language, Jung was describing PROJECTIVE IDENTIFICATION in which a part of the personality is projected into the object, and the object is then experienced as if it were the projected content.

Participation mystique or projective identification are early defences which also appear in adult PATHOLOGY. They enable the subject to control the external object or 'colour' it according to an inner world view. In this way, archetypal inheritance exerts its influence on the external world so that we can speak of subjective experience or the subjective environment. In day-to-day circumstances, *participation mystique* may be the condition in which two people can anticipate each other's needs, finish each other's sentences, each depending on the other to become what he or she is. (See ARCHETYPE; IDENTITY; OBJECT RELATIONS; PARANOID-SCHIZOID POSITION; PSYCHIC REALITY.)

part object   See OBJECT RELATIONS.

pathology   Pathology is defined as the study of disease with the aim both of understanding its cause and applying that knowledge to the treatment of patients. Although Jung's life-long concern was with pathology, after the initial years spent as a young psychiatrist and psychoanalyst, he directed less attention to the definition of so-called pathological states and he no longer relied upon a medical model which excluded his own empirical observations and conclusions. He saw distinct differences between a medical and a psychotherapeutic approach to pathology even though he regarded PSYCHOTHERAPY as one of the medical disciplines. It was precisely because the techniques of ANALYSIS unlock doors otherwise tightly closed in the person and thereby can reveal latent illness that he insisted lay analysts work in collaboration with doctors (see PSYCHOSIS).

In 1945, in a lecture addressed to the Senate of the Swiss Academy of Medical Science, Jung drew the attention of his fellow doctors to differences between the medical doctor and the psychotherapist in their approaches to pathology. Whereas the doctor proceeds to *treat* pathology, the psychotherapist must remain mindful that the ailing psyche encompasses the whole of man. Therefore, though diagnosis is of primary importance to the medical practitioner, it may prove to be of relatively little value to the psychotherapist. Likewise, so far as psychoneurosis is concerned, a full history is well nigh impossible to compile, since the contributing factors to the situation are initially unconscious for the patient and often hidden from the therapist. Finally, rather than attacking the symptom, psychotherapy has to be conducted psychologically; that is, with awareness of the psychic images which lie at the root of the disturbances. When such images are unacceptable both to the person and to SOCIETY, they may be seen as masking themselves as illnesses (see HYSTERIA; MENTAL ILL-NESS; NARCISSISM; NEUROSIS; SCHIZOPHRENIA).

patient See ANALYST AND PATIENT.

persona The term derives from the Latin word for the mask worn by actors in classical times. Hence, persona refers to the mask or face a person puts on to confront the world. Persona can refer to gender identity, a stage of development (such as adolescence), a social status, a job or profession. Over a lifetime, many personas will be worn and several may be combined at any one moment.

Jung's conception of the persona is of an ARCHETYPE, meaning in this context that there is an inevitability and ubiquity to persona. In any society, a means of facilitating relationship and exchange is required; this function is partly carried out by the personas of the individuals involved. Different cultures will establish different criteria for persona and there will be alteration and evolution over time since the underlying archetypal pattern is susceptible to infinite variation (see CULTURE; IMAGE). Sometimes, the persona is referred to as the 'social archetype', involving all the compromises appropriate to living in a community.

It follows that persona is not to be thought of as inherently pathological or false. There *is* a risk of PATHOLOGY if a person identifies too closely with his/her persona. This would imply a lack of awareness of much beyond social role (lawyer, analyst, labourer), or gender role (mother), and also a failure to take account of maturation (for instance, an apparent failure to adapt to having grown up). Persona identification leads to a form of psychological rigidity or brittleness; the UNCONSCIOUS will tend to erupt into consciousness rather than emerging in a manageable way. The EGO, when it is identified with the persona, is capable only of an external orientation. It is blind to internal events and hence unable to respond to them. It follows that it is possible to remain unconscious of one's persona.

These last comments point to the place Jung assigned to persona in the structure of the PSYCHE. That was as a mediator between the ego and the external world (in much the same way as ANIMA AND ANIMUS mediate between the ego and the internal world). Persona and anima/animus can therefore be thought of as OPPOSITES.

Whereas persona is concerned with conscious and COLLECTIVE adaptation, anima/animus are concerned with adaptation to that which is personal, interior and individual.

personal unconscious See SHADOW; UNCONSCIOUS.

personification A fundamental psychological activity whereby all that one experiences is spontaneously and involuntarily personified, i.e. becomes a psychic 'person'. We meet our personifications in DREAMS, FANTASY and in PROJECTION.

Jung's first reference to personification provides us with an example. It is part of his interpretation of a patient's fantasy and he says: 'It was Miss M's spirituality, which, personified as the Aztec, was far too exalted for her ever to find a lover among mortal men' (CW 5, para. 273). A psychic content that is of sufficient intensity or mass to have broken away from the personality as a whole can be perceived only when objectified or personified, according to Jung (see APPERCEPTION; ARCHETYPE; COMPLEX). Personification thus enables one to see the Psyche functioning as a series of autonomous systems. It depotentiates the threatening power of what has broken away and makes INTERPRETATION possible (see POSSESSION; PSYCHOSIS).

A natural psychic process, personifying was first observed by depth psychologists in pathological states such as DISSOCIATION, hallucination or break-up into multiple personalities. Later, Jung spoke of it in connection with the psychology of PRIMITIVES and he likened it to unconscious IDENTIFICATION or the PROJECTION of an unconscious content into an object until such time as it could be integrated into CONSCIOUSNESS. Freud translated concepts into personified images; i.e. the censor, the super-ego, the polymorphously perverse child. He was not the first physician or scientist to do so, however, as Jung pointed out in his work on the physician/philosopher Paracelsus and in elaborating the VISIONS of Zosimos, the alchemist (see ALCHEMY). Jung himself personified those concepts that he observed empirically (SHADOW; SELF, GREAT MOTHER, WISE OLD MAN/WOMAN, ANIMA AND ANIMUS), saying, 'the fact that the unconscious spontaneously personifies ... is the reason why I have taken over these personifications in my terminology and formulated them as names' (CW 9i, para. 51).

He was, in fact, writing of fantasy images. His radical formulation was that psychological behaviour proceeds by way of changing patterns between personified images (see IMAGE; IMAGO). De-personalisation can be spoken of as LOSS OF SOUL. A patient who cannot personify tends merely to personalise everything. ANALYSIS can be seen as an exploration of the patient's relationship to his or her personifications. Since the ability to personify underlies all psychic life, it ultimately provides us with the imagery of RELIGION and MYTH.

Among Jung's followers, Hillman (1975) has written at greatest length and depth about personifying as a natural and essential psychological process. He notes that: (1) it protects the psyche from domination by any one single power; (2) it provides a useful therapeutic tool by establishing a perspective whereby a person can admit that these figures belong to him and at the same time recognise they are also free of his identity and control; (3) as Jung pointed out, by personifying, the figures acquire objectivity and they are also differentiated not only from unconsciousness but from one another as well. That is to say, they no longer coalesce or adhere to one another; yet (4) personifying encourages relationship between and among psychic components; (5) it has an advantage over conceptualisation in that it evokes a living response in contrast to intellectual nominalism.

pleroma A Gnostic term used by Jung to designate a 'place' beyond time-space category boundaries and where all tension between opposites is extinguished or resolved (see OPPOSITES). To be distinguished from WHOLENESS or INDIVIDUATION by virtue of the fact that the pleroma is a given and not an achievement. The state of 'oneness' present therein is different from the wholeness derived from a bringing together of previously disparate elements of personality. Nevertheless, the condition of wholeness, along with certain mystical states, may also be understood as an apperception of the pleroma.

The pleroma corresponds to what the physicist Bohm has referred to as an 'implicate' or 'enfolded' order of reality lying within, behind, underneath reality as we ordinarily perceive it (1980).

See OPPOSITES; PSYCHOID UNCONSCIOUS; SYNCHRONICITY; *UNUS MUNDUS*; UROBOROS.

polytheism Belief in or worship of several gods instead of one god. Although commonly spoken of as the opposite of monotheism, it is generally recognised by theologians to be an expression of monotheism in the sense that it presupposes some kind of supraordinate principle, whether that be chaos or otherwise.

Jung applied the word within an historical context, i.e. the chaos of polytheism preceded the order of Christianity. Viewed psychologically, however, the multiplicity of archetypes, specifically referred to more than once as having the status which in former times might have been accorded to gods or daemons, may be seen as 'polytheistic', although in a state of constant tension with a supraordinate 'monotheistic' SELF.

Such considerations have become relevant with the extension of the concepts of analytical psychology into archetypal psychology (Hillman, 1983). Here, 'the soul's inherent multiplicity' is stressed and, Hillman writes, demands 'a theological fantasy capable of equal differentiation'.

possession In common usage, 'to possess' means 'to own' and carries connotations of holding, occupation and control. In psychological terminology, 'possession' means an ownership, a take-over or occupation of the EGO-personality by a COMPLEX or other archetypal content (see ARCHETYPE). Since bondage and possession are synonymous, the ego is the subject of a *coup d'état*. Because of the strength and obstinacy of the neurotic or psychotic symptom, a person is deprived of choice and is powerless to dispose of his WILL. A restraining effect is placed on CONSCIOUSNESS proportional to the strength of the invading autonomous psychic content and an acute one-sidedness results (see COMPENSATION; NEUROSIS). This imperils not only conscious freedom but also psychic equilibrium. Individual aims are falsified in favour of the possessing psychic agent whether it be a mother-complex or an IDENTIFICATION with the PERSONA or ANIMA/ANIMUS principle, for example.

In an article written for a Basle newspaper at the time of the death of Freud (CW 15), Jung gives a concise explication of the development of ANALYTICAL PSYCHOLOGY, linking it historically with Charcot's discovery 'that hysterical symptoms were the consequence of certain ideas that had taken possession of the patient's "brain"'. From this, according to Jung's account, Breuer substantiated a theory which Freud declared as one that 'coincides with the mediaeval view (of possession) once we substitute a psychological formula for the "demon" of priestly fantasy'. Jung found an analogy between the search for the causal factor of possession in order to cure the patient and mediaeval attempts to exorcise the EVIL spirits once and for all (see AETIOLOGY (OF NEUROSIS); HYSTERIA; PATHOLOGY).

From that analogy, Jung went on to delineate his own work further. After Freud's recognition that modern neurosis bears characteristics analogous to mediaeval possession, the Freudian interpretation of dreams was an attempt to investigate the root causes of such possession. But, according to Jung, this was an approach to the possessed psyche in order to dethrone the occupier or repressing agent. He found such an approach admirable but limited. In a crucial talk with Freud, he reports, he posed the question whether one might not be able to discover individual implication and, eventually, MEANING to falling victim to a neurotic possession. Here is the essence of Jung's TELEOLOGICAL POINT OF VIEW.

power Jung's early psychological formulations need to be seen in relation and reaction to theories advanced by his fellow pioneers and closest colleagues in the field of PSYCHOTHERAPY as well as representative of his own creative insights. Foremost among those with whom he established a dialogue were Alfred Adler and Freud. Adler's work was specifically based upon the will to power as a motivating principle of human behaviour and at one time Jung categorically stated that he saw the work of both men as built on the premise that man drives ahead and asserts himself with a will to succeed or be on top. Eventually, he took exception to this as a limited point of view, excessively 'masculine' and incomplete. He was convinced that along with other archetypal images, there is also a GOD-IMAGE in man's PSYCHE and he assigned a prior place to the urge for fulfilment or 'the instinct for WHOLENESS'. Words he used in response to Adler are expressive of his own religious orientation. He said that he found Adler's insistence upon man's will to power as a driving force to be an acceptance of man's 'moral inferiority' (CW 16, para. 234).

Jung does not deny that the will to power (i.e. the desire to subordinate all other influences to the EGO) is an INSTINCT. Neither did he see it as purely negative. It is a strong and determinative factor in the development of CULTURE. Likewise, without it, man would have no incentive to build a sufficiently strong ego to withstand either the vicissitudes of outer life itself or, more particularly, confrontations with the SELF in his own personality.

Conceptually, Jung regarded power as equivalent to the idea of SOUL, SPIRIT, daemon, godliness, health, strength, MANA, fertility, MAGIC, prestige, medicine, influence – a form of psychic ENERGY. He spoke of the archetypes as 'autonomous centres of power'. He saw in the ARCHETYPE not only a readiness to reproduce similar mythical ideas but also a deposit of power, i.e. 'determinative energy'.

Jung defined the power COMPLEX as the sum of all those energies, strivings and ideas aimed at the acquisition of personal power. When it dominates the personality, all other influences are subordinated to the ego, whether they are influences emanating from other people and external conditions or arising from the person's own impulses, thoughts and feelings. Someone may *have* power without being power-driven or the victim of a complex, however. An increase in the conscious ability to use power is a goal of psychotherapy (CW 8, para. 590).

primal scene   See INFANCY AND CHILDHOOD; MARRIAGE.

primary and secondary process   See DIRECTED AND FANTASY THINKING.

primitives   Jung wrote:

> In travelling to Africa to find a psychic observation post outside the sphere of the European, I unconsciously wanted to find that part of my personality which had become invisible under the influence and pressure of being European. This part stands in unconscious opposition to myself, and indeed I attempt to repress it. In keeping with its nature, it wishes to make me unconscious (force me under water) so as to kill me; but my aim is, through insight, to make it more conscious, so that we can find a common *modus vivendi* (1963).

His preoccupation with the world of so-called 'primitives'; his field work among them, his fascination with their rites and ceremonies, observations on their psychology, appreciation of their fears, their analogic thinking, the seriousness which they accorded phenomena of the soul, the respect they showed for the SYMBOL – all inform Jung's statements about the psychological residues of primitivity in modern man. But these elements must be seen from differing vantage points. The first is from within the man himself. This was, as the opening quotation attests, an experiment compelled by Jung's own psychic nature, a prompting from his own UNCONSCIOUS. It was not an intentional focus any more than were his PAINTINGS or sculptures, his active FANTASY, sequences of DREAMS or dialogues between No. 1 and No. 2 personalities. Quite the opposite; these were experiences of his own interiority motivated by something he could not explain except in the most general terms. He went to Africa not to meet native Africans or tribal people but, by way of observation, to meet a counterpart of the native, unfettered, tribal, sometimes savage person within himself.

The second vantage point is also a perspective arising from Jung's subjective orientation. Although it was never openly stated, his interest in so-called primitives was his first attempt to find verification of his psychological observations in collective PROJECTION. The later, more scholarly and sophisticated attempt was ALCHEMY. His preoccupation with the study of primitives was an extrapolation backward in time to find the COLLECTIVE origins of phenomena he was observing in his study of the unconscious in modern man.

The third perspective is one which brought him into methodological conflict with scientists and doctors of his time. This was research which granted to subjectivity the same status as that granted to objectivity in modern science.

The fourth is that this provided a meeting *in the flesh* of collective as opposed to individuated man. His hypothesis about the style of thinking of primitives was that they reasoned by way of projection because their minds were collectively oriented.

Because of the inadequacy of his field work by an anthropologist's standards and what looked like his over-reliance on a few sources, and also because so much of his research was conducted by way of dialogue, some social scientists of his time and since have discounted it. He has also been criticised by those who saw him as exploiting native peoples and under-valuing their worth. This he did not deliberately do; it is only when one looks for traces of exploitation as defined from a conscious and political point of view that he is at all suspect.

Jung's definition of 'primitives' was based upon the theories of Lévy-Brühl. However, although he relied upon Lévy-Brühl for a theoretical foundation, his was not the only influence. From reading, travel, dialogue and introspection, Jung's ideas of 'the primitive' became co-equal with an IMAGE of a liminal being and we have here one of the most complete portrayals of any of his *own* images. Therefore, a look at his study of so-called primitives is integral to any thoroughgoing acquaintance with or assessment of his work, clinical or otherwise. The psychological image of the primitive coincides with his conceptualisation of emerging CONSCIOUSNESS in an individual.

See LOSS OF SOUL; MANA PERSONALITIES; *PARTICIPATION MYSTIQUE*; PLEROMA; RELIGION.

primordial image See ARCHETYPE.

projection Jung's approach to projection builds upon a psychoanalytic base. Projection may be seen as normal or pathological and as a defence against anxiety. Difficult emotions and unacceptable parts of the personality may be located in a person or object external to the subject (see PERSONIFICATION). The problematic content is thereby controlled and the individual feels a (temporary) release and sense of well-being. Alternatively, aspects of the personality sensed to be good and valuable may be projected so as to protect them from the ravages of the rest of the personality, fantasised as bad or destructive. In terms of experience, a person feels something about another person (or institution or group) which he regards as applicable to that person; later he may realise that this is not the case. An impartial observer, an analyst, perhaps, may realise this sooner rather than later. The general result of projection beyond an optimum level is an impoverishment of personality. Normal levels of projection in infancy are considered pathological in an adult.

In ANALYTICAL PSYCHOLOGY, stress has also been laid on projection as the means by which the contents of the inner world are made available to ego-consciousness (see EGO). The assumption is that an encounter between the ego and such unconscious contents is of value (see UNCONSCIOUS). The external world of persons and things serves the internal world by providing the raw material to be activated by projection. This can be seen most clearly when what is projected is also representative of a part of the psyche. ANIMA AND ANIMUS projections are 'carried' by real women and men; without the carrier there would be no meeting. Similarly, the SHADOW is frequently encountered in projection. By definition, the shadow is the repository of what is unacceptable to consciousness. It is therefore ripe for projection.

For anything of value to be gained, though, it is necessary for some re-integration or re-collection of that which is projected to take place. Jung suggested that, for convenience of understanding, this process could be divided into five phases:

(1) The person is convinced that what he sees in the other is the case.

(2) A gradual recognition dawns of a differentiation between the other as she/he 'really' is and the projected image. The dawning of such awareness may be facilitated by DREAMS or, equally, events.

(3) Some kind of assessment or judgment is made of the discrepancy.

(4) A conclusion is reached that what was felt was erroneous or illusory. (Jung argued that this was as far as psychoanalysis went.)

(5) A conscious search for the sources and origin of the projection is undertaken. This includes COLLECTIVE as well as personal determinants of the projection (see ARCHETYPE).

Jung noted the role of projection in empathy, though estimating that of INTROJECTION as greater. Projection may be required to draw the object into the orbit of the subject; but it will be introjection of the object which facilitates the empathic response. A contemporary parallel is with Kohut's definition of empathy as 'vicarious introspection'. In Kohut's theory, projection and introjection are more or less evenly weighted.

A similar debate arises with Jung's insistence that one function of projection is to effect a *separation* of subject and object, leading to an isolation of the subject. The Kleinian emphasis on defensive control of the object by projective identification emphasises the *elimination* of whatever separation there might be (see PARTICIPATION MYSTIQUE).

projective identification   See PARTICIPATION MYSTIQUE.

prospective viewpoint   See TELEOLOGICAL POINT OF VIEW.

psyche Used by Jung interchangeably with the German word *Seele* which has no single English equivalent, as the translator of the *Collected Works* noted (*CW* 12, para. 9n).

By his basic definition of the psyche as the 'totality of all psychic processes, conscious as well as unconscious' (*CW* 6, para. 797), Jung intended to delineate the area of interest for ANALYTICAL PSYCHOLOGY. This would be something different from philosophy, biology, theology and a psychology limited to the study of either INSTINCT or behaviour. The somewhat tautological nature of the definition emphasises a particular problem with psychological exploration: the overlap of subjective and objective interest. Jung makes frequent references to the 'personal equation', the impact that the personality and context of the observer make on his observations. In addition to the linking of conscious and unconscious processes, Jung specifically included within 'psyche' the overlap and tension between the personal and COLLECTIVE elements in man (see UNCONSCIOUS).

The psyche can also be seen as a perspective on phenomena. That is characterised first by an attention to depth and intensity and, hence, the difference between an experience and a mere event (see DEPTH PSYCHOLOGY). Here the word 'SOUL' becomes relevant and it is in connection with such a depth perspective that Jung uses it rather than in a conventionally Christian manner (see ANIMA AND ANIMUS). Then there is the issue of the plurality and fluidity of the psyche, the existence of relatively autonomous components within it, and its tendency to function via imagery and associative leaps (see ASSOCIATION; COMPLEX; IMAGE; METAPHOR; PERSONIFICATION). Finally, the psyche as a perspective contains intimations of pattern and MEANING, not to the extent of a fixed predestination but, nevertheless, discernible by the individual.

To state the pluralism of the psyche leads to questions of its structure. His tendency to organise his thought in terms of OPPOSITES led Jung to map psyche in a way that may be somewhat too pat. For instance, ANIMA and ANIMUS balance PERSONA, EGO and SHADOW are paired, and ego and SELF defined in ways which stress their complementarity. On the other hand, Jung's thinking about the psyche is also systemic and flexible in that developments at one point send ripples throughout the entire system. What we see is a tension in Jung's ideas between structure and dynamic. To some extent, this is resolved in Jung's description of the psyche which suggests that it is a structure made for movement, growth, change and TRANSFORMATION. He refers to these capacities of the human psyche as its distinguishing characteristics. A degree of evolution towards self-realisation is therefore embedded in all psychic processes. This idea brings its own problem. Is man to be seen as developing out of some original, unconscious state of wholeness, realising more and more of his potential? Or as moving with greater or lesser regularity towards a goal that is, as it were, marked out for him – the 'person he was intended to be' (see TELEOLOGICAL POINT OF VIEW; WHOLENESS)? Or as proceeding in an anarchic manner from crisis to crisis, struggling to make sense of what is happening to him? To say that all three possibilities are intermingled is simple. But each has its own psychological impact and contribution. The weighting given to each plays a crucial part in debates concerning the self and INDIVIDUATION.

The psyche, like most natural systems such as the body, struggles to keep itself in balance. It will do this even when the attempt throws up unpleasant symptoms, frightening DREAMS or seemingly insoluble life problems. If a person's development has been one-sided, the psyche contains within it whatever is necessary to rectify this (see COMPENSATION; INFANCY AND CHILDHOOD). Here, over-optimism or blind faith must be avoided; keeping in balance requires work and painful or difficult choices often have to be made (see MORALITY; SYMBOL; TRANSCENDENT FUNCTION).

Jung's speculations on the nature of the psyche led him to consider it as a force in the universe. The psychological takes its place as a separate realm in addition to the biological and spiritual dimensions of existence. What is important is the relationship between these dimensions which comes into being in the psyche (see PSYCHIC REALITY; RELIGION). Jung's ideas on the relationship of psyche and body do not involve the psyche as based on, derived from, analogous to or correlated with BODY but as a partner with it (see PSYCHOID UNCONSCIOUS). A similar relationship is proposed with the non-organic world (see SYNCHRONICITY).

The conceptual overlap between the psyche and the self may be resolved as follows. Though the self refers to the totality of the personality, as a transcendent concept it also enjoys the paradoxical capacity to relate to its various components, for example, the ego (see EGO-SELF AXIS). The psyche encompasses these relationships and may even be said to be made up of such dynamics.

Jung's constant references to the ultimate unknowability of the psyche exemplify his readiness to include within it those phenomena often referred to as parapsychological or telepathic.

psychic reality This is a key concept of Jung's and he may be seen to have approached it in different ways; as experience, as IMAGE, and as suggesting the nature and function of the PSYCHE (see OBJECTIVE PSYCHE).

As experience, psychic reality embraces everything that strikes a person as real or with the force of reality. According to Jung, one experiences life and its events in terms of narrative truth rather than historical truth (the 'personal MYTH'). What is experienced as psychic reality may be a form of self-expression and, ultimately, contribute in a cybernetic manner to the accretion of further layers of psychic reality. A specific illustration of this is to be found in the tendency of the UNCONSCIOUS to personify its contents (see PERSONIFICATION). The resultant figures become real in the sense that they have an emotional impact on the EGO and undergo change and development. Personification was, for Jung, an empirical demonstration of psychic reality.

The existence of opinions, beliefs, ideas and fantasies does not mean that what they refer to is accurate to the degree and in the manner which may be claimed. By way of illustration, the psychic realities of two people will differ markedly. And a delusionary system, psychically real, will not have objective validity. Nevertheless, that is not the same thing as saying that *nothing* exists or is true.

In this first usage (that of a subjective level of reality), the relation of psychic reality to a hypothetical external or objective reality is relevant from a clinical rather than a theoretical viewpoint.

As image. It is now generally agreed that the structure of the BRAIN (its neurophysiological make-up) and the cultural context affect what is perceived and, still more, interpretations of those perceptions. Personal bias and desire also play what can be seen as a distorting role. These factors bring the conventional distinction between 'reality' and 'fantasy' into question and, in doing this, Jung stands in the Platonic, Idealist philosophical tradition. He may also be contrasted with Freud, whose idea of 'psychical reality' never overcame his belief that there was an objective reality which could be discovered and then measured scientifically.

Jung was among the first to point out that all CONSCIOUSNESS is of an indirect nature, mediated by the nervous system and other psycho-sensory processes, not to mention linguistic operations. Experiences, e.g. of pain or excitement, reach us in secondary form. In Jung's lexicon, this immediately suggests images and that both inner and outer worlds are experienced by and as imagery (see METAPHOR).

The notions of inner and outer worlds are themselves images, here used metaphorically. Such spatial entities have no existence save as psychic reality permits. Here Jung is using the term 'image' in an inclusive manner to denote the absence of a direct link between stimulus and experience. When using the word this way, somatic manifestations may also be seen as images along with the whole physical world as it is experienced in consciousness (see below). The image is what presents itself to consciousness directly. Put another

117

way, we become aware of our experience through an encounter with an image of it.

These arguments led Jung to conclude that, because of its imaginal composition, psychic reality is the only reality we can experience directly, a view which serves to introduce the third way in which 'psychic reality' is employed.

As suggesting the nature and function of the psyche. According to Jung, the psyche (and psychic reality) function as an intermediate world between the physical and spiritual realms, which may meet and mingle therein (see SPIRIT). Problems of translation from German intrude here and it is necessary to add that by 'physical' is meant both the organic and inorganic aspects of the material world and that 'spiritual' includes developed thoughts and cognitions. This means that the psyche appears to stand midway between such phenomena as sense impressions and plant or mineral life on the one hand and, on the other, intellectual and spiritual ideation (see FANTASY, also said to function as a 'third' factor between intellect and the material/sensual world). Acceptance of the idea of psychic reality brings to an end the easy acceptance of an inherent conflict between mind and matter or spirit and nature in which these are looked upon as radically different.

By way of example, Jung suggested a comparison between the fear of fire and the fear of ghosts. In terms of psychic reality, fire and ghosts (apparently quite different) occupy identical positions, activating the psyche in the same way. He is careful to point out that this argument says nothing about the ultimate origin of matter (fire) or spirit (ghosts); these remain as unknown as before. While Jung would not dispute that the negative consequences of contact with fire are usually different from those of contact with ghosts, it is the phenomenon of *fear* which leads us to an understanding of psychic reality.

In its acceptance of matter without distinction of its organic and inorganic aspects, this view of psychic reality is more comprehensive than Jung's suppositions about the PSYCHOID UNCONSCIOUS or SYNCHRONICITY. In the former, the overlap between psychological and physiological processes is highlighted. In the latter, it is the psyche and inorganic matter that are discussed as if enmeshed. Though the organic/inorganic distinction is a matter of emphasis, the all-embracing nature of psychic reality, as a metapsychological category, may more accurately be compared with the idea of the UNUS MUNDUS.

psychoanalysis There will be few readers completely unacquainted with the sequence of the Freud-Jung relationship: that Jung read *The Interpretation of Dreams* (Freud, 1900) in 1900 and re-read it in 1903;

that Jung sent Freud a copy of his *Studies in Word Association* in 1906 and a correspondence began; that this speedily became of great importance to both men; that they met in 1907 and talked for thirteen hours; that Freud saw Jung as the Crown Prince of the psychoanalytic kingdom (Freud was nineteen years the elder); that Jung's non-Jewishness was a boon to Freud, for he feared that psychoanalysis would become a 'Jewish science'; that they visited the USA together in 1909; that personal tensions and conceptual disputes crept in; that relations were difficult by 1912 when Jung published *Wandlungen und Symbole der Libido* (later to become *Symbols of Transformation*, CW 5); that Jung anticipated a final break with that publication; and that the break took place in 1913. After this, Jung designated his approach to psychology as 'Analytical Psychology' (see ANALYTICAL PSYCHOLOGY; DEPTH PSYCHOLOGY).

The two men interacted with one another. Freud provided Jung with the experience of a father-figure of strong conviction and moral courage that he had lacked (Jung, 1963). In addition, Freud's thought served as a structural framework within which to explore and criticise. Further, Jung received the status of the one on whom the mantle was laid. Finally, Freud's influence on Jung as a commentator upon his clinical work, with all that implied, was considerable. Jung's contribution to psychoanalysis, as Freud saw it, has been summarised by Papadopoulos (1984):

(1) introducing empirical, experimental methods (see EMPIRICISM);
(2) the concept of the COMPLEX;
(3) the institution of training analysis;
(4) the use of mythological and anthropological amplifications (see AMPLIFICATION; MYTH);
(5) the application of psychoanalytic theory and therapy to PSYCHOSIS (see PSYCHOTHERAPY).

Assessments of the Freud-Jung break vary greatly. Certain staunch adherents of one side or the other see the break as resulting in the purity of ideas having been preserved (Glover, 1950; Adler, 1971). Others regard what happened as catastrophic, seeing Freud and Jung as having exerted a balancing influence on each other, an influence that was therefore lost (Fordham, 1961). Similarly, there have been many interpretations of why the break took place and psychobiography has provided further speculations involving homoerotic problems, father/son conflicts, Jung's inability to cope with sexuality, Freud's power-complex, the TYPOLOGY of the two men. Sometimes Freud and Jung are recognised as writing from the perspectives of two different world views.

It is possible to identify six areas of disagreement out of which sprang a large part of Jung's subsequent thought and which serve to delineate the on-going differences between psychoanalysis and analytical psychology.

First, Jung could not agree with what he saw as Freud's exclusively sexual interpretation of human motivation. This view led him to modify Freud's theory of libido (see ENERGY).

The *second* of Jung's disagreements was with Freud's general approach to the PSYCHE which was, in Jung's view, mechanistic and causal. Human beings do not live according to laws analogous to physical or mechanical principles (see REDUCTIVE AND SYNTHETIC METHODS).

The *third* criticism Jung had of Freud was that there was too rigid a distinction made between 'hallucination' and 'reality'. Throughout his writings, Jung's concern is for psychological reality as experienced by the individual (see PSYCHIC REALITY). In this context, the unconscious is not to be seen as an enemy but rather as something potentially helpful and creative (see TELEOLOGICAL POINT OF VIEW). DREAMS, for instance, cease to be regarded, in Jung's perspective, as somehow deceitful, requiring decoding. Instead, dreams are claimed to reveal the unconscious situation in the psyche just as it is; quite often the opposite of what pertains in consciousness (see COMPENSATION). Lying behind these differences over dreams is a differing approach to SYMBOLS (see OPPOSITES; TRANSCENDENT FUNCTION) and to INTERPRETATION.

The *fourth* area of disagreement concerned the balance of innate (constitutional) factors in contrast to the environment in the formation of personality. This balance was perceived differently by each man. Jung was later to refine his statements about innate patterns but it is interesting to speculate what might have happened had Freud continued to develop his notion that some elements in the unconscious have never been conscious, a point which would have led to some such concept as 'ARCHETYPE' (Freud, 1916-17). Instead, both before and after his major theoretical revisions of the 1920s, Freud emphasised the unconscious as a repository of repressed but once-conscious material. Though the id is stated to be, in part, hereditary and innate, this idea was not fully taken up until Melanie Klein's use of it somewhat later (Klein, 1937). Similarly, Freud's early references to 'primal phantasies' as a 'phylogenetic endowment' are not emphasised in subsequent expositions of his thought (*ibid.*, pp. 370-1).

Fifth, there was a difference of opinion which became sharper over time regarding the origin of conscience and morality (see MORALITY; SUPER-EGO).

The *sixth* area of disagreement concerned the nodal status of the Oedipus complex in personality development. Jung's emphasis came to lie more on the primal relationship of infant and mother (see INFANCY AND CHILDHOOD; OBJECT RELATIONS).

In his objections to some of Freud's ideas, Jung shows a remarkable prescience for he anticipated many of the developments that were to take place later within psychoanalysis, as other views were developed (see Samuels, 1985a). The pioneering nature of Jung's contribution makes one question the 'credibility gap' which has attended him (Hudson, 1983).

Analytical psychology's borrowing from psychoanalysis has, of course, been immense. Jung himself seems to have stayed with his impression of psychoanalysis as it was when he left the movement. This leads him into what now seems simplistic criticism and occasionally his dependence on psychoanalytic ideas as he knew them leads to error (see EGO). Contemporary analytical psychologists have leant most heavily on psychoanalysis as regards analytic technique and for coherent schemas of early development (see ANALYST AND PATIENT; INFANCY AND CHILDHOOD; OBJECT RELATIONS). Kohut's self-psychology is becoming a major influence as well.

The recent publication (1983) of the papers Jung gave to a student discussion group at Basle University (the Zofingia Club) has, to a degree, thrown open the question of Freud's influence on Jung. At that time (1896-7), Jung had never heard of Freud. Prior to a thorough study of these lectures, analytical psychology's roots were assumed to lie solely within psychoanalysis. Many of Jung's later interests find early expression in these lectures and we can also take from them the clearest possible picture of the conceptual background to Jung's work. In 1897 Jung read a paper entitled 'Some thoughts on psychology'. Here, after setting the scene with quotations from Kant and Schopenhauer, he discusses the existence of 'SPIRITS' beyond the body and 'in another world'. The ideas are remarkably similar to those which later appear as the theory of the autonomous psychic principle; this is the 'SOUL' which is greater than our consciousness. Later in Jung's development, these seeds blossom into the theory of PSYCHIC ENERGY and the concept of the SELF.

In summary, as von Franz writes in her introduction to the *Zofingia Lectures*, 'here Jung first mentions indirectly the idea of an unconscious psyche'. What is more, the 'unconscious' is stated to be purposeful in its behaviour (see TELEOLOGICAL POINT OF VIEW) and outside of space-time logic (see SYNCHRONICITY). Jung then ranges the fields of spiritualistic and telepathic phenomena to underpin what he would later call PSYCHIC REALITY. The lecture concludes with a plea for morality in science (on this occasion a condemnation of vivisection) and for an approach to RELIGION which allows for its irrational aspects.

In addition to the philosophers already mentioned, Nietzsche exerted an influence on Jung. And Jung's work stands in the Platonic tradition. When considering further non-Freudian influences on Jung, the names of Flournoy and Bleuler should be mentioned. The latter was Jung's superior at Burghölzli, the mental hospital of Zurich, where Jung worked from 1900 to 1909 (see WORD ASSOCIATION TEST). Bleuler created an atmosphere in which Freud's ideas were welcomed and actively used. Up to about 1908, Bleuler was regarded by Freud as the most important adherent to the cause of psychoanalysis. However, Jung was able to convince Freud that Bleuler was ambivalent and not to be trusted and so the link gradually eroded. Jung scarcely mentions Bleuler in his autobiography (1963) and seems to have had rather a low opinion of him (but see SCHIZOPHRENIA). Janet, Charcot and James should also be mentioned as significant influences on Jung.

Finally, though out of sympathy with their overall viewpoint, Jung made use of the work of Wundt and the other German experimental psychologists of the late nineteenth century.

psychoid unconscious The idea of the psychoid unconscious was first put forward by Jung in 1946. His formulation has three aspects:
(1) It refers to a level of, or in, the UNCONSCIOUS which is completely inaccessible to consciousness.
(2) This most fundamental level of the unconscious has properties in common with the organic world; the psychological and the physiological worlds may be seen as two sides of a single coin. The psychoid level is neutral in character, being neither wholly psychological nor wholly physiological.
(3) When Jung applied the notion of the ARCHETYPE to the psychoid unconscious, the psychic/organic link was expressed in the form of a mind/body connection. An archetype can be depicted as a spectrum, ranging from an 'infra-red', physiological, instinctual pole to an 'ultra-violet' spiritual or imagistic pole. The archetype embraces the two poles and can be experienced and comprehended through either. Biological or ethological approaches to the archetype may be characterised as 'infra-red'; mythological or imaginal approaches as 'ultra-violet' (see IMAGE; METAPHOR; MYTH).

Contrast and compare PSYCHIC REALITY; SYNCHRONICITY; *UNUS MUNDUS*.

psychopomp The figure which guides the soul at times of INITIATION and transition; a function traditionally ascribed to Hermes in Greek MYTH for he accompanied the souls of the dead and was able to pass between polarities (not only death and life, but night and day, heaven and earth). In the human world the priest, shaman, medicine man and doctor are some who have been recognised as fulfilling the need for spiritual guidance and mediation between sacred and secular worlds. Jung did not alter the meaning of the word but he used it to describe the function of the ANIMA AND ANIMUS in connecting a person with a sense of his ultimate purpose, calling or destiny; in psychological terms, acting as a go-between connecting EGO and UNCONSCIOUS (see SELF).

See MANA PERSONALITIES.

psychosis A personality state in which an unknown 'something' takes POSSESSION of the PSYCHE to a greater or lesser degree and asserts its existence undeterred by logic, persuasion or WILL (see DISSOCIATION). The UNCONSCIOUS invades, assuming control of the conscious EGO, and, since the unconscious has no organised or centralised functions, the consequence is that there is psychic confusion and chaos (see ARCHETYPE). If the strange metaphorical language of the unconscious can be communicated to CONSCIOUSNESS, however, psychosis may have a curative effect (see METAPHOR; SYMBOL). When the repressed ENERGY thus released can be usefully channelled, the conscious personality has access to new sources of power for regeneration.

These ideas, presented originally by Jung in 1917, but reconsidered and restated several times, represent an approach to psychosis from the perspective of DEPTH PSYCHOLOGY; and, although in recent decades, psychotic behaviour has proved to be amenable to the administration of modern drugs, the psychic conditions associated with such states are not altered. The onset of psychosis may be very sudden, even though the eruption may have been preparing for a long time. And, although a neurosis may conceal a psychosis, the material thrown up by a neurosis is generally understandable in human terms while that of a psychosis is not. Here uncontrollable fantasy is let loose.

As far as aetiology is concerned, Jung was at pains to say that he saw in the innate psychological predisposition of a person certain of the determinants of later symptoms but not the sole cause of the psychosis (see PATHOLOGY; SCHIZOPHRENIA). If a psychotic condition is accessible to psychotherapy, an attempt may be made to strengthen the ego sufficiently so that psychic contents can be integrated. If left to itself, however, Jung's view was that in all probability the symbolic process would remain chaotic and out of control. Although it is often possible for an outsider, analyst or psychiatrist, to make sense of psychotic utterances, the usual compensatory mechanism of the psyche is upset in such a way that there is a forceful intrusion of unconscious imagery (see COMPENSATION). Paradoxically, the same baffling process of intrusion by unconscious symbolism occurs at times of intense creative inspiration and religious conversion; but, in both instances, there is a non-personal container of sufficient strength (work of art or RITUAL) so that stability and a sense of purpose can be maintained until individual balance is restored and MEANING becomes apparent (see INITIATION; RELIGION).

psychotherapy   Treatment of PSYCHE; when applying the methodology of ANALYTICAL PSYCHOLOGY, by way of investigating the UNCONSCIOUS.

Considered a relatively modern term and practice, psychotherapy, nevertheless, had its counterparts in ancient ceremonials of healing (Ellenberger, 1970). When Jung defines it as treatment of SOUL (CW 16, para. 212), we must be reminded that he refers to something other than a religious practice. Similarly, though related to the medical sciences, the domain of psychotherapy is that of NEUROSIS as distinct from MENTAL ILLNESS or nervous disorder. When making an address to his colleagues in 1941 (relatively late in his career and in the midst of a world-wide war), Jung stated that the prime task of psychotherapy was to pursue with singleness of purpose the goal of individual development and he traced its origin to restitution ceremonies of various kinds in which 'a man becomes what he always was'.

Fathered by psychoanalysis, modern psychotherapy has derived much from Freudian methodology. But, as Jung developed his own theories, differing characteristics began to emerge in the consulting rooms of analytical psychologists. Yet, psychotherapy remains a discussion between two persons (see ANALYST AND PATIENT). Since psyche cannot be treated compartmentally, for in psychic disturbances everything hangs together and the entire person is affected, it is a dialectical process between two psychic systems reacting and responding to one another.

The psychotherapist is not simply an agent of treatment but a fellow participant in the work. He deals with symbolic manifestations having multiple implications and, to say the least, temptations. This requires the 'moral differentiation' of the therapist himself, for a neurotic psychotherapist will invariably treat his own neurosis in the patient (CW 16, para. 23; also Guggenbühl-Craig, 1971).

In the foreground of the psychotherapeutic process is the personality of the practitioner himself as a curative or harmful factor (see ANALYST AND PATIENT). Work is based upon the principle that when symbolic fragments offered by the unconscious are assimilated into conscious life, a form of psychic existence results which is not only more healthy but also 'works' because it corresponds more fully to the individual's own personality. During psychotherapy the recuperative process of the patient activates archetypal and COLLECTIVE contents alive in himself. The cause of neurosis is seen as the discrepancy between the conscious attitude and the trend of the unconscious. This DISSOCIATION is ultimately bridged by the assimilation or INTEGRATION of unconscious contents. The 'CURE', as suggested earlier, is for the patient to become what he really is.

Jung distinguished between 'major psychotherapy' which deals with cases of pronounced neuroses or borderline psychotic states and 'minor psychotherapy' where suggestion, good advice or an explanation may suffice. With this delineation, he came close to the present-day differentiation between dynamic and supportive psychotherapy. He did not regard either medical training or academic psychology as sufficient in itself as a background for the practice of psychotherapy, stating that 'one cannot treat the psyche without touching man as a whole'. As a consequence, he held strong convictions about the necessity for thorough and ongoing treatment of would-be therapists and was the first to insist upon this procedure.

Post-Jungians have concerned themselves more explicitly with the conduct of psychotherapy and there are notable differences in practice among various schools (Samuels, 1985a). With overtones of Jung's own differentiation between major and minor psychotherapy, certain analysts speak of analysis as pertaining to work of considerable duration and frequency, while the term 'psychotherapy' is reserved for less frequent or long-term (though no less regular) work. However, Jung himself did not make this distinction and was more random in his methodology. He maintained that therapy must be devised, paced and evaluated in the individual's own terms. In cases of doubt, or if proceeding in an unorthodox manner, he was willing to submit what was done to the ultimate arbitration of the unconscious, his own along with that of his patient.

See ANALYSIS; PSYCHOSIS.

puer aeternus   The eternal youth; referred to as an ARCHETYPE, seen as a neurotic component of the personality, viewed as an archetypal dominant or IMAGE of one of a matched pair of extremes active in the human psyche and in search of union (the other of the two being the SENEX).

Jung saw the *puer aeternus* as referring to the child archetype and speculated that its recurring fascination springs from man's projection of his inability to renew himself. The capacity to risk detachment from one's origins, to be in a perpetually evolving state, to redeem by innocence, to visualise new beginnings are all attributes of this nascent saviour. The figure of the *puer aeternus* becomes fascinating

125

(even to himself in real life) as a symbol for the possibility of reconciling the warring OPPOSITES.

The most striking characteristic of the *puer aeternus* when looked at as a personality disorder, is his over-emphasis upon SPIRIT. Von Franz (1971) used the term *puer* to describe men who had difficulty settling down, were impatient, unrelated, idealistic, ever starting anew, seemingly untouched by age, appearing to be without guile, given to flights of imagination.

But the *puer* has a positive side as well. Along with the perennial adolescence that leads to the provisional life, Hillman (1979) saw in the *puer* a vision of 'our own first natures, our primordial golden shadow ... our angelic essence as messenger of the divine'. From the *puer*, he concludes, we are given our sense of destiny and meaning.

Corresponding attributes in women are only beginning to be observed and the imagery explored (e.g. Leonard, 1982).

R

rebirth   A psychic experience of transcendence and/or transformation that is not observable from an exterior perspective but is nevertheless a reality felt and attested to by those who have experienced it (see PSYCHIC REALITY). It is the subjective result of an encounter with the ARCHETYPE of TRANSFORMATION.

Experiences of *transcendence* are connected with sacred rites of renewal, whether in the process of INITIATION or other religious and sacramental ceremonies (see RITUAL). VISIONS, mystical or otherwise, can have a somewhat similar effect in that the spectator can be involved though his nature is not necessarily altered. He may be aesthetically or even ecstatically impressed but he registers no lasting change in his being (see RELIGION).

Subjective *transformations*, on the other hand, involve changes in one's very being. They can be psychopathological (for example, ABAISSEMENT DE NIVEAU MENTAL; IDENTIFICATION, INFLATION, POSSESSION). They can be connected with altered states of consciousness induced by drugs, incantation, mesmerisation or other magical procedures (see MAGIC). But they may also occur as the result of the natural process of INDIVIDUATION in which one feels reborn as a 'larger' personality.

The inner figure that personifies the larger self is traditionally found in PROJECTION. It has been represented as the stone of the alchemists, Christ, a cult god, guru, guide, leader or other MANA PERSONALITY. Jung illustrated the rebirth process by interpretation

of the figure of Khidr from Islamic mysticism (*CW* 9i, para. 240 ff).
Such tales grip us, he said, because they both express the archetype
of transformation and parallel our own unconscious processes.

reductive and synthetic methods Jung questioned the operation of
causality and determinism in human psychology.

> The psychology of an individual can never be exhaustively ex-
> plained from himself alone ... No psychological fact can ever be
> explained in terms of causality alone; as a living phenomenon, it
> is always indissolubly bound up with the continuity of the vital
> process, so that it is not only something evolved but also contin-
> ually evolving and creative (*CW* 6, para. 717).

Jung used the word 'reductive' to describe the central feature of
Freud's method of attempting to reveal the primitive, instinctual,
infantile bases or roots of psychological motivation. Jung is critical
of the reductive method because the full MEANING of the unconscious
product (symptom, DREAM, IMAGE, slip of the tongue) is not dis-
closed. By connecting an unconscious product to the past, its present
value to the individual may be lost. A further objection is the tendency to over-simplify by reduction, bypassing what he saw as deeper
implications. In particular, reductive interpretations may be couched
in excessively personalistic terms, linked far too closely with the
supposed 'facts of the case'.

Jung was more interested in where a person's life was leading him,
rather than the supposed causes of his situation. His was a TELEO-
LOGICAL POINT OF VIEW. Jung described this orientation as 'synthetic',
with the implication that it was what emerged from the starting
point that was of primary significance. Developing this idea, he argued that what a patient might tell the analyst should not be regarded
as *historically* true but as subjectively so (see PSYCHIC REALITY).
Thus, accounts of sexual molestation or of events claimed to have
been witnessed were quite possibly fantasies but nevertheless psychologically 'true' for the persons involved (see FANTASY).

Jung pointed out that the synthetic method is taken for granted in
everyday life where we tend to disregard the strictly causal factor. For
example, if a man has an opinion and expresses it, we want to know
what he means, what he is getting at. Use of the synthetic method involves considering psychological phenomena *as if* they had intention
and purpose – i.e. in terms of goal-orientedness or teleology. To the
UNCONSCIOUS is granted the possession of a kind of knowledge or, even,
foreknowledge (*CW* 8, para. 175). Such methodology was consistent
with Jung's basic view of the OPPOSITES which, however widely
separated, constantly tend toward or seek synthesis (see *CONIUNCTIO*).

It must be emphasised that Jung never eschewed the analysis of infancy and childhood as such – he regarded this as essential in some cases though limited in scope (*CW* 16, paras 140–8). Reductive and synthetic approaches can also co-exist. For example, fantasy can be reductively interpreted as an encapsulation of a personal situation, the outcome of antecedent events. It can also be interpreted from a symbolic, synthetic viewpoint as tracing out a line of future psychological development (*CW* 6, para. 720). See SYMBOL.

Jung is less than fair to the reductive standpoint which requires something more than the mentality of an archivist. It is not simply a question of *reconstructing* the events of infancy but of using imagination to reflect on the import of such events. Occasionally, analytical psychologists themselves are guilty of using archetypes and complexes in a crudely reductive manner.

Jung's critique is shared by several contemporary psychoanalysts (Rycroft, 1968; Schafer, 1976). Causality, as a principle of explanation in psychology, is now open to question.

reflection   Jung identified various areas of instinctive activity (see ARCHETYPE; LIFE INSTINCT; TRANSFORMATION). Among them was reflection: a bending backwards or turning inward from consciousness so that instead of an immediate and unpremeditated reaction to objective stimuli, psychological deliberation intervenes. The effect of such deliberation is unpredictable and, as a consequence of the freedom to reflect, individualised and relativised responses are possible. Reflection 're-enacts the process of excitation', referring the impetus to a series of internalised, intrapsychic images before action is taken. By way of the reflective instinct, a stimulus becomes a psychic content, an experience through which a natural or automatic process may be transformed into a conscious and creative one.

Jung also advanced the hypothesis that reflection, though consciously oriented, has its subliminal counterpart in the UNCONSCIOUS as well since *all* experience is reflected by way of psychic imagery (see IMAGE; PSYCHIC REALITY). Such a hypothesis follows logically from his theory of ARCHETYPE and COMPLEX. However, the reflective process itself, though instinctive, is mainly a conscious one which involves bringing imagery (with its attendant affect) to the threshold of decision and action.

Psychologically speaking, reflection is the act of 'producing consciousness'. Jung speaks of it as 'the cultural instinct *par excellence*', its strength being shown in the power of CULTURE to manifest itself as superior to nature and to maintain itself in face of it (*CW* 8, para. 243). Left alone at the near instinctual level, however, reflection is automatic. Early researches using the WORD ASSOCIATION TEST corroborated this. When raised to conscious awareness, however, reflection transforms an otherwise compulsive act into one which is both purposive and individually oriented.

It is reflection that makes possible the balancing of OPPOSITES. But, for this to happen, consciousness has to be recognised as more than knowledge and the reflective process accepted as 'seeing within'. Here our individual freedom is manifested most strikingly. Reflection involves one with DREAM, SYMBOL, and FANTASY.

Just as Jung identified the ANIMA as giving relatedness to a man's consciousness, he stated that the ANIMUS gives to a woman's consciousness the capacity for reflection, deliberation and self knowledge. The tension between these two principles is not an either/or but would appear to require confrontation and INTEGRATION which will manifest itself creatively in a TRANSFORMATION of the relationship between them. Jung expressed this himself when writing near the end of his life: 'At this point the fact forces itself on my attention that beside the field of reflection there is another equally broad if not broader area in which rational understanding and rational modes of representation find scarcely anything they are able to grasp. This is the realm of Eros' (1963).

regression   Jung's attitude towards regression differed markedly from Freud's. For the latter, regression was almost always a negative phenomenon. Even as a defence, it was often a failure ('out of the frying pan, into the fire', Rycroft, 1972). Regression was something to be fought off and overcome. From 1912 onwards, Jung insisted on the therapeutic and personality enhancing aspects of periods of regression (without denying the harmful nature of prolonged and unproductive regression). Regression may be seen as a period of regeneration, or retrenchment prior to subsequent advance. Because of this, ANALYSIS and PSYCHOTHERAPY may have to support regression – even to a 'pre-natal level'. Maduro and Wheelwright (1977) summarize Jung as advocating 'creative regression within the transference' (see ANALYST AND PATIENT).

Incestuous fantasy may be seen as a particular form of regression; an attempt to make contact with the grounds of being, represented by the figure of a parent. For such regression to have value, it must eventually be lived onward. The cost or SACRIFICE inherent in progression is a loss of the security that merger with a parent figure provides. Jung's emphasis upon progression out of regression is consistent with his emphasis upon death and REBIRTH (see DEATH INSTINCT; INCEST; LIFE INSTINCT; TRANSFORMATION).

Contemporary psychoanalysis has revised Freud's rather harsh view (what Kohut, 1980, called his 'maturation morality'). Kris coined the slogan 'regression of ego in the service of ego' (1952); Balint referred to 'benign' regression (1968): Winnicott wrote of the 'valuable resting place of illusion' (1971).

religion Jung's statements about religion have been looked at from many points of view and inquiries have been made about them from the perspectives of medicine, psychology, metaphysics and theology. He has been examined both for evidence of subjective bias in his work and avoidance of acknowledging a credo. Within his own writings, however, there is consistency. For him, religion was an attitude of mind, a careful consideration and observation in relation to certain 'powers'; spirits, demons, gods, laws, ideals – or, indeed, an attitude toward whatever has impressed a person sufficiently so that he is moved to worship, obedience, reverence and love. In Jung's own words: 'We might say, then, that the term "religion" designates the attitude peculiar to a CONSCIOUSNESS which has been changed by experience of the NUMINOSUM' (CW 11, para. 9).

Yet critics, especially clergymen, continued to question because he staunchly refused to say from whence the numinosum itself sprang excepting that it corresponded to a GOD-IMAGE in the individual with an archetypal propensity both to provoke expression and, when expressed, to take a recognisable form. This form, Jung observed, was approximate to that which has characterised the relationship between human beings and the so-called divine throughout the ages (see AR- CHETYPE). He felt man to be naturally religious, the religious function being as powerful as the instinct for sex or aggression. Being a natural form of psychic expression, religion was also, in his view, an appropriate subject for psychological observation and ANALYSIS.

Affirming a psychological standpoint, Jung was at pains to make clear that by religion he did not mean code, creed or dogma. 'God is a mystery', he said, 'and everything we say about it is said and believed by human beings. We make images and concepts, but when I speak of God I always mean the IMAGE man has made of him. But no one knows what he is like, or he would be a god himself' (1957).

The psychological carrier of the God-image in a person Jung called the SELF. He saw it as something which acted as an ordering principle of the personality, reflecting the potential wholeness of the individual, prompting life enhancing encounters and verifying MEANING. Almost anything that connects a person with these attributes can be used as a SYMBOL of the self, he noted, but certain time-honoured and basic forms such as the cross and the MANDALA are acknowledged collective expressions of man's highest religious value; i.e. the cross symbolising the tension of the ultimate opposition of human and divine and the mandala representing the resolution of that

opposition (see OPPOSITES). Psychologically, Jung saw the TRANSCEN-
DENT FUNCTION as fulfilling the task of linking man and God, or a
person and his ultimate potential by way of symbol formation.

The idea of the EGO's being enjoined to respond to the demands
of the self is central to Jung's concept of INDIVIDUATION, the process
of fulfilling oneself. Such fulfilment becomes of religious significance
inasmuch as it conveys meaning to individual endeavour. All lives,
Jung felt, involve the bringing together and resolution of heterogeneous and conflicting impulses. He saw a union between the individual and the collective psyche as being possible only when an alive
and valid religious attitude exists.

Speaking of his personal religious views, Jung wrote: 'I don't *be-
lieve* but I do *know* of a power of a very personal nature and an
irresistible influence. I call it "God"' (1955). Speaking explicitly of
Christianity, he accounted himself as a Lutheran and a Protestant. In
his autobiography he conveyed that he not only wanted to leave the
door open for the Christian message but that he considered it of
central importance for Western man. He emphasised, however, that
it needed to be seen in a new light and in accordance with the
changes wrought in and by the contemporary spirit. Otherwise, he
felt, it would stand apart from the times and have no constructive
effect. He admitted that his view of religion was that it linked us to
an eternal MYTH but it was precisely this connection that gave it its
universality and its human validity.

ritual   A service or ceremony enacted with a religious purpose or
intent, whether such a purpose or intent is conscious or UNCONSCIOUS
(see ENACTMENT; RELIGION). Ritual performances are based upon
mythological and archetypal themes, express their messages symbolically, involve a person totally, convey a sense of heightened MEANING
for the individual and, at the same time, rely upon representations
congenial to the SPIRIT of the times (see ARCHETYPE; MYTH; SYMBOL).
When individual and COLLECTIVE rites no longer embody the spirit
of the times, new archetypal representations are sought or new interpretations are given to old forms in order to compensate the
altered state of CONSCIOUSNESS.

Ritual functions as a psychic container for TRANSFORMATION (i.e.
INITIATION; MARRIAGE) when the psychological balance of a person
is threatened by the unexpected power of the NUMINOSUM during a
period of change from one status or way of being to another. Jung
believed that man expressed his most important and fundamental
psychological conditions in ritual and that if appropriate rituals were
not provided, persons spontaneously and unconsciously devised
rituals to safeguard the stability of the personality as the transition

from one psychological condition to another was affected. The ritual itself does not affect the transformation, however; it merely contains it.

Jung's interest in ritual occasioned his journeys to Africa, India, and to the Indian tribes in the south-western part of the United States. He was especially attracted to rituals of initiation, finding in them parallels of psychological processes and progressions made by the individual at different STAGES OF LIFE. In work with his patients he observed that a reliance upon ritual was an aspect of each increase in consciousness. His work on the psychology of the transference (CW 16) can be seen as an INTERPRETATION of the ritual symbolism of a psychological metamorphosis.

M. Eliade, anthropologist and student of comparative religion, was a resource and colleague for Jung in this field of investigation. Henderson has related rites of initiation to clinical findings (1967), as has Perry (1976).

S

sacrifice   In his writings on sacrifice Jung comes close to a disclosure of his own theology. In common usage the word sacrifice has two meanings; one is to forgo and the other to renounce. Both are relevant to sacrifice when thought of psychologically but neither takes fully into account the original meaning of the word which is to sanctify, make sacred. The act of renunciation is equivalent to the recognition of an ordering principle supraordinate to one's present consciousness.

Jung acknowledges that at some point in life each of us will be called up to sacrifice; that is to renounce a cherished psychological attitude, neurotic or otherwise. In each case, the demand is greater than that for casual adjustment. One consciously forgoes an EGO position in favour of another which appears to hold greater MEANING and significance. The choice involved and the transition from one point of view to the other is difficult and Jung saw this as the pattern implied whenever UNCONSCIOUS contents present themselves and OPPOSITES conflict (see TRANSFORMATION, INITIATION). Sacrifice is the price we pay for CONSCIOUSNESS.

The sacrificial gift that one makes symbolises a part of one's personality and self-esteem; yet, one can never be fully aware of the implications of his sacrifice at the time when it is made. In traditional mythological and religious terms, all that is given must be given as if it were to be destroyed. Therefore, it is impossible to consider sacrifice without suggesting directly or indirectly that it has meaning in relation to a GOD-IMAGE as well. Jung sees the necessity for sacrifice not as a remnant of archaic superstition but as an essential part of the cost we pay for being human. To say the SELF requires it of me is to give a logical answer but one may still remain unmindful of the relationship that is involved.

Analytic awareness of such an exchange necessitates making conscious the religious function of the psyche and many analysts shy away from it, perhaps erroneously equating ANALYSIS of the religious function with an analysis of RELIGION. An understanding of sacrifice affirms, however, the presence of meaning in loss and often reverses the effect of disintegration.

schizophrenia   From his early days as a student, Jung was interested in schizophrenia (then known as *dementia praecox*). As he developed his concept of the collective unconscious and the theory of archetypes, he moved to the position that psychosis in general and schizophrenia in particular could be explained as (a) an overwhelming of the EGO by the contents of the collective unconscious and (b) the domination of the personality by a split-off COMPLEX or complexes (see ARCHETYPE; UNCONSCIOUS).

The crucial implication of this was that schizophrenic utterance and behaviour could be seen as meaningful, if only it were possible to work out what the meaning might be. This was where the technique of ASSOCIATION was first used and, later, AMPLIFICATION as a method of seeing the clinical material in conjunction with cultural and religious motifs. This led, firmly and finally, to Jung's break with Freud which occurred with the publication of *Symbols of Transformation*, an analysis by association and amplification of the prelude to a case of schizophrenia (CW 5).

But what of the causation of schizophrenia? The evolution of Jung's thought reveals his uncertainty. He is clear that schizophrenia is a psychosomatic disorder, that changes in body chemistry and personality distortions are somehow intertwined. The issue was which of these should be regarded as primary.

Jung's superior, Bleuler, thought that some kind of toxin or poison was developed by the body which then led to psychological disturbance (see PSYCHOANALYSIS). Jung's crucial contribution was to estimate the importance of PSYCHE sufficiently to reverse the elements: psychological activity may lead to somatic changes (CW 3, para. 318). Jung did attempt to combine his ideas with those of Bleuler's, however, by use of an ingenious formula. While the mysterious toxin might well exist in all of us, it would only have its devastating effect if psychological circumstances were favourable to this. Alternatively, a person might be genetically predisposed to develop the toxin and this would inevitably attach itself to one or more complexes.

That schizophrenia was anything other than an innate, neurological abnormality was, in its time, revolutionary. That its causation was psychogenic within an overall psychosomatic framework (Jung's final position, CW 3, paras 553ff.) enabled him to propose that psychological treatment (PSYCHOTHERAPY) was appropriate. The decoding of schizophrenic communication and treatment within a therapeutic *milieu* form central strands in the existential-analytic approaches developed by Binswanger (1945), Laing (1967) and, to an extent, are recognisable in contemporary psychiatric endeavours.

One contemporary and controversial approach to schizophrenia is the idea that schizophrenia is not really an illness but rather a measure of what our society considers normal and tolerable. Hence, as psychiatrists opposed to conventional psychiatry suggest, it is nothing more than a psychiatric classification: the map is not the territory (cf. Szasz, 1962). Jung's thought does not go as far as this, but he stressed that 'latent psychosis' was much more prevalent than is generally accepted and that 'normal' can never be descriptive of an individual (see ADAPTATION). A further refinement, which also strikes a chord with a contemporary view, is that apparent breakdown might in fact be a form of breakthrough, a necessary initiatory prelude to further development (see INITIATION; PATHOLOGY; REBIRTH; SELF-REGULATION).

Jung's experience of schizophrenia seems to have been mainly of its florid form (delusions, serious thought disorders, ideas of reference, etc.). He does not write much about the characteristic schizophrenic 'flatness of AFFECT' so marked in psychiatric hospitals now. It is known that mental illnesses change their character according to cultural shifts – it is one reason why their existence is disputed. For instance, the prevalence of hysterical paralyses in Germany and Austria during the 1890s might have something to do with the introduction of insurance schemes for railway accidents around that time.

Schizophrenic withdrawal can be seen as a reaction to the meaninglessness and alienation of modern industrial society and, in particular, to the experience of extreme psychological deprivation attendant upon poverty. In socially impoverished circumstances, the effort required to keep the lid on the unconscious, so to speak, means that emotion of any sort is repressed or split off from the personality. The element of depression in such 'acute situational psychosis' is also something not explored by Jung. Here we must read him as a man of his times (see COLLECTIVE; CULTURE; SOCIETY).

Several analytical psychologists (e.g. Perry, 1962; Redfearn, 1978) have applied a developmental framework to schizophrenia. The contents of the schizophrenic mind remain archetypal in tone because of the mother's failure to mediate them for her infant – i.e. somehow reduce them to a human scale so that they might be integrated. That is why the 'flatness' comes into being – as an unconscious form of self-control. Working with schizophrenic or seriously damaged patients requires an analyst to make considerable use of his counter-transference (see ANALYST AND PATIENT).

self An archetypal IMAGE of man's fullest potential and the unity of the personality as a whole. The self as a unifying principle within the human psyche occupies the central position of authority in relation to psychological life and, therefore, the destiny of the individual.

At times Jung speaks of the self as initiatory of psychic life; at other times he refers to its realisation as the goal. He stressed this was an empirical concept and not a philosophical or theological formulation but the similarity of his views and a religious hypothesis have needed clarification. One cannot consider the concept of the self apart from its similarity to a GOD-IMAGE and, consequently, ANALYTICAL PSYCHOLOGY has been confronted both by those who welcome acceptance of it as an acknowledgment of man's religious nature and others, whether doctors, scientists or religious dogmatists, who find such a psychological formulation unacceptable.

'The self is not only the centre', Jung writes, 'but also the whole circumference which embraces both conscious and UNCONSCIOUS; it is the centre of this totality, just as the EGO is the centre of the conscious mind' (CW 12, para. 444). In life, the self demands to be recognised, integrated, realised; but there is no hope of incorporating more than a fragment of such a vast totality within the limited range of human CONSCIOUSNESS. Therefore, the relationship of ego to self is a never-ending process. The process carries with it a danger of inflation unless the EGO is both flexible and capable of setting individual and conscious (as opposed to archetypal and unconscious) boundaries. The life-long interaction of ego and self, involving an ongoing process of ego-self referral, is expressed in the individuality of a person's life (see EGO-SELF AXIS; INDIVIDUATION).

Lest the self appear to be entirely benign, Jung emphasised that it should be likened to a daemon, a determining power without conscience; ethical decisions are left to man (see MORALITY). Therefore, in relation to interventions of the self, which may come by way of DREAMS, for example, Jung warned that a person must be aware, insofar as possible, of what he decides and what he does. Then, if he responds positively, he is not merely submissive to the ARCHETYPE nor following his own whim; or, if he turns aside, he is conscious that he may be destroying not just something of his own intervention but an opportunity of indeterminate worth. The power of exercising such discrimination is the function of consciousness.

Following Jung conceptually, the self can be defined as an archetypal urge to coordinate, relativise and mediate the tension of the OPPOSITES. By way of the self, one is confronted with the polarity of good and EVIL; human and divine (see SHADOW). Interaction requires exercise of the maximum human freedom in face of life's seemingly inconsistent demands; the sole and final arbiter being the discovery of MEANING. A person's ability to integrate such an image without priestly mediation has been questioned by the clergy, and theologians have been critical of the inclusion of both positive and negative elements in the God-image. But Jung staunchly defended his position by pointing out that Christian emphasis upon 'the good' alone had left Western man estranged and divided within himself.

Symbols of the self often possess a numinosity (see NUMINOSUM) and convey a sense of necessity which gives them transcendent priority in psychic life. They carry the authority of a God-image and Jung felt there was no doubt that alchemists' statements about the *lapis*, considered psychologically, describe the archetype of the self (see ALCHEMY). Although he claimed to have observed intent and purpose in psychic manifestations of the self, he nevertheless eschewed making any statement in regard to the ultimate source of that purpose (see RELIGION).

Jung's theoretical work on the self has been extended and used as a developmental concept (Fordham, 1969, 1976). See DEVELOPMENT. A primary or original self is hypothesised as existing at the outset of life. This primary self contains all the innate, archetypal potentials that may be given expression by a person. In an appropriate environment, these potentials commence a process of *deintegration* emerging from the original unconscious integrate. They seek correspondences in the outer world. The resultant 'mating' of an active infant's archetypal potential and the mother's reactive responses is then *reintegrated* to become an internalised object. The deintegrative/reintegrative process continues throughout life.

In infancy, the degree of excitement created by deintegration requires lengthy periods of reintegrative sleep. Gradually, ego fragments present in the deintegrates cohere to form the ego. The primary self is said to have its own defensive organisation which operates most markedly in situations when, from the infant's point of view, there has been an environmental lack. Such defences protect the self, not only from a sense of outer attack and persecution, but also from the fear of implosion generated by an uncontrollable level of anger corresponding to unmet expectation, deprivation being experienced as attack.

Like ego defences, defences of the self may be regarded as normal, in Fordham's view. But, if they persist or become over-determined, a tendency toward omnipotence develops which leads to grandiosity and rigidity; i.e. resulting in a narcissistic personality disorder (see NARCISSISM). On the other hand, autism may result. In either case, the individual is cut off from the satisfactions of relationship because it is *otherness* itself which feels persecutory.

A second application of Jung's thesis to development was advanced by Neumann (1973, written in 1959–60). Neumann sees the mother as carrying the image of the baby's self in unconscious PROJECTION or even functioning 'as' the baby's self. Since in infancy the child cannot experience the characteristics of an adult self, the mother reflects or acts as 'mirror' of her child's selfhood. The first conscious experiences of the self derive from perceptions of her and interactions with her. Extending Neumann's thesis, the baby's gradual separation from his mother may be compared with the ego's emergence from the self and the image he develops of his relationship to his mother forms the basis of his subsequent attitude toward the self and the UNCONSCIOUS in general (see GREAT MOTHER; IMAGO).

It is clear that a conceptual difference exists among analytical psychologists. Some tend to define the self as the original state of organismic integration. Others see it as an image of a supraordinate unifying principle. Both groups make use of Jung's frequent references to the individual personality as 'emerging from' the archetypal potentials contained within the self. Neumann's work represents an imagistic approach; Fordham's provides a model.

(CW 9ii is devoted to the phenomenology of the self. For a comparison of the views of Fordham and Neumann, see Samuels, 1985a.)

self-regulatory function of the psyche   See COMPENSATION.

senex   An archetypal rather than a developmental concept (Hillman, 1979). Latin for 'old man', but not to be confused with the 'wise old man' (see MANA PERSONALITIES). Used in analytical psychology to refer to a personification of certain psychological features usually attributed to the aged, though even babies may display *senex* features – balance, generosity towards others, wisdom, far-sightedness. See ARCHETYPE; DEVELOPMENT; INFANCY AND CHILDHOOD.

Senex is often mentioned in contradistinction to the PUER AETERNUS. Puer pathology can be described as excessively daring, over-optimistic, given to flights of imagination and idealism, and excessively spiritualised. *Senex* pathology may be characterised as excessively conservative, authoritarian, over-grounded, melancholic and lacking in imagination.

See OPPOSITES.

sex The innate, biological characteristics of males and females, thereby constituting the difference between male and female. Jung had a tendency to confuse sex with GENDER. He did not agree with Freud's idea of a fundamental inborn bisexuality. However, he did allow for the fact that true heterosexuality takes time to develop and is not present in its adult form in infants (see HOMOSEXUALITY; IN-FANCY AND CHILDHOOD).

Emphasis upon what he regarded as innate gender differences rather than sexuality *per se* distinguished his work from that of Freud, and there is no doubt that, after the break with Freud, Jung concentrated upon this further. He deplored the reduction of the possibilities of individual development to any one general principle such as sexuality and counterposed the concept of WHOLENESS as consistent with INDIVIDUATION which he saw as the goal and end of psychic life (see ARCHETYPE; BODY; PSYCHOANALYSIS; TELEOLOGICAL POINT OF VIEW).

shadow In 1945 Jung gave a most direct and clear-cut definition of the shadow: 'the thing a person has no wish to be' (CW 16, para. 470). In this simple statement is subsumed the many-sided and re-peated references to shadow as the negative side of the personality, the sum of all the unpleasant qualities one wants to hide, the inferior, worthless and primitive side of man's nature, the 'other person' in one, one's own dark side. Jung was well aware of the reality of EVIL in human life.

Over and over again he emphasises that we all have a shadow, that everything substantial casts a shadow, that the EGO stands to shadow as light to shade, that it is the shadow which makes us human.

> Everyone carries a shadow, and the less it is embodied in the individual's conscious life, the blacker and denser it is. If an in-feriority is conscious, one always has a chance to correct it. Furthermore, it is constantly in contact with other interests, so that it is continually subjected to modifications. But if it is re-pressed and isolated from CONSCIOUSNESS, it never gets corrected, and is liable to burst forth suddenly in a moment of unawareness. At all counts, it forms an unconscious snag, thwarting our most well-meant intentions (CW 11, para. 131).

It is to Freud that Jung gives credit for calling the attention of modern man to the split between the light and dark sides of the human psyche. Approaching the problem from a scientific angle and innocent of any religious aim, he felt that Freud uncovered the abyss of darkness in human nature that the enlightened optimism of Western Christianity and the scientific age had sought to conceal. Jung spoke of Freud's method as the most detailed and profound analysis of the shadow ever achieved.

Jung professed to deal with the shadow in a way different from the Freudian approach which he said that he found limited. Recognising that the shadow is a living part of the personality and that it 'wants to live with it' in some form, he identifies it, first of all, with the contents of the personal UNCONSCIOUS. Dealing with these involves one in coming to terms with the INSTINCTS and how their expression has been subject to control by the COLLECTIVE (see ADAPTATION). Moreover, the contents of the personal unconscious are inextricably merged with the archetypal contents of the collective unconscious, themselves containing their own dark side (see ARCHETYPE; OPPOSITES). In other words, it is impossible to eradicate shadow; hence, the term most frequently employed by analytical psychologists for the process of shadow confrontation in ANALYSIS is 'coming to terms with the shadow'.

Given that the shadow is an archetype, its contents are powerful, marked by AFFECT, obsessional, possessive, autonomous – in short, capable of startling and overwhelming the well-ordered ego. Like all contents capable of entering consciousness, initially they appear in PROJECTION and when consciousness is in a threatened or doubtful condition, shadow manifests as a strong, irrational projection, positive or negative, upon one's neighbour. Here Jung found a convincing explanation not only of personal antipathies but also the cruel prejudices and persecutions of our time.

So far as shadow is concerned, the aim of PSYCHOTHERAPY is to develop an awareness of those IMAGES and situations most likely to produce shadow projections in one's individual life. To admit (to analyse) the shadow is to break its compulsive hold (see INDIVIDUATION; INTEGRATION; POSSESSION).

sign See SYMBOL.

society In contrast to the COLLECTIVE, which Jung saw as the repository of the psychic potential of mankind, his use of the word society suggests the presence of a civilising influence, the result of an interaction between individal persons and mankind as a whole, a development made possible by CONSCIOUSNESS. He states that the collective PSYCHE bears the same relation to the personal psyche as society does to the individual.

See ADAPTATION; CULTURE.

soul In the 'Definitions', published relatively early among Jung's writings (*CW* 6, 1921), he has under the entry for psyche: 'see "soul"'. On balance, Jung refers more often to PSYCHE rather than soul when discussing the totality of all psychic processes and ANALYSIS. But it is also possible to tease out certain specific usages of 'soul':
(1) Used by Jung (and analytical psychologists) instead of psyche especially when it is wished to underline movement at depth, emphasising plurality, variety and the impenetrability of the psyche in contrast to any pattern, order or meaning discernible therein (cf. SELF). In reference to plurality, Jung describes cultures where one speaks of 'multiple souls'.
(2) Used instead of SPIRIT when it is wished to refer to the non-material aspect of humans – their core, heart, centre (Samuels, 1985a, pp. 244–5).
(3) Used by some post-Jungian analytical psychologists to indicate a particular perspective on the world, one which concentrates on depth imagery and the way in which the psyche converts events into experiences – 'soul-making' (Hillman, 1975).

spirit Jung applied the word 'spirit' to the non-material aspect of a living person (thought, intention, ideal) as well as to an incorporeal being detached from a human body (ghost, shade, ancestral soul). He wrote extensively on both subjects, an interest in the latter involving him in some of his earliest psychic researches. In both instances, spirit is conceived of as the opposite of matter (see OPPOSITES). This explains the elusive and evanescent quality of FANTASY, for example, as well as the transparency of apparitions.

Spirit as the non-material aspect of man can neither be described nor defined. It is infinite, spaceless, formless, imageless. It lives of itself, neither subject to our human expectations nor the demands of will. It is *other* worldly or *non*-worldly, arrives unbidden, and the usual response is one of AFFECT, whether positive or negative.

Jung goes on, however, to link spirit with purpose, a kind of intuitive force which connects and influences disparate events and endeavours (see SYNCHRONICITY). He wonders whether there are laws of the spirit. His prolonged study and interest in the *I Ching* was stimulated by the 'spirit wisdom' he felt it contained and the relevance of such wisdom to human life which he affirmed had been amply demonstrated over thousands of years in China. Hence, he gave credence to spirit but without stipulation of a creed (see GOD-IMAGE). Jung's concept of the SELF, however, comes close to expressing a universal ARCHETYPE of spirit and he acknowledged that spiritual goals must be embodied for fulfilment. Hence, there is an interdependence of the opposites of spirit and matter.

Although one way of looking at Jung's work is as a psychological survey of evidence for belief in spirit, he applied himself most directly to the subject when he wrote 'The Psychological Foundations of Belief in Spirits' (CW 8, 1948). This was based upon empirical observations of the presence of and belief in incorporeal beings – ghosts, ancestral spirits and the like. In short, in his work on the psychological foundations of man's belief in spirits, Jung highlighted the necessity for man's conscious relationship to spirit.

The phenomenon of spirits, he states, is verification of the reality of a spirit world. One of the most important evidences of an other-than-body realm, whether reported by so-called primitives or contemporary Western man, is the presence of DREAMS and VISIONS. Jung does not address himself to the question of whether spirit exists in and of itself – that would be a metaphysical inquiry, he admits. His interest is in how people perceive and react to the appearance of spirit and this is a psychological concern.

Belief in soul is not necessarily a correlative of a belief in spirits. SOUL is universally perceived as having its home in a particular individual while spirits dwell in a place apart, estranged from the EGO. He observes that spirits make their appearance when a person has lost his adaptive powers or their appearance causes him to do so. It is because of their disturbing effect that spirits are most often feared. Consequently, Jung concluded, spirits are either pathological fantasies or new but as yet unknown and challenging ideas. 'Spirits, viewed from a psychological angle', he concluded, 'are UNCONSCIOUS autonomous COMPLEXES which appear as PROJECTIONS because they have no association with the ego' (CW 9i, para. 285). Furthermore, they may be manifestations of complexes belonging to the COLLECTIVE which alter or replace the attitude of a whole people, enabling a new one to be realised. The interventions of so-called spirits seem to demand an increase in CONSCIOUSNESS.

The latter suggests why spirit manifests itself, psychologically, as superior and more powerful than ego; perhaps conceived as an idea, conviction or hunch but most frequently personified in someone with clarity of insight, a kind of prophet or visionary (see MANA PERSONALITY; HERO). We hear spirits referred to as 'the spirit of the past', i.e. belonging to our dead ancestors; the spirit personified by an individual, i.e. a high-spirited man; an idea that captures the spirit of a nation, or represents the spirit of an age, and in a different vein: 'the spirit of evil abroad in the world'. It is what they symbolise that accounts for the attraction and repulsion of spirits, their numinous power and the effectiveness of their interventions.

The appearance of spirits is symbolic of heightened tension between material and non-material worlds. They are borderline or threshold phenomena which seem to want to be given life in some form.

See TRANSCENDENT FUNCTION.

stages of life   Jung has been recognised as a forerunner of the developing field of whole of life psychology (sometimes referred to as adult development) (Levinson, 1978). In his paper 'The stages of life', written in 1931 (CW 8), Jung laid emphasis on the psychological transition he saw as occurring at midlife. This he describes as a 'crisis' or problem period and he illustrates his thesis with case material which demonstrates the consequences of a failure to anticipate and adapt to the demands of the second half of life. Jacobi (1965) followed Jung by writing of two phases of the process of INDIVIDUATION as corresponding to the first and second half of life. M. Stein (1985) has concerned himself with the midlife transition.

Ideally, the psychological achievements of the first half of life include separation from the mother and achievement of a strong EGO, the giving up of the status of INFANCY AND CHILDHOOD and the acquisition of an adult identity. Such accomplishments suggest the achievement of a social position, relationship or MARRIAGE, parenthood, and employment. In the second half of life, the accent shifts from the interpersonal or external dimension to a conscious relationship with intrapsychic processes. Dependence upon the ego has to be replaced by relationship to the SELF; dedication to outer success modified to include a concern for MEANING and spiritual values. Jung's emphasis for the second half of life is on CONSCIOUSNESS of a sense of purpose. In the second half of life, the approach of death becomes a reality. Ultimately, what is involved is a degree of self-acceptance, a natural fullness or flowering and a sense of a life satisfyingly lived in accord with one's potential (see INDIVIDUATION).

From the point of view of psychic structure, this can be expressed as bringing to consciousness the function of ANIMA AND ANIMUS and integration of the inferior function (see PSYCHE; TYPOLOGY).

While the overall accuracy of Jung's description is not to be doubted, there are a number of problems with his schema: (1) Why, in a psychology that is not otherwise based upon PSYCHOPATHOLOGY, is the midlife transition regarded as so traumatic and crisis-ridden? When Rank wrote of the 'birth trauma', Jung dismissed the idea on the grounds that nothing universal could possibly be regarded as traumatic. It may be that Jung generalised too freely from his own personal experience of breakdown following the separation from Freud when he was in his late thirties (see PATHOLOGY; PSYCHOANALYSIS). (2) It is questionable whether the achievement of goals of the first half is always at the cost of a 'diminution of personality' (CW

8, para. 787). Again, how can what is natural be damaging? In any case, social achievement is not always a product of one-sided development, though it may be (see NEUROSIS). (3) Jung's adherence to the theory of OPPOSITES makes the division somewhat pat and rigid.

suggestion   When writing a review of a book by Moll, Jung quoted the author's definition of suggestion as: 'a process whereby, under inadequate conditions, an effect is obtained by evoking the idea that such an effect will be obtained' (CW 18, para. 893). This is essentially the definition he himself employed when speaking of suggestion in relation to hypnosis, parapsychological phenomena, PSYCHOSIS, ANALYSIS and PSYCHOTHERAPY.

He strongly cautioned psychotherapists against the use of suggestion, pointing out its obvious effect upon the therapeutic relationship: keeping the patient in a weak and subordinate position. UNCONSCIOUS suggestion cannot be avoided but it is the continuing responsibility of both ANALYST AND PATIENT to remain as conscious as possible of what is happening in the analysis.

So far as Jung was concerned, suggestion therapy was not limited to counselling or the giving of advice, however, but extended to all therapies which either simply employ diagnostic terms and thereby stop short of disclosing unconscious causes or those which attempt actively to intercede or interfere with unconscious processes. He saw all such attempts as educational rather than psychological. Moreover, suggestive methods are opposed to the disclosure of individuality because their use presupposes that the end product is predictable and achievable rather than spontaneous and unique (see INDIVIDUATION). So far as INTERPRETATION of DREAMS is concerned, Jung stated that if one seeks to avoid suggestion, every interpretation must be considered invalid until such time as a formula can be found which wins the assent of the patient himself.

super-ego   Jung used this term infrequently and usually in discussion of Freud's views. This was because of Jung's emphasis on the innate nature of MORALITY, there being, in his METAPHOR, a pre-existing moral channel to accommodate the flow of psychic ENERGY. Hence, there is less need to postulate a learning process in connection with conscience.

When Jung does write of the super-ego as such, he equates it with COLLECTIVE morality, buttressed by CULTURE and tradition. Against the background of such collective morality, a person has to work out his or her own system of values and ethics (see INDIVIDUATION).

In PSYCHOANALYSIS, a recognition of innate super-ego capacities is part of the Kleinian approach to early OBJECT RELATIONS. Contemporary analytical psychologists (e.g. Newton, 1975) have examined the harsh, archetypal (i.e. powerful, primitive, extreme) nature of the early super-ego and stressed the manner in which this is modified, rather than accentuated, by parental introjects (see ARCHETYPE).

See RELIGION.

superior function   See TYPOLOGY.

symbol   Jung's theoretical break with Freud was partly over the issue of what is to be meant by 'symbol'; the concept, its intent or purpose and content.

Jung explains the *conceptual difference* as follows:

> Those conscious contents which give us a clue to the unconscious background are incorrectly called *symbols* by Freud. They are not true symbols, however, since according to his theory they have merely the role of *signs* or *symptoms* of the subliminal processes. The true symbol differs essentially from this, and should be understood as an intuitive idea that cannot yet be formulated in any other or better way (CW 15, para. 105).

Earlier he had written as a definition of the symbol: 'A symbol always presupposes that the chosen expression is the best possible description or formulation of a relatively unknown fact, *which is nonetheless known to exist or is postulated as existing*' (CW 6, para. 814).

At another point, but without specific reference to Freud, he expresses appreciation for the subtlety and challenge of the symbol which to him is so much more than an expression of repressed sexuality or any other definitive content. Speaking of works of art that are openly symbolic, he says:

> Their pregnant language cries out to us that they mean more than they say. We can put our finger on the symbol at once, even though we may not be able to unriddle its meaning to our entire satisfaction. A symbol remains a perpetual challenge to our thoughts and feelings. That probably explains why a symbolic work is so stimulating, why it grips us so intensely, but also why it seldom affords us a purely aesthetic enjoyment (CW 15, para. 119).

Conceptual struggles on the subject of symbolisation did not end with Jung's break with Freud; within ANALYTICAL PSYCHOLOGY the debate continues. The discipline as a whole demonstrates a wide range of theoretical understanding and practice in regard to symbolic conceptualisation, purpose and content. However, even when some-one is most literal in interpreting a prevailing image or prone to see the symbolism as manifestly sexual, even then it is possible to dis-cover breadth and diversity of implication consistent with Jung's definition *provided* the symbol is not confused with its content and, thereby, assumed to have an intellectual, expository and allegorical function, rather than to play a psychological mediatory and tran-sitional role.

As far as the ultimate *intent of the symbol* is concerned, Jung saw it as having goals which, though functioning in a definite manner, are hard to verbalise. Symbols express themselves in analogies. The symbolic process is an experience *in images and of images*. Its de-velopment is consistent with the law of ENANTIODROMIA (i.e. in accord with the principle that a given position eventually moves in the direction of its opposite, see OPPOSITES) and gives evidence of COMPENSATION at work (i.e. that the attitude of CONSCIOUSNESS is being balanced by movement from within the UNCONSCIOUS). 'From the activity of the unconscious there now emerges a new content, constellated by thesis and anti-thesis in equal measure and standing in a *compensatory* relation to both. It thus forms the middle ground on which the opposites can be united' (*CW* 6, para. 825). The sym-bolic process begins with a person's feeling stuck, 'hung-up', forcibly obstructed in pursuit of his aims and it ends in illumination, 'seeing through', and being able to go ahead on a changed course.

What unites the opposites partakes of both sides and can easily be judged from one side or the other. But, if we take up either position, we simply reaffirm the opposition. The symbol itself helps here, for though it is not logical, it encapsulates the psychological situation. Its nature is paradoxical and it represents the third factor or position that does not exist in logic but provides a perspective from which a synthesis of the opposing elements can be made. When confronted with this perspective, the EGO is freed to exercise REFLECTION and choice.

The symbol, therefore, is neither an alternative point of view nor a compensation *per se*. It attracts our attention to *another* position which, if appropriately understood, adds to the existing personality as well as resolving the conflict (see TRANSCENDENT FUNCTION). It follows that though there undoubtedly are symbols of totality, they are of a different order. It is possible that all symbols become symbols of totality after a fashion (see SELF).

Symbols are captivating pictorial statements (see NUMINOSUM; VISIONS). They are indistinct, metaphoric and enigmatic portrayals of psychic reality. The *content*, i.e. the meaning of symbols, is far from obvious; instead, it is expressed in unique and individual terms while at the same time partaking of a universal imagery. Worked upon (that is, reflected upon and related to), they can be recognised as aspects of those IMAGES that control, order and give MEANING to our lives. Their source, therefore, can be traced to the archetypes themselves which by way of symbols find more full expression (see ARCHETYPE).

The symbol is an unconscious invention in answer to a conscious problematic. Hence, analytical psychologists often speak of 'unifying symbols' or those which draw together disparate psychic elements, 'living symbols' or those which are interwoven with one's conscious situation, and 'symbols of totality' which pertain and adhere to realisation of the self (see MANDALA). Symbols are not allegorical for they would then be about something already familiar but they are expressive of something intensely alive, one might say 'stirring', in the SOUL.

Although it is commonly assumed that the symbolic contents which appear in an individual analysis are similar to those of other analyses, that is not the case. Regular and recurring psychic patterns can be represented by manifold and diverse images and symbols. Apart from this clinical application, symbols can be amply interpreted from a historical, cultural or generalised psychological context.

See ALCHEMY; AMPLIFICATION; FAIRY TALE; INTERPRETATION; MYTH.

synchronicity Repeated experiences that indicated events do not always obey the rules of time, space and causality led Jung to search for what might lie beyond those rules. He developed the concept of synchronicity which he defined in several ways:

(1) as an 'acausal connecting principle';

(2) as referring to events meaningfully but not causally related (i.e. not coinciding in time and space);

(3) as referring to events that coincide in time and space but can also be seen to have meaningful psychological connections;

(4) as linking the psychic and the material worlds (in Jung's writings on synchronicity, often, but not always, the inorganic material world).

Jung tried to demonstrate a synchronistic principle by examining a possible correspondence between astrological birth signs and choice of marriage partners. He concluded that there was neither a statistical connection, nor was the pattern due to chance; so in 1952 synchronicity was proposed as a third option (CW 8). See REDUCTIVE AND SYNTHETIC METHODS; UNCONSCIOUS.

The experiment has been much criticised. The sample was based on a group who took astrology seriously and, therefore, it was not a random sample. The statistics have been challenged, and, most importantly, whatever else it may be, astrology is not considered to be acausal. Nevertheless, the experiment shows clearly that Jung was attempting to cut across the chance/cause dualism. Phenomena assumed to be linked by chance or coincidence may, in fact, be connected by synchronicity.

At times, Jung applied synchronicity to a wide range of phenomena which are, perhaps, more accurately seen as psychological or parapsychological, for example, telepathy. However, most people have experienced meaningful coincidences or detected some sort of purposeful trend in their affairs, and it is in connection with that type of experience that Jung's synchronistic hypothesis may have direct relevance on a personal level.

He suggested that synchronistic phenomena may be more apparent when the level of consciousness is low (see ABAISSEMENT DU NIVEAU MENTAL). What occurs may then have therapeutic value in analysis, directing attention to problem areas which, because unconscious, may as yet be untouched. Keeping synchronicity in mind protects the analyst from the twin perils of feeling that everything is due to fate or of falling back on purely causal explanations which 'serve only to debunk the patient's experience instead of letting it work towards change' (Williams, 1963b). The synchronistic experience occurs where two kinds of reality (i.e. 'inner' and 'outer') intersect.

Synchronicity should be compared and contrasted with PSYCHIC REALITY; PSYCHOID UNCONSCIOUS; UNUS MUNDUS.

synthetic method   See REDUCTIVE AND SYNTHETIC METHODS.

syzygy   A term applied to any pair of OPPOSITES when spoken of as a pair, whether in conjunction or opposition. Jung used the word most frequently in relation to the linkage of ANIMA AND ANIMUS. He wrote of that linkage as being psychologically determined by three elements: 'The femininity pertaining to the man and the masculinity pertaining to the woman; the experience man has had of woman and vice versa (here early childhood events are of prime importance); and the masculine and feminine archetypal image' (CW 9ii, para. 41 n. 5). See IMAGO.

Jung concluded that images of the pairing of male-female syzygy were as universal as the existence of man and woman, citing the recurring motif of male-female pairs in mythology and pointing to the pair of concepts designated as Yang and Yin in Chinese philosophy. In early alchemical illustrations the male and female are conjoined symbolically, suggesting that as part of the process they must be differentiated and then reunited as an androgynous pair (see ALCHEMY; CONIUNCTIO). Bisexuality is not implied, however; rather, the complementary functioning of otherwise opposing elements (see ANDROGYNE; HERMAPHRODITE; SEX).

T

teleological point of view   An orientation to ends or purposes rather than causes; it characterises Jung's observation about the UNCON-SCIOUS, NEUROSIS and most especially INDIVIDUATION. This point of view distinguished his method and conclusions from those of psychoanalysis but led to criticisms that he had adopted a quasi-religious stance.

Lively discussion was provoked on this issue. Jung was suspect to those trained in the traditional schools of medicine and science. At the same time, certain theologians felt they found in him an ally, though others blamed him for his psychologism and, most especially, his terminology. Among theologians, Jung maintained the most prolonged dialogue with Father Victor White (1952).

Jaffé pointed out that Jung's words 'it is not I who create myself, rather, I happen to myself' (CW 11, para. 391) posit the SELF as an a priori existent. Whether known or unknown, it is the hidden operator behind our lives. Man cannot escape being destined by the self even in his freedom, but the possibility of an experience of MEANING lies in recognising its imprint (1971). Jung saw the incarnation of Christ as symbolising the fulfilment of what he, as a psychologist, called 'the process of indiduation'. The figure of Christ fully realised his potential and achieved his destiny.

Among contemporary analytical psychologists, Edinger (e.g. 1972) pays the most attention to the teleological point of view which he sees as consistent with that Christian standpoint.

See AETIOLOGY (OF NEUROSIS); REDUCTIVE AND SYNTHETIC METHODS; RELIGION.

temenos   A word used by the early Greeks to define a sacred precinct (i.e. a temple) within which a god's presence can be felt.

Jung's use of the word adds nothing to its original meaning but gives it a psychological application. He applied it quasi-metaphorically to describe: the psychically charged area surrounding a COM-PLEX, unapproachable by CONSCIOUSNESS and well-guarded by defences of the EGO; an analytic precinct (i.e. of the transference) within which ANALYST AND PATIENT feel themselves to be in the presence of a potentially overwhelming UNCONSCIOUS and daemonic force; the area of the psyche most foreign to the ego and characterised by the numinosity of the SELF or GOD-IMAGE (see NUMINOSUM); and the psychological container shaped by analyst and patient during ANALYSIS and distinguished by mutual respect for unconscious processes, confidentiality, a commitment to symbolic ENACTMENT and trust in one another's ethical judgment (see ETHICS; MORALITY).

A synonym for temenos is 'the hermetically sealed vessel'. This is an alchemical term used for the closed container within which OPPO-SITES transform (see ALCHEMY). Because of the presence of a sacred and unpredictable hermetic element, there could be no assurance that the process would be positive. By analogy, the psychological temenos may be experienced as either a womb or a prison. The presence of an erratic and unpredictable element within the psychological temenos caused Jung to remark *vis-à-vis* analytic containment that PSYCHO-THERAPY succeeds, when it does, *'Deo concedente'* (an alchemical epithet meaning 'with God's consent').

theory   Many of Jung's statements regarding theory strike one as being negative. For example: 'theories in psychology are the very devil'. Or 'scientific theory has ... less value from the point of view of psychological truth than religious dogma'. However, on balance, Jung's main emphasis was on the *integration* of theory. The analyst should not practise on the basis of ideas which are foreign to him or with which he has had no experiential contact. The patient should not be regarded as fitting or not fitting the theory. Indeed, it is virtually true that each patient will require modification of the analyst's pre-existing theory (see ANALYST AND PATIENT).

Jung was also at pains to underline the empirical nature of his approach. He felt that his hypotheses stemmed from observations of real people; the enormous amount of comparative, amplificatory data served to illustrate the hypotheses (see AMPLIFICATION; EMPIRICISM). As far as scientific methodology is concerned, Jung would probably have liked to think that he participated in the evolution of theory rather than applying it. His concern was hardly ever to predict, more to illuminate and make clear whatever it was that was under observation and discussion.

From a traditional standpoint, DEPTH PSYCHOLOGY cannot have the status of scientific theory, being neither provable nor unprovable. However, this point of view may be changing. In particular, a methodology in which an hypothesis is developed *before* hard evidence for or against it is amassed may be equal in validity to one in which data is collected and patterns in it are subsequently detected. If this is so, then it does not damn Jung's confession that his theories originated in his own thought processes, for few, if any, investigators have empty minds at the start of their work. Jung's continuing and defensive assertion of his empiricism may no longer be as necessary as it once was.

Accidental and unintended discoveries will always take place. Sometimes, Jung argued, these are on the basis of the activation of an archetypal structure (cf. Pauli, 1955, for a scientist's account of this phenomenon).

transcendent function   The function which mediates OPPOSITES. Expressing itself by way of the SYMBOL, it facilitates a transition from one psychological attitude or condition to another.

The transcendent function represents a linkage between real and imaginary, or rational and irrational data, thus bridging the gulf between CONSCIOUSNESS and the UNCONSCIOUS. 'It is a natural process', Jung writes, 'a manifestation of the energy that springs from the tension of opposites and it consists in a series of fantasy-occurrences which appear spontaneously in DREAMS and VISIONS' (CW 7, para. 121).

Standing in compensatory relationship to both, the transcendent function enables thesis and antithesis to encounter one another on equal terms. That which is capable of uniting these two is a metaphorical statement (the symbol) which itself transcends time and conflict, neither adhering to nor partaking of one side or the other but somehow common to both and offering the possibility of a new synthesis (see METAPHOR). The word *transcendent* is expressive of the presence of a capacity to transcend the destructive tendency to pull (or be pulled) to one side or the other.

Jung considered the transcendent function to be the most significant factor in psychological process. He insisted that its intervention was due to conflict between the opposites but he did not address himself to *why* this happened, concentrating instead upon the question 'what for?'. This he found answerable in psychological rather than metaphysical or religious terms. That meant analysing the appearance of a particular symbol in terms of its unique significance rather than regarding it as either a judgment from on high or a matter for self-congratulation.

From a TELEOLOGICAL POINT OF VIEW, however, Jung argued strongly that the transcendent function does not proceed without aim and purpose. At the very least, it enables a person to move beyond pointless conflict and avoid one-sidedness (see INDIVIDUATION; MEANING). Its role in the stimulation of conscience is significant (see MORALITY). It supplies a perspective other than one which is purely personal. It surprises one by asserting, often as if from a more objective position, a possible solution.

As a psychiatrist, Jung observed a variation of the same process in the initial stages of schizophrenia. In CW 14 he interprets alchemical symbolism applied to periods of transition that activate the transcendent function. Subsequent to his early theorisations, he discovered that the transcendent function is also a term employed in higher mathematics, being the function of real and imaginary numbers.

transference See ALCHEMY; ANALYST AND PATIENT; COMPENSATION; CONIUNCTIO; HERMAPHRODITE; MANA PERSONALITIES; OPPOSITES.

transformation A psychic transition involving REGRESSION and temporary 'loss of ego-hood' in order to bring to CONSCIOUSNESS and fulfil a psychological need hitherto unrecognised. As a consequence, the person becomes more complete. Not to be equated with achievement, transformation is an ongoing process and, Jung warned, even the stages of transformation should not be given hard and fast names lest something alive be made static. Spoken of as the goal of PSYCHO-THERAPY, the psychological opposite of repression; in ANALYSIS transformation involves a careful investigation of the SHADOW in all its aspects.

The symbolism of transformation is mirrored in primitive INITIA-TION rites, ALCHEMY and religious RITUAL, all of these being ceremonies designed to avert the psychic injuries liable to occur at times of transition (see PRIMITIVES; SYMBOL). All transformation includes experiences of transcendence and mystery and involves symbolic death and REBIRTH. Although there is a tendency to speak somewhat exaggeratedly of complete renewal, such is not the case. There is only a relative change so that continuity of person and PSYCHE are preserved. Otherwise, Jung notes, transformation would bring about a splitting of the personality, amnesia or other psychopathological state.

There can be negative transformation (see LOSS OF SOUL; PSY-CHOSIS). Yet, Jung was convinced that we naturally seek to obtain what we need; therefore, he referred to an INSTINCT for WHOLENESS or to transformation as being a natural process which involves an ongoing dialogue between the EGO and the SELF (see EGO-SELF AXIS). This process he also referred to as INDIVIDUATION.

The theme of transformation runs throughout Jung's work. His break with Freud was signalled by his analysis and publication of the transformation symbolism of an individual case (CW 5). His alchemical studies are an amplification of this basic psychic process (CW 12, 13, 14). Transformation rite and mystery are explored in 'Transformation symbolism in the mass' (CW 11).

See MANA PERSONALITIES.

trauma See PSYCHOANALYSIS; REDUCTIVE AND SYNTHETIC METHODS.

Trickster When Jung first encountered the IMAGE of the Trickster, he was reminded of the tradition of carnival with its striking reversal of hierarchic order and medieval observances where the devil appeared as 'the ape of God'. He found in the Trickster a striking resemblance to the alchemical figures of Mercurius with his fondness for sly jokes and malicious pranks, power to change shape, a dual nature (half animal/half divine), the urge for unremitting exposure to privation and torture as well as an approximation to the figure of a saviour. An altogether negative HERO, the Trickster yet manages to achieve through his stupidity what others fail to achieve by concentrated effort.

As Jung discovered, however, the Trickster is both a mythical figure and an inner psychic experience (see MYTH). Wherever and whenever he appears and in spite of his unimpressive exterior, he brings the possibility of transforming the meaningless into the meaningful. Hence, he symbolises the propensity for ENANTIODROMIA; and, gauche, UNCONSCIOUS creature though he may be, his actions inevitably reflect a compensatory relationship to CONSCIOUSNESS (see COMPENSATION). 'In his clearest manifestations', Jung writes, 'he is a faithful reflection of an absolutely undifferentiated human consciousness, corresponding to a PSYCHE that has hardly left the animal level' (CW 9i, para. 465). He may be seen as inferior even to the beasts because he is no longer dependent upon instinct alone; yet, for all his eagerness to learn, he hasn't achieved the full measure of human awareness. His most frightening aspect is probably not connected simply with his unconsciousness but also with his unrelatedness.

Psychologically, Jung saw the Trickster-figure as equivalent to the SHADOW. 'The Trickster is a COLLECTIVE shadow figure, a summation of all the inferior traits of character in individuals' (CW 9i, para. 484). However, his appearance is more than evidence of a residual trace inherited from primitive forebears. As in *King Lear*, his appearance owes itself to a dynamic existing in the actual situation. When the King wanders deranged as a result of his own arrogantly conscious blunders, his companion is the 'wiser' Fool.

Nevertheless, for the Trickster image to be active means that a calamity has happened or a dangerous situation has been created. When the Trickster appears in DREAMS, in PAINTINGS, in synchronistic events, slips of the tongue, in fantasy projections and personal accidents of all kinds, a compensatory energy has been released (see SYNCHRONICITY). Recognition of the figure is only the first step in its INTEGRATION, however. With the emergence of the SYMBOL, attention is called to the original destructive unconscious state but it is not yet overcome. And, since the individual shadow is an enduring component of the personality, it can never be eliminated. The collective

Trickster-figure reconstructs itself continually, manifesting the ener-
gising power and numinosity of all would-be saviour images (see
MANA PERSONALITIES; NUMINOSUM).

Jung's introduction to the Trickster-figure was Bandelier's *The
Delight Makers*. He wrote his own commentary entitled 'On the
Psychology of the Trickster-Figure' as a contribution to the German
edition of Radin's *The Trickster: A Study in American Indian
Mythology* (1956). Willeford (1969) is generally regarded as having
written the definitive work on the subject in contemporary ANALYTICAL
PSYCHOLOGY.

typology Jung was interested in illustrating how CONSCIOUSNESS
works in practice, and also in explaining how it is that consciousness
works in different ways in different people (1963, p. 233). He formulated a general theory of psychological types hoping to distinguish
the components of consciousness. This theory was first published in
1921 (CW 6).

Some individuals are more excited or energised by the internal
world and others by the external world; these are *introverts* and
extraverts respectively. But in addition to these basic *attitudes* to the
world, there are also certain properties or *functions* of consciousness.
Jung identified these as *thinking* – by which he meant knowing what
a thing is, naming it and linking it to other things; *feeling* – which
for Jung means something other than affect or emotion, a consideration of the value of something or having a viewpoint or perspective
on something; *sensation* – which represents all facts available to the
senses, telling us that something is, but not what it is; and, finally,
intuition, which Jung uses to mean a sense of where something is
going, of what the possibilities are, without conscious proof or knowledge. A further refinement is that these four functions divide into
two pairs – a *rational* pair (thinking and feeling) and an *irrational*
pair (sensation and intuition). What Jung means by these categories
and, in particular, the use of the word 'feeling' is a problematic issue
(see AFFECT).

We are now in a position to describe a person's overall style of
consciousness and his orientation towards inner and outer worlds.
Jung's model is carefully balanced. A person will have a primary (or
superior) mode of functioning; this will be one of the four functions.
The superior function will come from one of the two pairs of rational
or irrational functions. Of course the person will not depend exclusively on this superior function but will utilise a second, or *auxiliary*
function as well. This, according to Jung's observations, will come
from the opposite pair of rational or irrational functions depending
on whether the superior function came from the rational or irrational

pair. Thus, for example, a person with a superior function of feeling (from the rational pair) will have an auxiliary function of either sensation or intuition (from the irrational pair).

Using the two attitudes and the superior and auxiliary functions, it is possible to produce a list of sixteen basic types. Jung sometimes represented the four functions on a cross-like diagram. The EGO has energy at its disposal which can be directed into any of the four functions; and of course the extraversion-introversion possibility provides another dimension (see ENERGY). Jung felt that the number 4, although arrived at empirically and psychologically, was symbolically apt for the expression of something intended to be as encompassing as a description of consciousness.

Further, Jung then puts forward a proposition which transforms his typological theory from being merely a descriptive, academic exercise into something of value in diagnosis, prognosis, assessment and in connection with psychopathology generally.

We have so far allotted two of the four functions of consciousness; what of the other two? Jung observed that the other function from the pair that provided the superior function often caused a good deal of difficulty for the individual. Let us say that an individual has a superior function of feeling. If Jung is right, then he may have a problem with the other function from the same, rational category – namely, thinking. We can see how this approach of Jung's works out in practice. We all know of people who have a mature, balanced attitude to life and seem stable; they are at home with emotions and value personal relationships. But they may lack the capacity for sustained intellectuality or systematic thinking. They may even regard such thinking as a terrible thing, hate logic and proudly talk of themselves as innumerate and so on. But the pride may hide feelings of inadequacy and the problem may not be so easily resolved. Jung names the problematic function the *inferior function*. This will be the area of consciousness that is difficult for a person. On the other hand, the inferior function, which remains for the most part in the unconscious, contains enormous potential for change which can be brought about by attempts to integrate the contents of the inferior function into ego-consciousness. Doing this, realising one's inferior function, is a prime element in INDIVIDUATION because of the 'rounding out' of the personality that is involved.

It is important to realise that Jung is applying his theory of OPPO-SITES in the construction of this system. Within the broad category of 'rationality', thinking and feeling are opposites and this fact struck Jung more forcibly than the more obvious opposition between rational and irrational, e.g. between thinking and intuition. It is the very *link* of their shared rationality that enables thinking and feeling to be conceived of as opposites. Jung felt that, as a person is more likely to be rational *or* irrational, the important question typologically would have to be answered from within either the rational or the irrational category. The point needs stressing because, in a way, it conflicts with commonsense which would assert that the true opposites would be rational and irrational tendencies.

Jung speculated that in maturation and individuation these various typological opposites merge so that a person's conscious attitudes, and, hence, a great part of his experience of himself, will become richer and more variegated. One interesting question is the chronology of type formation. Jung describes a two-year-old child who would not enter a room before he had been told the names of the pieces of furniture there. Jung took this as, among other things, an example of early introversion. The issue of timing leads to the conundrum of how fixed or changeable is a person's type.

Jung thought that the functions have a physiological base with a psychic component which is partially controllable by the ego (see BODY; PSYCHE). To some extent a person can choose how to operate, but the limits are probably innate. No one can dispense with any of the four functions; they are inherent to ego-consciousness. But the use of one particular function may become habitual and exclude the others. The excluded function will remain untrained, undeveloped, infantile or archaic and possibly completely unconscious and not integrated into the ego. But it is possible for each function to be differentiated and, within limits, integrated. Nevertheless, for social, educational, or familial reasons one function may become one-sidedly dominant in a way that is not in tune with the person's constitutional personality.

U

unconscious Like Freud, Jung uses the term 'unconscious' both to describe mental contents which are inaccessible to the ego and to delimit a psychic place with its own character, laws and functions.

Jung did not regard the unconscious solely as a repository of repressed, infantile, personal experience but also as a locus of psychological activity which differed from and was more objective than personal experience, since it related directly to the phylogenetic, instinctual bases of the human race. The former, the *personal unconscious*, was seen as resting upon the latter, the *collective unconscious*. The contents of the collective unconscious have never been in consciousness and reflect archetypal processes (see ARCHETYPE). Inasmuch as the unconscious is a psychological concept, its contents, as a whole, are of a psychological nature, whatever their root connection to instinct may be. Images, symbols and fantasies may be termed the *language* of the unconscious (see FANTASY; IMAGE; METAPHOR; SYMBOL). The collective unconscious operates independently of the EGO on account of its origin in the inherited structure of the BRAIN. Its manifestations appear in CULTURE as universal motifs with their own degree of attraction (see NUMINOSUM).

It has been pointed out that such a distinction of Jung's is somewhat academic in that the contents of the collective unconscious require the involvement of elements of the personal unconscious for their manifestation in behaviour; the two kinds of unconscious are therefore indivisible (Williams, 1963a). On the other hand, the concept of the collective unconscious may be used in analysis to go beyond or behind personal experience to ascertain its non-personal connections (see AMPLIFICATION; ASSOCIATION). The ego may then relate differently to these (Hillman, 1975). The dialogue within analytical psychology is between a personal perspective and the reality of a non-personal perspective (see OBJECTIVE PSYCHE).

In terms of *psychic structure*, the anima or animus is conceived of as connecting the ego with the unconscious (see ANIMA AND ANIMUS; PSYCHE; PSYCHOPOMP). The relation between consciousness and the unconscious is usually expressed by Jung in terms of COMPENSATION.

REFLECTION upon the unconscious leads to a consideration of why it is that some parts become conscious and some do not. Jung's tentative conclusion was that (a) the quantum of energy alters and (b) the strength of the ego determines what may pass over into CONSCIOUSNESS. With regard to the ego, the crucial factor is its ability to maintain dialogue and interact with possibilities revealed in the unconscious. If the ego is relatively strong, it will permit the selective passage of unconscious contents into consciousness (see TRANSCENDENT FUNCTION). Over time, such contents may be seen as enhancing personality development in a unique and individual way (see INDIVIDUATION; TRANSFORMATION). It can be seen that there is a difference of emphasis between Freud and Jung in relation to the unconscious. Jung's view is that the unconscious is primarily, or potentially, creative, functioning in the service of individual and species. (For a discussion of Freud's views on phylogenetic aspects of the unconscious, see ARCHETYPE.)

So far it has been mentioned that the unconscious has its place in psychic structure, its own internal structure, its language and an overall cast of creativity. In addition, though some decoding may be necessary, Jung ascribes to the unconscious a form of knowledge, even of thought. This may be expressed in the language of philosophy as containing the 'final cause' of a psychological tendency or line of development. We could regard this as the reason or purpose for something happening, the 'sake' for which it happens or is brought about. In consciousness, a final cause would be a hope, aspiration or intention. It is hard to name the final causes which operate in the unconscious but these may be experienced by a person as promoting the expression and MEANING of his or her individual life. This aspect of the unconscious involves the so-called TELEOLOGICAL POINT OF VIEW. It should be noted that Jung is neither saying that the unconscious *causes* things to happen, nor that its operation and influence are *necessarily* beneficial (see SYNCHRONICITY).

For discussion of unconscious thought see DIRECTED AND FANTASY THINKING.

unus mundus   Jung's research into ALCHEMY and the evolution of concepts such as PSYCHIC REALITY, the PSYCHOID UNCONSCIOUS and SYNCHRONICITY, led him to bring in the pre-Newtonian idea of the *unus mundus* or unitary world. This concept, or IMAGE, is used by Jung to suggest that each stratum of existence is intimately linked with all the other strata, rather than that there is a transcendent or supraordinate plan for the coordination of separate parts. For example, BODY and PSYCHE are interrelated, and psyche and matter may also be related as well.

In using the *unus mundus* as a working concept for psychological discourse, an analogy was drawn between the operation of the UNCONSCIOUS and what is known of sub-atomic particle physics. In both we observe rapid interaction and interchange of the entities involved; and in both there are patterns and probabilities to be found. For example, what relativity theory tells us about the fluidity and 'symbolic' nature of the physical world may be compared with the similar characteristics of intrapsychic activity. When the sub-atomic physicist accepts that something can be simultaneously particle and wave, he is required to take a more or less psychological attitude to his work (see SYMBOL). Physicists search for an underlying force in nature, perhaps one which would unify electromagnetism, nuclear forces and gravity. Similarly, the non-Einsteinian notion of 'action-at-a-distance', in which two distinct sub-atomic particles behave harmoniously, as though each 'knew' what the other is doing, may be compared to the theory of archetypes and/or the operation of the transpersonal SELF (see ARCHETYPE).

The *unus mundus* is a world view which is essentially at odds with causal explanation. The focus is on relations existing between 'things' rather than on the 'things' themselves, and, further, on the relations between relations. It is necessary to remember that the *unus mundus* is not a device but the background of attempts to discern MEANING (see REDUCTIVE AND SYNTHETIC METHODS; TELEOLOGICAL POINT OF VIEW). Discernment requires EGO involvement and personal authority. Dependence on codices, such as the *I Ching* or astrological charts, must, according to Jung, be strictly monitored. Nevertheless, the vision of a unitary world, perhaps of a world permeated by a divine intelligence, is, to a degree, a transcendent one. Nowadays there is talk of the 'mysticism of physics' and of an 'implicate order' underlying the fragmentation apperceived by ordinary CONSCIOUS-NESS (cf. Capra, 1975; Bateson, 1979; Bohm, 1980).

Not all analytical psychologists accept Jung's view of the *unus mundus*. What is lost is the vitality of the pluralistic psyche, which tends to find expression in 'sparks' or fragments. Search for a ground-plan cuts us off from what may be gained from a full emotional and imaginative investment in, and exploration of such fragments (Hillman, 1971). Jung's use of *unus mundus* as a defence against his own intense anxiety has also been suggested (Atwood and Stolorow, 1979).

uroboros Universal motif of a serpent coiled into a circle, biting its own tail. As such, it 'slays, weds and impregnates itself. It is man and woman, begetting and conceiving, devouring and giving birth, active and passive, above and below, at once' (Neumann, 1954). As a symbol, the uroboros suggests a primal state involving darkness and self-destruction as well as fecundity and potential creativity. It portrays the stage which exists before delineation and separation of the OPPOSITES.

Following Jung and Neumann, the uroboros is used by some analytical psychologists as a primary METAPHOR for an early stage of personality DEVELOPMENT. The LIFE INSTINCT and the DEATH INSTINCT are not delineated, nor are love and aggression; GENDER identity is unformed; a lack of PRIMAL SCENE experience suggests fantasies of parthenogenesis or immaculate conception; there is no distinction between feeder and fed, simply a perpetually devouring mouth. These fantasies may be assumed to constitute such a great part of an infant's psychological life that this early stage of development is characterised as *uroboric*. Subsequent phases are termed by Neumann as *matriarchal* and *patriarchal*.

It is important to bear the metaphorical nature of this description in mind for it is essentially an empathic construction. That is, external observations of an empirical nature suggest that a baby is a great deal more related, active and initiatory than the uroboric focus on solipsism and fantasy would suggest. However, both the internal and external perspectives are valid in their differing ways (see INFANCY AND CHILDHOOD).

Contemporary psychoanalysis has moved towards the idea that if the mother and/or the environment do not fit in with an infant's quite normal illusions of grandiosity and omnipotence, then he tends to feel impinged upon or persecuted. This may lead to the development of a false self organisation, as Winnicott (1960) suggested. Or the failure to 'mirror' him may lead to feelings of deprivation, tending toward possible narcissistic personality disorder later in life (Kohut, 1971).

An adult's religious sense may be seen as an involvement with the image of the uroboros – recognition of God's encompassing power on the one hand and, on the other, moments of oneness with Him (see RELIGION; SELF).

V

vision An irruption of an unconscious content which intrudes upon the field of consciousness in the form of an impressive personal experience portrayed in visual and pictorial terms. This happens when one is in the waking state and excepting for rare instances is accompanied by an *ABAISSEMENT DU NIVEAU MENTAL*. As a general rule, visions are born of extreme personal alienation. They are compelling and have an uncanny force of persuasion. It is because mystical visions have so powerfully recalled to persons what they felt to be their own true natures that they have been so indelibly impressed.

Though visions are not themselves evidence of mental disturbance, some visions are pathological and occur in PSYCHOSIS. Jung's early work with schizophrenic patients alerted him to mythological motifs (i.e. of the Sun God) that were commonly repeated in reported visions (see MYTH; SCHIZOPHRENIA). He later identified these motifs as archetypal fragments belonging to the collective UNCONSCIOUS. Once such contents break through into consciousness, the question arises as to how the individual will respond.

There is no special merit in the seeing of visions; their value depends upon the attitude that the recipient takes toward them. When a primordial idea presents itself in visionary terms, the task of the individual is to translate the spontaneous and symbolic picture or dramatic sequence into an individual statement. Otherwise, the vision is no more than a natural phenomenon against which he is powerless to defend himself. The danger is then that the weak EGO will be subject to INFLATION.

Visions may be grotesque or transcendentally beautiful. Some are of such a nature as to suggest the designs of a super-conscious power. However, as Jung points out, it is impossible to imagine such a consciousness without an identity. Since the existence of such a super-conscious identity is not provable other than a subjective way, no further psychological statement can be made on the subject. Here psychology ends and some sort of belief in SPIRIT takes over (see GOD-IMAGE; NUMINOSUM; RELIGION).

W

wholeness The fullest possible expression of all aspects of the personality, both in itself and in relation to other people and the environment.

According to Jung, wholeness is to be equated with health. As such, it is both a potential and a capacity. We are born possessing fundamental wholeness but, as we grow, this breaks down and reforms into something more differentiated (see SELF). Expressed in this way, the achievement of conscious wholeness may be regarded as the goal or purpose of life. Interaction with others or the environment may or may not facilitate this, as the case may be. Wholeness, however, is to be seen in all its aspects as individually relevant and, hence, a qualitative rather than a quantitative achievement.

While wholeness cannot be actively sought or pursued *per se*, it is possible to see how often life's experience has that end as its secret goal. The connection with creativity underlines that wholeness (and health) are relative terms, distinguishable from normality or conformism (see ADAPTATION; HEALING; INDIVIDUATION). As Jung used the word, 'wholeness' speaks more of 'completeness' than of 'perfection'.

The idea of wholeness is linked to the theory of OPPOSITES. If two conflicting opposites come together and synthesise, the result partakes of a greater wholeness (see CONIUNCTIO; MANDALA). Jung was concerned that Western culture in general, and Christianity in particular, have ignored two elements which are vital to wholeness: the feminine (see ANIMA AND ANIMUS; ASSUMPTION OF THE VIRGIN MARY; GENDER) and EVIL or man's destructiveness (see SHADOW).

Jung was aware that a person can acquire a patina of wholeness which is spurious (CW 7, para. 188) and that a too-eager devotee will confuse his wish with his actual state. A greed for wholeness can be an escape from psychological conflict.

Jung's ideas, in common with many developments in twentieth-century thought, show a holistic cast of mind (though Jung does not

use the word). See PLEROMA; PSYCHIC REALITY; PSYCHOID UNCON-
SCIOUS; SYNCHRONICITY; *UNUS MUNDUS.*

will Used by Jung to denote the energic aspect of CONSCIOUSNESS,
i.e. the power of consciousness in relation to the UNCONSCIOUS in
general and, in particular, to the instincts. For Jung, consciousness
was never a neutral factor but rather an active intervention in the
affairs of the psyche (see COMPLEX; EGO). He defined will as the
energy available to consciousness, stressing the role played by motivation in the release of such energy. Motivation he saw as effected
by COLLECTIVE forces such as education, CULTURE and the church as
well as by psychic determinants such as DEPRESSION or NEUROSIS.

In relation to instinct, will may be seen as capable of altering (a)
its intensity and (b) its orientation. However, will itself must draw
upon instinctual energy. Here Jung comes close to Freud's early
formulation of 'ego-instincts' (1910). These instincts are at the service
of the ego and in opposition to the sexual instinct. The main difference is the emphasis in Freud's theory on the conflicts created by the
sexual instinct compared to Jung's stress on TRANSFORMATION of it
(see ENERGY; EROS; INCEST).

One implication of Jung's use of 'will' is that consciousness is
instinctual, hence an inherent, definitory aspect of humanity and not
a secondary, learnt, factor. Further, there is a form of 'consciousness'
in the unconscious (see ARCHETYPE; SELF). Sometimes Jung speculates
on the possibility of a form of BODY consciousness.

The realm of will is a limited one: will 'cannot coerce instinct nor
has it power over the SPIRIT' (*CW* 8, para. 379).

See RELIGION.

wise old man/wise old woman See MANA PERSONALITIES.

word association test An experimental method for the identification
of personal complexes by the investigation of associations or chance
psychological linkages (see ASSOCIATION). Jung concentrated upon
research with the word association test for several years during the
first decade of this century when he was a young psychiatrist working
at the Burghölzli Clinic (a mental hospital in Zurich) where the test
had been introduced by Bleuler and was used for the clinical assessment of patients (see PSYCHOANALYSIS).

The test had been invented by Galton and taken over and changed
by Wundt, who wanted to discover and establish the laws governing
the association of ideas. Aschaffenburg and Kraepelin introduced
distinctions between verbal or 'clang' (sound) associations and those
related to meaning and they observed the effect of fatigue upon

responses. Fever patients, alcoholics and mental patients were tested. Next, Ziehan discovered that reaction times were longer if the stimulus words related to something that the patient felt was unpleasant. Delayed responses were found to be related to a 'common underlying representation' or 'emotionally charged complex of representations'. It was at this point that the test was taken up for use at the Burghölzli and Jung was entrusted with the research which, in the first instance, was concerned with the loosening or release of tension surrounding associations at the onset of SCHIZOPHRENIA.

Jung perfected the test, his main purpose being the detection and analysis of complexes. During these investigations, he became convinced that the patient might be cured if he could be helped to conquer and overcome his COMPLEX. Among his first findings (published in 1907 as *The Psychology of Dementia Praecox*, CW 3) Jung distinguished different kinds of complexes, depending upon whether they were related to single, ongoing or repeated events; whether they were conscious, partly conscious or unconscious and whether they revealed strong charges of AFFECT. Jung's investigations caused a divergence with Bleuler regarding hypotheses concerning the genesis of schizophrenia and Jung also enunciated his seminal supposition that the delusional ideas of the psychotic were attempts to create a new vision of the world (CW 3, paras 153–178).

Throughout his work on the word association test, Jung regarded Freud as an authority. Freud himself was not unaware of research on association and he used a number of terms such as chain, thread, train or line of association to describe the pathways of so-called 'free association'. Jung felt his own researches upon complexes and complex indicators confirmed constellations of unconscious repressed contents and gave support to Freud's discoveries of traumatic reminiscences. But, whereas Freud continued to apply his method of free association largely to contents of the patient's personal unconscious (Jung's term), Jung's interest in complexes carried him further to investigation of archetypes residing in the collective unconscious (again Jung's term). See ARCHETYPE; COLLECTIVE; UNCONSCIOUS.

For a brief time, Jung speculated that the word association test might be a tool of social value for use in crime detection as well as in therapy. But after several years of intense work on the problems involved, he ceased to use the word association test altogether and abandoned any further attempts at experimental psychology.

wounded healer   See HEALING.

References

Adler, G. (1971), 'Analytical psychology and the principle of complementarity', in *The Analytical Process*, ed. Wheelwright, J., Putnam, New York.

Atwood, G. and Stolorow, R. (1979), *Faces in a Cloud: Subjectivity in Personality Theory*, Jason Aronson, New York.

Balint, M. (1968), *The Basic Fault: Therapeutic Aspects of Regression*, Tavistock, London.

Bateson, G. (1979), *Mind and Nature: A Necessary Unity*, Dutton, New York.

Binswanger, L. (1945), 'Insanity as life historical phenomenon and as mental disease: the case of Ilse', in *Existence*, eds May, R., Angel, E., Ellenberger, H., Basic, New York, 1958.

Bohm, D. (1980), *Wholeness and the Implicate Order*, Routledge & Kegan Paul, London.

Capra, F. (1975), *The Tao of Physics*, Wildwood House, London.

Corbin, H. (1972), '*Mundalis imaginalis*, or the imaginary and the imaginal', *Spring*.

Corbin, H. (1983), 'Theophanies and mirrors: idols or icons?', *Spring*.

Dictionary of Modern Thought (1977), Fontana, London.

Edinger, E. (1972), *Ego and Archetype*, Penguin, New York.

Eliade, M. (1968), *The Sacred and the Profane*, Harcourt, Brace & World, New York.

Ellenberger, H. (1970), *The Discovery of the Unconscious*, Allen Lane, London; Basic, New York.

Ford, C. (1983), *The Somatizing Disorders: Illness as a Way of Life*, Elsevier, New York.

Fordham, M. (1961), 'C. G. Jung', *Brit. J. Med. Psych.*, 34.

Fordham, M. (1969), *Children as Individuals*, Hodder & Stoughton, London.

Fordham, M. (1976), *The Self and Autism*, Heinemann, London.

Freud, S. (1900), *The Interpretation of Dreams*, Std Edn, 4–5, Hogarth, London.

Freud, S. (1901), *The Psychopathology of Everyday Life*, Std Edn, 6, Hogarth, London.

Freud, S. (1905), 'Jokes and their relation to the unconscious', Std Edn, 8, Hogarth, London.

Freud, S. (1910), 'The future prospects of psycho-analytic therapy', Std Edn, 11, Hogarth, London.

Freud, S. (1912), 'Recommendations to physicians practising psycho-analysis', Std Edn, 12, Hogarth, London.

REFERENCES

Freud, S. (1913), 'The disposition to obsessional neurosis', Std Edn, 12, Hogarth, London.

Freud, S. (1915), 'Instincts and their vicissitudes', Std Edn, 14, Hogarth, London.

Freud, S. (1916–17), *Introductory Lectures on Psychoanalysis*, Std Edn, 15–16, Hogarth, London.

Freud, S. (1920), *Beyond the Pleasure Principle*, Std Edn, 18, Hogarth, London.

Freud, S. (1937), 'Analysis terminable and interminable', Std Edn, 23, Hogarth, London.

Glover, E. (1950), *Freud or Jung*, Allen & Unwin, London.

Goldberg, A. (1980), Introduction to *Advances in Self Psychology*, ed. Goldberg, A., International Universities Press, New York.

Gordon, R. (1978), *Dying and Creating: A Search for Meaning*, Society of Analytical Psychology, London.

Greenson, R. and Wexler, M. (1969), 'The non-transference relationship in the psychoanalytic situation', *Int. J. Psychoanal.*, 50, pp. 27–39.

Guggenbühl-Craig, A. (1971), *Power in the Helping Professions*, Spring, New York.

Guggenbühl-Craig, A. (1977), *Marriage – Dead or Alive*, Spring, Zürich.

Guggenbühl-Craig, A. (1980), *Eros on Crutches: Reflections on Psychopathy and Amorality*, Spring, Dallas.

Hall, J. (1977), *Clinical Uses of Dreams: Jungian Interpretation and Enactments*, Grune and Stratton, New York.

Heimann, P. (1950), 'On counter-transference', *Int. J. Psychoanal.*, 31.

Heisig, J. (1979), *Imago Dei: A Study of C. G. Jung's Psychology of Religion*, Bucknell University Press, Lewisburg; Associated Universities Press, London.

Henderson, J. (1967), *Thresholds of Initiation*, Wesleyan University Press, Middleton, New York.

Henderson, J. (1982), 'Reflections on the history and practice of Jungian analysis', in *Jungian Analysis*, ed. Stein, M., Open Court, La Salle and London.

Henry, J. (1977), Comment on 'The cerebral hemispheres in analytical psychology' by Rossi, E., *J. Analyt. Psychol.*, 22:2, pp. 52–8.

Hillman, J. (1971), 'Psychology: monotheistic or polytheistic?', *Spring*.

Hillman, J. (1972), *The Myth of Analysis*, Northwestern University Press, Evanston, Illinois.

Hillman, J. (1975), *Revisioning Psychology*, Harper & Row, New York.

Hillman, J. (1979), *The Dream and the Underworld*, Harper & Row, New York.

Hillman, J. (1980), 'On the necessity of abnormal psychology: Ananke and Athene', in *Facing the Gods*, ed. Hillman, J., Spring, Dallas.

Hillman, J. (1983), *Archetypal Psychology: A Brief Account*, Spring, Dallas.

Hudson, L. (1983), Review of *Jung: Selected Writings* ed. Storr, A., Fontana, London, in *Sunday Times*, 13 March, London.

Isaacs, S. (1952), 'The nature and function of phantasy', in *Developments in Psychoanalysis*, ed. Riviere, J., Hogarth, London.

Jacobi, J. (1965), *Complex/Archetype/Symbol in the Work of C. G. Jung*, Princeton University Press, 2nd edition (orig. 1959).

Jacoby, M. (1981), 'Reflections on H. Kohut's concept of narcissism', *J. Analyt. Psychol.*, 26:1, pp. 19–32.

Jaffé, A. (1971), *The Myth of Meaning*, Putnam, New York.

Jaffé, A. (1979), *C. G. Jung: Word and Image*, Princeton University Press.

Jung, C. G. (1955), In *C. G. Jung Letters*, ed. Adler, G., Vol. 2, p. 274, Routledge & Kegan Paul, London.

Jung, C. G. (1957), In *C. G. Jung Letters*, as above, Vol. 2, p. 383.

Jung, C. G. (1963), *Memories, Dreams, Reflections*, Collins and Routledge & Kegan Paul, London.

Jung, C. G. (1964), *Man and His Symbols*, Dell, New York.

Jung, C. G. (1983), *The Zofingia Lectures*, CW Supplementary Volume A, ed. McGuire, W., Routledge & Kegan Paul, London; Princeton University Press.

Jung, C. G. (1984), *Dream Analysis*, CW Seminar Papers, Volume 1, ed. McGuire, W., Routledge & Kegan Paul, London; Princeton University Press.

Jung, E. (1957), *Animus and Anima*, Spring, Irving, Texas.

Kirsch, T. (1982), 'Analysis in training', in *Jungian Analysis*, ed. Stein, M., Open Court, La Salle and London.

Klein, M. (1937), *Love, Hate, and Reparation*, Hogarth, London.

Klein, M. (1957), *Envy and Gratitude*, Tavistock, London.

Kohut, H. (1971), *The Analysis of the Self*, International Universities Press, New York.

Kohut, H. (1977), *The Restoration of the Self*, International Universities Press, New York.

Kohut, H. (1980), 'Reflections', in *Advances in Self Psychology*, ed. Goldberg, A., International Universities Press, New York.

Kraemer, W. (ed.). (1976), *The Forbidden Love: The Normal and Abnormal Love of Children*, Sheldon Press, London.

Kris, E. (1952), *Explorations in Art*, International Universities Press, New York.

Lacan, J. (1949), 'The mirror stage as formative of the function of the I as revealed in psychoanalytic experience', in *Écrits*, trans. Sheridan, A., Tavistock, London, 1977.

Laing, R. (1967), *The Politics of Experience*, Penguin, Harmondsworth.

Lambert, K. (1981), *Analysis, Repair and Individuation*, Academic Press, London.

Langs, R. (1978), *The Listening Process*, Jason Aronson, New York.

Laplanche, J. and Pontalis, J.-B. (1980), *The Language of Psychoanalysis*, Hogarth, London.

Layard, J. (1945), 'The incest taboo and the virgin archetype', in *The Virgin Archetype*, Spring, Zürich (1972).

Layard, J. (1959), 'On psychic consciousness', in *The Virgin Archetype*, Spring, Zürich (1972).

Ledermann, R. (1979), 'The infantile roots of narcissistic personality disorder', *J. Analyt. Psychol.*, 26:4, pp. 107–26.

REFERENCES

Leonard, L. (1982), *The Wounded Woman: Healing the Father–Daughter Relationship*, Swallow, Athens.

Levinson, D. *et al.* (1978), *The Seasons of a Man's Life*, Knopf, New York.

Little, M. (1957), ' "R": the analyst's total response to his patient's needs', *Int. J. Psychoanal.*, 38:3.

Maduro, R. and Wheelwright, J. (1977), 'Analytical psychology', in *Current Personality Theories*, ed. Corsini, R., Peacock, Ithaca.

Mattoon, M. (1978), *Applied Dream Analysis: A Jungian Approach*, Winston, Washington.

Meier, C. (1967), *Ancient Incubation and Modern Psychotherapy*, Northwestern University Press, Evanston, Illinois.

Micklem, N. (1980), 'The removable eye: reflections on imagination in neurosis', *Dragonflies*, Winter, 1980.

Money-Kyrle, R. (1978), *Collected Papers*, ed. Meltzer, D., Clunie Press, Strath Tay, Perthshire.

Neumann, E. (1954), *The Origins and History of Consciousness*, Routledge & Kegan Paul, London

Neumann, E. (1955), *The Great Mother: An Analysis of the Archetype*, Routledge & Kegan Paul, London.

Neumann, E. (1973), *The Child*, Hodder & Stoughton, London.

Newton, K. (1975), 'Separation and pre-oedipal guilt', *J. Analyt. Psychol.*, 20:2, pp. 183–93.

Newton, K. and Redfearn, J. (1977), 'The real mother, ego-self relations and personal identity', *J. Analyt. Psychol.*, 22:4, pp. 295–316.

Odajnyk, V. (1976), *Jung and Politics: The Political and Social Ideas of C. G. Jung*, Harper & Row, New York.

Otto, R. (1917), *The Idea of the Holy*, Oxford University Press (1923).

Papadopoulos, R. (1984), 'Jung and the concept of the Other', in *Jung in Modern Perspective*, eds Papadopoulos, R. and Saayman, G., Wildwood House, Hounslow.

Pauli, W. (1955), 'The influence of archetypal ideas on the scientific theories of Kepler', in *The Interplay of Nature and the Psyche* by Jung, C. G. and Pauli, W., Bollingen, New York and London.

Perry, J. (1962), 'Reconstitutive processes in the psychopathology of the self', *Annals* of the New York Academy of Sciences, Vol. 96, article 3, pp. 853–76.

Perry, J. (1974), *The Far Side of Madness*, Prentice-Hall, Englewood Cliffs, New Jersey.

Perry, J. (1976), *Roots of Renewal in Myth and Madness*, Jossey-Bass, San Francisco.

Radin, P. (1956), *The Trickster: A Study in American-Indian Mythology*, Routledge & Kegan Paul, London.

Redfearn, J. (1978), 'The energy of warring and combining opposites: problems for the psychotic patient and the therapist in achieving the symbolic situation', *J. Analyt. Psychol.*, 23:3, pp. 231–41.

Rossi, E. (1977), 'The cerebral hemispheres in analytical psychology', *J. Analyt. Psychol.*, 22:1, pp. 32–58.

Rycroft, C. (1968), *Psychoanalysis Observed*, Penguin, Harmondsworth.

Rycroft, C. (1972), *A Critical Dictionary of Psychoanalysis*, Penguin, Harmondsworth.

Samuels, A. (1985a), *Jung and the Post-Jungians*, Routledge & Kegan Paul, London and Boston.

Samuels, A. (1985b), 'Countertransference, the *mundus imaginalis* and a research project', *J. Analyt. Psychol.*, 30:1, pp. 47–71.

Sandner, D. (1979), *Navaho Symbols of Healing*, Harcourt, Brace, Jovanovich, New York and London.

Sandner, D. and Beebe, J. (1982), 'Psychopathology and analysis', in *Jungian Analysis*, ed. Stein, M., Open Court, La Salle and London.

Schafer, R. (1976), *A New Language for Psychoanalysis*, Yale University Press, New Haven.

Schwartz-Salant, N. (1982), *Narcissism and Character Transformation: The psychology of Narcissistic Character Disorders*, Inner City, Toronto.

Searles, H. (1968), *Collected Papers on Schizophrenia and Related Subjects*, Hogarth, London.

Sheldrake, R. (1981), *A New Science of Life*, Shambhala, Boulder and London.

Singer, J. (1972), *Boundaries of the Soul: The Practice of Jung's Psychology*, Gollancz, London.

Singer, J. (1976), *Androgyny: Towards a New Theory of Sexuality*, Doubleday, Garden City, New York.

Stein, M. (1982), 'The aims and goal of Jungian analysis', in *Jungian Analysis*, ed. Stein, M., Open Court, La Salle and London.

Stein, M. (1985), *In Midlife*, Spring, Dallas.

Stein, R. (1974), *Incest and Human Love*, Penguin, Baltimore.

Stevens, A. (1982), *Archetype: A Natural History of the Self*, Routledge & Kegan Paul, London.

Storr, A. (1983), *Jung: Selected Writings*, Fontana, London.

Sutherland, J. (1980), 'The British object relations theorists: Balint, Winnicott, Fairbairn, Guntrip', *J. Amer. Psychoanal. Assn.*, 28, pp. 829–59.

Szasz, T. (1962), *The Myth of Mental Illness*, Secker & Warburg, London.

Tolpin, M. (1980), Contribution to 'Discussion' in *Advances in Self Psychology*, ed. Goldberg, A., International Universities Press, New York.

Ulanov, A. (1981), *Receiving Woman: Studies in the Psychology and Theology of the Feminine*, Westminster, Philadelphia.

von Franz, M.-L. (1970), *The Problem of the Puer Aeternus*, Spring, New York.

von Franz, M.-L. (1971), 'The inferior function' in *Jung's Typology* by Hillman, J. and von Franz, M.-L., Spring, New York.

Watkins, M. (1976), *Waking Dreams*, Gordon & Breach, New York.

Weaver, M. (1964), *The Old Wise Woman*, Vincent Stuart, London.

Wheelwright, J. (1982), 'Termination', in *Jungian Analysis*, ed. Stein, M., Open Court, La Salle and London.

White, V. (1952), *God and the Unconscious*, Harvill, London.

Wilber, K. (ed.). (1982), *The Holographic Paradigm and Other Paradoxes: Exploring the Leading Edge of Science*, Shambhala, Boulder and London.

Willeford, W. (1969), *The Fool and His Scepter*, Northwestern University Press, Evanston, Illinois.

REFERENCES

Williams, M. (1963a), 'The indivisibility of the personal and collective unconscious', in *Analytical Psychology: A Modern Science*, ed. Fordham, M. *et al.*, Heinemann, London, 1973.

Williams, M. (1963b), 'The poltergeist man', *J. Analyt. Psychol.*, 8:2. pp. 123–44.

Winnicott, D. (1960), 'The theory of the parent–infant relationship', in *The Maturational Processes and the Facilitating Environment*, Hogarth, London, 1965.

Winnicott, D. (1967), 'Mirror role of mother and family in child development', in *Playing and Reality*, Tavistock, London, 1971

Winnicott, D. (1971), *Playing and Reality*, Tavistock, London.

List of entries